THE DIGITAL IS KID STUFF

The Digital Is Kid Stuff

*Making Creative Laborers
for a Precarious Economy*

- - - - - - -

JOSEF NGUYEN

 University of Minnesota Press
Minneapolis
London

The University of Minnesota Press gratefully acknowledges the financial assistance provided for the publication of this book by the School of Arts, Technology, and Emerging Communication at the University of Texas at Dallas.

Portions of the Introduction and chapter 2 were published in "How Makers and Preppers Converge in Premodern and Post-Apocalyptic Ruin," *Lateral: Journal of the Cultural Studies Association* 7, no. 2 (Fall 2018): https://csalateral.org/issue/7-2/makers-preppers-premodern-post-apocalyptic -ruin-nguyen/; licensed under CC BY-NC 4.0 (http://creativecommons.org/licenses/by-nc/4.0/). An earlier version of chapter 1 was published as "*Minecraft* and the Building Blocks of Creative Individuality," *Configurations* 24, no. 4 (December 2016): 471–500; copyright 2016 The Johns Hopkins University Press. An earlier version of chapter 2 was published as "*Make* Magazine and the Social Reproduction of DIY Science and Technology," *Cultural Politics* 12, no. 2 (July 2016): 233–52; reprinted by permission of Duke University Press.

Published by the University of Minnesota Press
111 Third Avenue South, Suite 290
Minneapolis, MN 55401-2520
http://www.upress.umn.edu

ISBN 978-1-5179-1115-7 (hc)
ISBN 978-1-5179-1114-0 (pb)

Library of Congress record available at https://lccn.loc.gov/2021025932

Printed in the United States of America on acid-free paper

The University of Minnesota is an equal-opportunity educator and employer.

CONTENTS

What We Are to Make of Creative Digital Youth

Much is believed to be at stake at the intersection of youth, digital media, and creativity.

In a 2010 *Newsweek* article titled "The Creativity Crisis," Po Bronson and Ashley Merryman find the decline of American creativity scores since the 1990s troubling.[1] Taking the tests that produce these scores at face value, Bronson and Merryman contend that "the potential consequences are sweeping," since they claim that "the necessity of human ingenuity is undisputed."[2] In attempting to identify root causes, the authors posit that "one likely culprit is the number of hours kids now spend in front of the TV and playing videogames," casting media and computing technologies as antithetical to the nation's future.[3]

Expressing a more optimistic view in their 2015 book *Creative Schools: The Grassroots Revolution That's Transforming Education,* Ken Robinson and Lou Aronica contend that "there are immense benefits in the digital revolution for the education of all young people," which includes fostering creative capacities.[4] Rather than framing digital technologies as absolute detriments to youth, Robinson and Aronica suggest that education must adapt to childhood undergoing transformation in digital culture. Youth today, they suggest, "are under intense pressure from their peers, from the wider cultural environment, from the relentless demands of the digital world and social media, and from the incessant noise of advertising that badgers them for their attention, sense of identity, and money."[5]

And Mark Yarm explores the question "Does Screen Time Stunt Kids' Creativity?" in an article included in the 2018 *Time* magazine special edition on "The Science of Creativity."[6] Alongside presenting experts who assert that screens negatively impact children's creative development, Yarm also emphasizes that other "experts stress that the quality and content of a child's screen viewing matter as much as or more than the quantity."[7] Rather than view screens as inherently dangerous to children's creativity, these experts focus on the function of screen time, such as whether screen engagements encourage play and self-expression. Having explored competing positions on the issue, Yarm concludes that "until there's more research available, parents and teachers will just have to rely on their gut when it comes to kids and screens and creative play," ultimately placing the onus on parents and teachers to decide for themselves in lieu of conclusive research showing whether screen engagements foster children's creative development.[8]

Much is believed to be at stake at the intersection of youth, digital media, and creativity.

But little consensus exists over how exactly youth should encounter digital media to support their creative development.

In *The Digital Is Kid Stuff: Making Creative Laborers for a Precarious Economy,* I examine how contemporary American culture constructs youth in the era of digital media as inextricable from creativity. At a time when creativity operates as a principal political and economic value through discourses of the creative economy, discussions of contemporary youth—figured as intrinsically creative and technologically savvy—characterize them as poised to produce innovations that will ensure economic growth, increased democratization, and national prosperity. I argue that contemporary American culture mediates ambivalences and contradictions of a precarious creative labor economy constituted by and dependent on digital technologies through constructions of creative digital youth as well as in debates over their development into productive creative workers.

This book is a study of images and discourses about youth rather than a study of actual youth per se. In investigating constructions of youth as sites of cultural expression and negotiation, I unpack particular ideologies of creativity prominent in the United States instead of treating creativity as a naturally individualistic trait or an unequivocal good, as much of contemporary creativity discourses do. I analyze cultural depictions of creative digital youth in order to uncover how specific understandings of creativity are constructed as biologically inherent, socially necessary, and economically productive as well as requiring precise social and material arrangements for development through youth engagements with digital media. In so doing, I interrogate how constructions of contemporary youth as both naturally creative as well as inherently technological articulate autonomy, personal responsibility, entrepreneurship, and risk as necessary for both these future creative workers as well as the adults tasked to raise them.

The Digital Is Kid Stuff demonstrates how contemporary discourses about creativity refracted through figures of digital youth mediate changing conceptions of subjecthood, education, labor, civic engagement, and the nation under the dominance of neoliberal economic and political conditions in early twenty-first-century American digital culture. At stake is understanding not only who and what are valued through discussions of creative digital youth and those responsible for raising these future workers but also who and what are excluded from the future world promised by the creative economy.

Generating Digital Youth and Digital Culture

My investigation into youth, digital media, and creativity begins with understanding that there is little that is natural about the cultural coupling of youth and digital media. Belief that innate aptitude with computing technologies is a defining feature of youth, and often through the presumed exclusion (and confusion) of adults, demonstrates more how adult subjects grapple with the uncertainties, hopes, and fears that accompany emerging digital media technologies and the potential impacts such technologies might have rather than expressing some true relation between digital media and youth per se. After all, conceptions of youth are not necessarily or exclusively about actual youth subjects themselves. Conceptions of youth also function as vessels for adults' hopes and anxieties, reflecting social preoccupations of their respective times and contexts.[9] Youth in this regard can function as prime sites for adults to make sense of, celebrate, and dismiss emerging—that is, new and future—media technologies.

A cartoon by Benjamin Schwartz in a May 2016 issue of the *New Yorker,* for instance, depicts a forensic analyst and a police officer examining a headless and suited corpse seated in an office chair. Smoke fumes from the dead body's neck, as a mobile phone displaying the trademark ghost icon of the social media platform Snapchat rests in the lifeless left hand. The punch line that the situation "looks like another case of someone over forty trying to understand Snapchat" juxtaposes the serious crime scene investigation with what is ironically suggested to be the culprit: attempting to comprehend social media and youth culture, treated as one and the same. The illustration hyperbolizes an imagined insurmountable generational gap between adults, represented by the corpse and the investigators, and youth, suggested by Snapchat as the then-latest of a seemingly unending rotation of emerging social media platforms popular with and popularly associated with youth. This satirical treatment of social media and youth culture as deadly to adults renders both social media and youth culture as not only confounding but also dismissible, implying that it is not worth the effort to try to understand something inconsequential as well as figuratively (and fatally) incomprehensible to adults.

Since the 1990s, digital generation discourses prevalent in U.S. culture have explicitly coupled descriptions of contemporary youth intimately with emerging digital technologies and in distinct contrast with earlier generations. Terms such as the "digital generation," the "net generation," "cyberkids," "digital natives," the "app generation," and "iGen," for example, all attempt to characterize the cohort of contemporary children, adolescents, and other youth subjects as one born into and shaped by ubiquitous computing technologies, mobile screens, and social media platforms.[10] In particular, Don Tapscott's 1998 book *Growing Up Digital: The Rise of the Net Generation* has been an influential touchstone in contemporary discussions of digital youth.[11] Celebrating a generation he believes is equipped to be both more playful and more democratic, Tapscott contends that the contemporary youth growing up with digital technologies will prove to be a promising "force for social transformation."[12]

Subsequent constructions of a digital generation, however, often conflictingly portray the coupling of contemporary youth and digital technologies as both the hope for the future and the sign of end times. With regards to youth and social media platforms, for example, optimistic figures like Clay Shirky, who argues that digital technologies enable users new forms of ad hoc political organization, encounter pessimistic figures like Sherry Turkle, who argues that online interactions isolate users by devaluing face-to-face communication.[13] Although anchored to some degree in actual youth and technological practices, as David Buckingham contends, such discussions demonstrate how "the combination of childhood and technology serves as a powerful focus for much broader hopes and fears about social change."[14]

From the Silent Generation and Baby Boomers to Generation X and Millennials, attempts to define generations have explored a range of factors of varying primacy in seeking to identify differences in social age believed to make a difference, including shared experiences of major historic events, psychological dispositions, and economic pressures and opportunities.[15] As such, marking contemporary youth through labels of "digital generation," "net generation," "cyberkids," and other similar terms expresses the desire to attribute primary influence to media technologies for dividing age populations into generations.[16] For instance, in constructing contemporary youth as a product of pervasive computing and internet technologies, Tapscott's argument about a net generation also differentiates the older Baby Boomer generation as a cohort whose members grew up through the dominance of television during the mid-twentieth century.[17]

Whether distinguished by different media technologies, wars, or other cultural factors, however, generations are discursive constructs deployed to discuss age-bounded populations in relation to others, which may not directly reflect the experiences of those they are imagined to characterize.[18] For example, contemporary constructions of Millennials as a generation demonstrate how generational discourses are not only attempts to explain existing differences in a population due to age but are also the deliberate product of market logics and advertising. As Michael Serazio shows, advertising forces and media industries beginning in the early twenty-first century strategically constructed a Millennial generation that attributed to U.S. teenagers "a perceived technological intimacy" in order to sell digital technologies, particularly to these supposed Millennial consumers.[19]

Additionally, broad generational claims risk essentializing differences between generations and effacing important variations among a generation presumed to be uniform as well as in the conditions of their emergence.[20] For instance, the term "digital native" has also been used widely alongside "digital generation" to characterize contemporary youth as organically part of an increasingly digital world. While often attributed to Marc Prensky for popularization of the term in 2001 or to John Perry Barlow or Douglas Rushkoff for early suggestions of a metaphoric distinction between native and immigrant computer users in 1996, Turkle's 1995 book *Life on the Screen: Identity in the Age of the Internet* suggests the logic of "digital nativism" through claims that "today's children are growing up in the computer culture; all the rest of us are at best its naturalized citizens."[21] Consequently, conceptions of digital natives treat computing technologies as increasingly constitutive of the present and the future, suggesting that the world must be understood as increasingly digital through the emergence of digital natives.

Despite its popularity, "digital native" has been criticized for eliding the work of acquiring technological literacies as well as for the citizenship framework it inscribes in order to mark generational age. danah boyd argues, for instance, that such a term ignores that "becoming literate in a networked age requires hard work, regardless of age," whether supposedly "native" or otherwise.[22] The label of "digital native," like "digital generation," presumes effortless and natural youth encounters with digital media, yet acquiring digital literacy requires access to computers, economic and cultural resources, and time that are unevenly distributed across gender, race, class, geography, and other factors.[23] Moreover, as Jodi A. Byrd argues, such use of "native" and related "tribal" language to mark different groups rehearses U.S. settler colonial discourses that conceive of "sovereign Indigenous nations [as] warring ethnic factions hindering the destiny of the United States," all while Indigenous subjects are often imagined as of the past and operating outside the modern digital world.[24]

Although explicit digital generation discourses gained prominence in the 1990s, interest in the intersection of youth and digital technologies predates the coining of such generational labels as the "digital generation," the "net generation," or "digital natives." Images of youth in popular media and in political debates beginning in the 1970s, for instance, were cultural sites of conflict for shaping public opinion over increasingly available computing technologies and computing practices to the public, suggesting how the public should understand, accept, or regulate a growing digital world. For example, while the film *WarGames* (John Badham, 1983) characterized computing networks and hacking as adolescent in nature and, thus, potentially dangerous without adequate paternalistic government intervention, 1980s magazines such as *Microkids* and *Family Computing* mobilized images of children to domesticate personal and home computing technologies and hacking as family-friendly.[25] These intersections of youth and digital media articulate and negotiate competing views over emerging technologies through their perceived relationship to, impact on, and associations with youth.

In particular, Neil Selwyn explains that "notions of children and technology have long been used to 'sell' technology to a society sometimes resistant to such change" by rendering that technology as beneficial to children and youth.[26] As one such example of this, Mizuko Ito demonstrates that the emergence of the category of "edutainment," which characterized consumer software aimed at combining education with entertainment and designed specifically for children, was instrumental in reframing the adult technology of the computer.[27] Previously understood as a tool of academic research, military operations, and business, edutainment software rendered computers as a technology suitable and necessary for children's education during the 1980s and early 1990s. While computing and childhood became increasingly linked together, however, this linking would privilege and prioritize boys' engagements with computing to the exclusion of girls'.[28] Carly A. Kocurek explores an element of this history by examining how the once family-centric arcade and digital gaming culture of the United States beginning in the 1970s would be revived and marketed as the domain of boys and young men following the 1983 industry-wide crash.[29] Such images of youth and digital technologies, in mediating public attitudes toward emerging computing technologies, were precursors to the ensuing digital generation discourses, which not only strove to normalize the presence of digital technologies and their relationship to youth but also shaped who counts among digital youth.

Generational discourses, including discourses about digital youth, manifest the preoccupations of those defining population-wide age differences to make sense of large-scale sociocultural and economic shifts, such as shifts in target consumer bases, in media technologies, and in dominant modes of work. Whether in favor of or anxious about computing technologies, debates over digital youth imagine the kinds of adult subjects that they can—or perhaps must—become through their encounters with digital media. Constructions of youth becoming innovative entrepreneurs inventing new mobile apps or becoming screen-addicted Instagrammers with millions of followers but no intimate friends suggest some of the hopes and fears about the subjects that emerging digital media technologies may produce. Informed by this, *The Digital Is Kid Stuff* examines what youth are expected to create within digital culture and how digital culture creates contemporary youth as a generation preparing to contribute to a creative economy. I demonstrate how creative economy discourses mobilize the supposed innate kinship between digital media and youth to negotiate and naturalize the economic insecurity and precarious labor pervasive under the auspices of creative work in an increasingly digital world.

Cultivating Creativity through the Creative Child

Today, creativity operates as an organizing value for political, economic, and cultural life in the United States. As Amy F. Ogata argues, "The pervasiveness of the creativity discourse suggests that [contemporary America] remains heavily invested in its promises."[30] In addition to its central role in business management literature, such as the work of marketing consultant and self-branding advocate Tom Peters, creativity has been characterized as the engine for social reform and revitalization at various scales.[31] Richard Florida, for example, has published influential work on the creative class, what he describes as the emerging population of flexible workers whose wealth of ideas hold potential for urban renewal.[32] And at the national level, President Barack Obama has argued during his presidency for the need to develop and express creativity for economic growth and national prosperity.[33]

Although figures since the mid-twentieth century have advocated for the economic and political value of creativity, presumed as a natural and good individual human quality, only more recently have critical studies interrogated the ideological and cultural histories informing contemporary understandings of creativity itself.[34] *The Digital Is Kid Stuff* engages with and contributes to this growing body of critical work by investigating how creative economy discourses hinge technological innovation, economic development, and nation-building on images of youth, specifically creative digital youth. In so doing, I suggest that constructions of naturally creative digital youth mediate the increasing uncertainty and precarity associated with the rise of a creative labor economy.

While a prominent concept in popular, political, and economic discourses today, modern conceptions of creativity coalesced and gained prominence in the United States during the mid-twentieth century through the confluence of a range of efforts that coupled creativity with both democracy and individualism. Drawing on earlier concepts of imagination, wonder, curiosity, invention, and originality, creativity as a description of individualistic thinking and expression was positioned against social convention and conformity, as it transitioned from being a subject of research first in the 1940s into a public national value by the 1970s.[35] Many figures during the early postwar period sought to understand and advocate for the value of individual autonomy as a national project against mass conformity and social dependence, suggestive of the perceived differences between democracy and its enemies—both fascism and communism. This would shape contemporary understandings of creativity as individual and autonomous, since the model "creative figure was an intuitive and independent character who was also natural, artistic, and conscientious."[36]

Concerted efforts in the 1940s by sociological, anthropological, and psychological experts along with Bauhaus artists who fled Europe during World War II constructed what Fred Turner defines as a democratic personality.[37] Psychologist Erich Fromm, anthropologist Margaret Mead, and architect Walter Gropius, among others, for instance, worked to create the aspirational image of a democratic personality that stressed integrated, critical, and creative individuality against the dangerous mass conformity that fascist and communist enemies represented. Moreover, psychologists including J. P. Guilford, Carl Rogers, and Abraham H. Maslow participated in research during the 1950s and 1960s that sought to account for creativity, helping to propel the term "creativity" itself to wider popular usage during the period. Such figures, in addition to studying creativity as a highly individualized and complexly developed psychological trait, further advocated the value of understanding creativity for economic and national prosperity.

By the close of the 1940s, constructions of children had already become increasingly vital to this emerging and evolving twentieth-century discourse of creativity.[38] For instance, Maslow articulated his influential understanding of individualistic creativity through descriptions of children as natural models of creativity itself.[39] This modern discourse of creativity as well as the modern image of the creative child evolved and was cemented during this period through the popularization of personality psychology, child development studies, parenting literature, and educational reforms in the United States that characterized

creativity and the development of the creative child as a national project during the Cold War.[40]

According to Ogata, "at an ideological level, creativity provided a
foil for the preoccupations of the age. Positioned against the critique
of social conforming, creativity stood for an admirable individuality"
and was manifest in the modern creative child, which joined several
earlier Western images of children and childhood together.[41] Drawing
on seventeenth- and eighteenth-century Enlightenment thinkers, including John Locke, Jean-Jacques Rousseau, and Maria and Richard
Lovell Edgeworth, the modern creative child was born malleable and
required the appropriate settings, tools, and training to develop into
proper adults. As an inspired creature, the modern creative child also
echoed William Wordsworth's and other Romanticists' views of the
naturally wondrous child. And as a figure who would secure the future
of the nation, the modern creative child grew to be seen as increasingly
precious, both socially and economically, across the twentieth and into
the twenty-first centuries.[42]

In contemporary discourses, the cultural significance attributed to
children, childhood, and youth as sites for mediating societal preoccupations and changes links youth intimately with the future—rendering
youth as a symbol for the future—which is particularly prevalent in the
rhetorical mobilization of imperiled youth. Images of imperiled youth
or youth in crisis suggest that youth subjects are vulnerable and at
risk, and, as youth is also linked to the future, so, too, is the future.[43]
According to Charles R. Acland, the image of youth in crisis "acts as a re-
pository for social concerns and serves as an impetus for debate. 'Youth'
is the location of social concern and social desire, fear, and pleasure."[44]
Constructions of youth in crisis not only express beliefs about the present and future impacts of social changes, whether hopeful or fearful,
but also prescribe specific attitudes and actions for adults to adopt in
the purported interest of saving imperiled youth.[45] As a result, following
Lee Edelman, constructions of children as they have become increasingly tied to the future also "[serve] to regulate political discourse,"
since "whatever refuses this mandate by which our political institutions compel the collective reproduction of the Child must appear as a
threat not only to the organization of a given social order but also, and
far more ominously, to social order as such."[46] Consequently, competing

views over what is best for society and for the future often find expression in competing claims over what is best for youth, and vice versa.

The modern creative child articulated during the midcentury was constructed as such an image of imperiled youth, one who needed to develop their own individual character under the guidance of adults through unrestrained but carefully directed self-expression and creativity, which embodied particular conceptions of an ideal creative and democratic subject as part of a national project. The future of the nation vis-à-vis the child was believed to depend on how adults would raise children. The future promise of the modern creative child can only be fulfilled through proper parenting and education. Insufficient nurturing or excessive restriction of the child in creative capacities would stunt psychological growth, undermine self-esteem, and perhaps foster, instead, the development of a fascist or totalitarian personality prone to mass conformity rather than a more democratically framed autonomous individuality. While the specific contours of the imperilment have shifted, such as in the particular threats believed to be present, the imperiled modern creative child and the unquestioned investment in creativity as a national U.S. project persist to this day, evinced in the contemporary intersection of youth, digital media, and creativity.

Although images of imperiled childhood and youth in the United States are central to contemporary cultural and political thought, axes of difference such as race, gender, sexuality, class, and ability impact the mobilization of distinct images of children and youth subjects as stand-ins for the future, since not all children are constructed equally as precious, valuable, or at risk. For instance, Robin Bernstein demonstrates how the predominant image of the vulnerable and innocent child in need of care is primarily constituted through whiteness at the historic denial of that same innocent childhood to Black youth.[47] Responding to Edelman, José Esteban Muñoz underscores the presumed whiteness of the child as political symbol in the United States by arguing that "this monolithic figure of the child . . . is indeed always already white."[48] While whiteness may constitute the normative conception of childhood as imperiled in the United States, however, this has not precluded images of nonwhite children to serve a similar albeit nonidentical function for particular purposes.[49] As such, the cultural politics of children, childhood, and youth is constituted through many diverse images of children and youth—aged, raced, gendered, classed, et cetera—operating in both coherent and incongruous ways within changing historical milieus.

Constructions of childhood and youth subjects growing up into adults have also served to negotiate and naturalize ideologies constructing social difference, including gender, race, and sexuality, through prescriptions of normative development. This is despite how, as Kathryn Bond Stockton demonstrates, children consistently "grow sideways" and, thus, complicate normative and simplistic linear expectations of development, growth, and maturation.[50] Beginning in the late nineteenth century, for instance, psychologist G. Stanley Hall proposed the racist developmental model of recapitulation theory, which claimed that individual development directly embodied, or recapitulated, evolutionary development such that all children were born "savages" (read: nonwhite) and that only white children were capable of growing into truly civilized adults. As Gail Bederman explains, recapitulation theory held that "children were not merely metaphoric savages; their somatic makeup made children physically recapitulate primitive evolutionary stages," which manifested white supremacist ideologies by positioning whiteness, adulthood, and modern civilization as developmentally more advanced both individually and evolutionarily compared to nonwhite races, children, and primitive savagery.[51] Providing another example, Jules Gill-Peterson traces how trans children were instrumentalized in the medicalization and naturalization of specific understandings of sex and gender via a racialized conception of plasticity beginning in the early twentieth century.[52]

While constructions of children as creative, innovative, and inventive were not new—nineteenth-century French poet Charles Baudelaire, for example, wrote about children as examples of originality to describe the individual and expressive qualities of painter Constantin Guy—the mid-twentieth century marked the first time that the modern creative child was discussed, commodified, and marketed widely to parents, largely to white middle-class parents who could afford to buy literally into the project of raising creative children.[53] Describing this midcentury image of the child, Ogata notes that "in the postwar era, the romantic child was given new life as an imaginative figure whose natural gifts could be developed through correct parenting, studied, quantified, and assessed in new postwar psychological research, and constituted materially in a wide variety of consumer goods and media."[54] In this way, the study and marketing of a modern creative child with a particular desired developmental trajectory at potential risk continues into the present, as the creative child still operates as an individualistic and nationalistic project in the United Sates, cementing particular understandings of what creativity is, how it works, what it can do, and how to cultivate it.[55]

Alongside the rise of computing technologies and digital media, images of midcentury creative children evolved into constructions of creative digital youth by the close of the millennium, a cohort of youth whose creativity was imagined to be shaped by and would need to be channeled into technological innovations for the benefit of all. But as the linking of youth with digital media is not a natural truth, so, too, is the cultural association of youth (and specifically children) with creativity. Images of children constructed as inherently creative subjects were central to articulating and disseminating the modern conception of creativity dominantly in operation today, advancing an individualistic understanding of creativity as something natural, necessary, and also requiring careful cultivation through the modern creative child in need of proper development. In this book, I examine ways in which debates over how this modern creative child is now expected to grow up in an increasingly digital world are instrumentalized and contested in creative economy discourses.

Working the Creative Economy

Having discussed the historic coupling of youth both to digital media and to creativity, I now turn to the rise of creative economy discourses, their celebration of youthful workers, and how they negotiate the increasing economic precarity that these youthful workers face in the creative labor economy itself. Creativity in the contemporary moment operates as "*the* critical paradigm of economic growth," following Oli Mould, manifest in pervasive discussions over the promise of the creative economy, creative labor, creative industries, the creative class, and creative workers for all.[56] The term "creative industries," in particular, emerged in the 1990s to describe the growing economic sector centered around cultural labor, such as in media production and publishing, design and advertising, as well as software development. Although

Australian Prime Minister Paul Keating first introduced the label "creative industries" during his term in the early 1990s, popularization of the language of "creative industries" and "creative economy" is typically attributed to UK Prime Minister Tony Blair and a pro-business New Labour administration in the late 1990s.[57] This rhetorical promotion of "creativity" as an economic concern appeared in key government documents such as the first *Creative Industries Mapping Document* report in 1998 and the 2001 green paper *Culture and Creativity: The Next Ten Years,* both of which were developed by what is now the UK Department for Digital, Culture, Media and Sport. As Andrew Ross asserts, Blair's adoption of the concept emphasized "technological enthusiasm, the cult of youth, branding and monetization fever, and ceaseless organizational change," which have become pervasive features of creative economy discourses.[58]

Through its coining, "creative industries" offered a celebratory spin on what the Frankfurt School had initially criticized in the early twentieth century as the "culture industry."[59] Theodor Adorno and Max Horkheimer articulated the concept of the culture industry to explain how popular culture was itself constituted through manufactured and standardized media and products for mass consumption by passive audiences, which would largely reinforce the continued operations of capitalism without critical attention.[60] Championing of the creative industries, then, manifests in the increasing economic and political investment in culture industries as key sources of value generation.

The ways in which creative industries and creative economy policies emerge and manifest in different geographies, whether national, regional, or by municipality, however, are not uniform. Although discourses of the creative economy, creative industries, and creative labor may seem ubiquitous and homogeneous, different geographic contexts participate in and influence such discourses and practices in varied and uneven ways. Ross notes, for instance, distinctions between the character of creative industries and creative economy policies in the larger European context compared to the U.S. variant.[61] Many European nations demonstrate deliberately temporary moves by the state to activate what is believed to be latent entrepreneurial and creative potential among their citizenry until they become autonomous. In contrast, the United States negotiates complicated relations to the First Amendment that would suggest that creative industry and economy policies ought "to maintain a strict constitutional separation between the state and cultural expression."[62] In addition to accounting for how countries negotiate their particular relationship to creative industries and creative economy policies, particular geographic contexts, typically those characterized under the Global South, have historically been excluded, by discourses or by material resources, from the privileged project of the creative industries that originate in and center primarily white American, European, and Commonwealth nations.

In his critique of contemporary creative industries in the West, Pascal Gielen traces how the understanding of creative labor developed alongside increasing neoliberalization starting in the 1970s.[63] Framed against the rigidity of conventional institutions and traditionally fixed models of work, creative labor encouraged a desire for autonomy among its workers to be in control of their individual lives alongside valuing creativity as an enduring capacity to produce novelty for the market. As Gielen notes, "the creative work ethic is against commitment to the rigid demands of an institution," which suggests that institutions as social organizations interfere with individual autonomy.[64] The idealized worker is autonomous and productive, best captured in the flexible, mobile, and self-sufficient creative individual free of staid institutions.

This construction of a self-sufficient and self-reliant worker, however, operates to mask and normalize the increasing socioeconomic precarity that accompanies increasing neoliberal governmental and economic practices. The creative labor economy is deeply coherent with neoliberalism, understood as interconnected economic practices and government policies that function to erode the securities previously offered by the welfare state, undermine worker securities and rights, advance privatization and free market ideologies, and welcome increasing entrepreneurial capitalist development and expansion.[65] Such shifts away from state-provided support and secure long-term career opportunities have resulted in increasing work options that are short-term, piecemeal, and contract-based. Long-term stable careers are now commonly replaced by temporary employment organized around projects and gigs as exemplified by the insecure work offered by the creative industries.[66]

Creative economy discourses typically offer creative labor and the identity of a creative worker as the highly desirable alternatives to work characterized as individually unfulfilling, such as work under the category of the service sector—including retail, waitstaffing, and other customer service-oriented professions. As Angela McRobbie demonstrates, "Many young working-class people now become self-employed in the cultural field (as 'stylists', make-up artists, or by setting up club nights, or making dance tracks at home in their bedrooms) as an escape from the inevitability of unemployment, or in preference to an unrewarding job in the service sector."[67] Moreover, creative labor enables freelance and self-employed workers the fantasy of owning their individual means of production in a world where stable employment is an increasing rarity.[68] Consequently, creativity operates as the prized resource for individual success, while "creative" serves as an aspirational label for individual workers seeking to survive increasingly precarious and unstable economic conditions under the logics of creative economy discourses by supposedly "doing what you love" rather than hating what you do.[69] The freelance or self-employed creative worker, then, serves as the optimistic spin on what Gerald Raunig terms the "precariat," the post-Fordist manifestation of the disempowered proletariat worker in a deeply precarious work world.[70]

As part of the logics of contemporary creative labor economies, creative workers as autonomous individuals are expected to support themselves in the face of precarity. This is especially true, since creativity is conceived as "inherent in personhood (childhood, adolescence and young adulthood; less often, old age), which has the potential to be turned into a set of capacities" productive for the market through forms of self-fashioning and self-regulation.[71] This creative "*dispositive* is encouraging rather than coercive, and the imperative to 'be creative' is an invitation to discover one's own capabilities, to embark on a voyage of self-discovery" but also to weather economic insecurity individually given the lack of social or state support for success.[72] The emphasis on the individual's responsibility to use their own creative capacities to secure economic and social success coheres tightly with enduring bootstrap ideology core to contemporary neoliberalism in the United States.[73]

Moreover, computing and digital technologies are central to the operations of the creative labor economy and the life of creative workers. Many of the desired qualities of creative workers and their labor, such as flexible work scheduling and mobility, rely on infrastructures of a networked and ubiquitous computing culture. Social media platforms and technologies, including YouTube, Twitter, and Facebook, are recognized as prized products of creative labor but also function as vital platforms for sharing creative products and for maintaining and improving employability, such as through self-branding and networking practices.[74] Additionally, debates about creativity and creative work are also often closely tied to discussions of digital computing technologies. Pierre Lévy, Lawrence Lessig, as well as Shirky, for example, each have argued that recent computing technologies are transforming the conditions for creativity itself.[75]

Buckingham argues that Tapscott and other optimistic commentators discussing digital technologies and youth "place a generational spin on what has come to be called the *Californian ideology*—the form of cyberlibertarianism favored not just by Internet activists, but also (perhaps paradoxically) by many marketing gurus."[76] Referencing Richard Barbrook and Andy Cameron's initial characterization of the Californian ideology, Buckingham identifies that discourses proclaiming the promise of digital media for improving social conditions through youth often echo the philosophical and political tenets of contemporary Silicon Valley computing culture.[77] As a brand of libertarianism with roots in mid-twentieth-century counterculture, the Californian ideology combines techno-utopian aspirations and American neoliberal politics into commitments to entrepreneurial risk-taking and free market capitalism largely through technological innovations. Where the image of the midcentury creative child reinforced postwar ideologies through the treatment of creativity both as an inherent quality of children and as a national project for economic and political prosperity during the Cold War, contemporary discussions of creative digital youth reinforce neoliberal ideologies informing digital and computing industries, especially through the intersections of creative economy discourses and the Californian ideology.

Additionally, the cultural mythology of Silicon Valley as the center of commercial digital technologies traffics in origin stories that champion creative young entrepreneurs as the primary drivers of innovation and economic growth.[78] Idolized figures of Silicon Valley, including Bill Gates, Steve Jobs, and Mark Zuckerberg, demonstrate how the tech industry celebrates images of the youthful creative male genius, often demonstrated in the emphasis on their successes despite all having dropped out of college.[79] As Stephanie Ricker Schulte contends,

"Representations of industry executives as anti-establishment teenagers were tempered by representations of those individuals as 'good capitalists,'" suggesting that in the cultural imagination the archetype of the genius college dropout could be harnessed productively through savvy business acumen toward technological innovation.[80]

However, dominant understandings of creative labor in Western digital culture often foreground individual white men centered largely in North America and in Europe, demonstrating how the privileged category of creativity is unevenly recognized and denied within the racial and gendered politics of technological innovation. As Lilly Irani argues, understandings of technology and of creativity are not divorced from histories of colonialism, racism, and gender politics.[81] For instance, the gendering and valuing of computing technologies and computing industries as the domain of men over the course of the twentieth century involved eliding women's early contributions during World War II.[82] Similarly, as Lisa Nakamura demonstrates, important work by Navajo women in the manufacture of computing technologies in the mid-twentieth century has largely been ignored by conventional histories of digital computing that center white men.[83] Such effacement omits the contributions of these Navajo women, which highlights how histories of colonialism, race politics, and gender enable and obfuscate the historic recognition of what constitutes and who possesses creativity in technological domains. In this case, Fairchild Semiconductor, the company that employed these women, commodified racialized understandings of these workers as Indigenous subjects and their cultural practices of weaving to market the intricate circuitry at the time. This also underscores how markers of identity and difference can also be purposefully instrumentalized and commodified to mark creativity and innovation in particular contexts.[84]

Exclusions from the history of computing and contributions to creative technological work also manifest in the ways that creative labor only comes to describe particular kinds of labor as privileged, both domestically and internationally, and at particular times or within specific industries. For instance, Anita Say Chan emphasizes that discourses that center Silicon Valley and the United States as the vanguard of computing elide the technological advancements, practices, and cultures vibrant in "peripheral" localities around the world, such as in Peru.[85] Additionally, conceiving of innovation as occurring largely in

the West relies on both externalizing labor conceived as "uncreative" to the Global South—including work in call centers and manufacturing plants—as well as racializing labor by naming and bifurcating the privileged creative work of design in the West from the supposedly "uncreative" manufacturing labor in East Asian geographies, such as China.[86]

Despite associations linking Japan with technological advancement, as many critics have demonstrated, U.S. discourses about modern Japanese innovation often express less a celebration of Japanese creativity and more concern over a looming threat of East Asian economic dominance, including persistent unease about Chinese development and innovation in particular.[87] As an example of this distrust of East Asian innovation, former editor-in-chief of *Wired* magazine Chris Anderson argues that the rise of new commercially available technologies for scalable manufacture, such as 3D printers, means that "manufacturing companies in the United States and Europe are increasingly able to compete with low-cost labor in China."[88] Anderson's comment depicts China as a competing manufacturing force that the United States must surpass, which continues American constructions of competition between U.S. and Chinese industries beginning in the Cold War. These constructions championed images of the individual ingenuity of the citizens of capitalist America against images of the racialized and uniform others engaged in mass industrial manufacture in communist China.[89] And yet amid anxieties over the perceived threat of East Asian innovation as a challenge to the United States, Japanese digital game designers have consistently been exalted as creative geniuses in the United States in ways "similar to the mythos generated around tech 'geniuses' like Steve Jobs, who put personality and artistry into products thought to be merely profit driven."[90] These histories of computing and digital technologies highlight how uneven and shifting negotiations, exploitations, and exclusions along racial, cultural, and gendered axes have functioned largely to privilege Western white masculinity in conceptions of creativity and creative labor that inform the relations among contemporary creative economy discourses and digital culture in the United States.

The contemporary celebration of creativity and creative labor masks the increasing economic insecurity, unstable employment, and uneven access to the privileges and prestige afforded to that creativity and creative labor constitutive of the rise of creative industries, creative economy policies, and creative economy discourses. In *The Digital Is Kid Stuff,* I examine how images of creative digital youth mediate and normalize these facets of a precarious creative labor economy in digital culture that maintains that creativity under neoliberal capitalism is essential now and for the future.

Investigating Creative Digital Youth

The Digital Is Kid Stuff draws on work in cultural histories of childhood and youth, studies in digital culture, literary and media studies, and critical and historical approaches to creativity in order to investigate contemporary images of creative digital youth as key sites of meaning making in the creative economy. While references to actual youth subjects may appear throughout my analysis, my primary interest is in how youth, digital media, and creativity are imagined closely together as part of broader creative economy discourses. I unpack how images of creative digital youth as well as debates over how they should be raised for a creative economy in an increasingly digital culture mediate our relationship to changes in social life under the dominance of neoliberal economic and political conditions in early twenty-first-century America, including changes in our understanding of subjecthood, education, labor, civic engagement, and the nation.

This book focuses primarily on the contemporary American context; however, the subjects, technologies, and discourses that constitute these discussions, while perhaps centered in and around, or at least pass through, the United States, are not confined to its geographic or cultural boundaries. Sarah Brouillette, for example, points to the central influence of mid-twentieth century American psychologists in contemporary creative economy discourses in her study of British creative industries.[91] Similarly, Buckingham's examination of digital generation discourse argues that his broad arguments have "international resonance" despite the fact that his primary case is British youth and technology.[92] And Barbrook and Cameron argue that the globalized economy enables the Californian ideology to spread worldwide as Silicon Valley computing serves as a model for high-tech industries and innovation abroad.[93] Consequently, this book treats the American context as a particularly rich though not totalizing site for understanding the contemporary intersection of youth, digital media, and creativity as a vital element of the rise of precarious creative labor economies. To do so, I anchor each chapter of *The Digital Is Kid Stuff* with a key media object or cultural practice that possesses a dominant or emerging association with creative youth subjects and digital culture, serving as exemplary touchstones for cultural debates at the intersection of youth, digital culture, and creativity. Specifically, I situate textual and formal analysis of the digital game *Minecraft* (Mojang, 2009/2011), the print magazine *Make,* the social media platform Instagram, and the speculative technological design practice of design fiction within broader discourses of creative labor and the creative economy. In so doing, I demonstrate how hopes and anxieties about the development and expression of creative digital youth negotiate underlying ideological contradictions I identify as part and parcel to creative labor economies more broadly: the relationship between the individual and the social in creative development and expression *(Minecraft),* regulating the self-governance of risk and responsibility toward amateur innovation *(Make),* the tension between authenticity and artificiality in self-branding on social media (Instagram), and the cultivation and restriction of the imagination toward productive ends in design work (design fiction). Ultimately, I explore how images of creative digital youth, especially as they are imagined predominantly through white middle-class masculinity, shape understandings of the impacts of precarious creative labor economies on both youth and adults as well as how they privilege particular gendered, racialized, and classed subjects, practices, and histories at the exclusion of others with regard to who can participate in the creative economy and what it might offer for the future.

I have organized the chapters into a developmental narrative of a creative worker, from childhood through adolescence and into adulthood, with each stage representing a particular problem for creative development and creative labor. Beginning with understanding how children are constructed as naturally creative and technological, the first chapter investigates the historic and ideological contours of the archetypal creative subject of digital culture by examining the increasing educational use of *Minecraft*—a digital game wherein players gather resources and build to survive on virtual islands. I argue that *Minecraft* weaves together two influential histories that tether modern creativity centrally to individual autonomy and precarity: construction toys and island narratives. I illustrate how *Minecraft* allows players to experiment with various social and environmental conditions that have long been central to debates about creativity, rooted in the island narrative as the generic site of negotiating enduring conflicts between individual autonomy and social dependence such as in Daniel Defoe's *Robinson Crusoe* (1719) and Francis Bacon's *New Atlantis* (1624). In situating *Minecraft* with other island narratives concerned with inventiveness, including Abraham H. Maslow's influential theories of psychological development, I demonstrate how modern creativity is conceived of as a highly individualistic character trait, one best developed and expressed through risk-taking amid precarious conditions and in direct opposition to social convention, through images of children as naturally creative subjects. I then show how *Minecraft* players not only become such creative individuals through a simulation of surviving Crusoe's island but also acquire computational literacies as they encounter the game as it is connected to other digital technologies and subjects. Through my analysis of *Minecraft* and player practices of creation, particularly modding, I suggest that modders function as the archetypal creative subjects of digital modernity, subjects that despite cultural and political desires to be understood as autonomous are inextricable from their social ties and dependencies.

The second chapter examines debates over how to raise children in order to cultivate what is believed to be their innate creativity toward producing future innovations. Specifically, this chapter explores how contemporary interests in maker, hacker, and do-it-yourself (DIY) cultures, in attempting to democratize technoscientific innovation without government interference, negotiate concerns over risk and responsibility through debates over child-rearing practices. I argue that *Make* magazine, an American periodical concerned with raising creative children under the banner of DIY, deploys constructions of children as naturally creative subjects to domesticate risk-taking by rendering it necessary for future innovations and by advocating personal responsibility for risks taken in the name of innovation. Through its parenting advice, *Make* encourages privatizing scientific education and research through creating domestic amateur workshops in order to raise children to become innovative and entrepreneurial risk-takers, individuals taught to self-govern their risks toward innovation responsibly. I show that *Make* reveals how the democratization of DIY science and technology intersects the politics of social reproduction through the creation of the workshop and the subjects who operate it when both are imaged as integral functions of the home rather than of the state. Furthermore, as I demonstrate, *Make*'s tethering of political legitimacy to domestic labor in support of amateur technoscientific innovation is distributed and recognized unevenly, since different adult subjects are privileged and excluded along gendered, racialized, and classed dimensions based on what is imagined as necessary for this work of DIY innovation and social reproduction. As part of a larger cultural interest toward forms of manual craftwork and expertise, *Make* as a product of Silicon Valley computing culture also expresses anxieties about raising creative children for an uncertain future.

In the third chapter, I explore anxieties regarding how adolescents individuate and socialize themselves through practices of creative self-presentation afforded by digital media. I begin by investigating the cultural imagination of social media as a specific source of public concern over the development of the creative self as adolescents mature into adults to inhabit an increasingly digital world, focusing on the amateur photography and social media platform Instagram in order to interrogate beliefs about the impact of social media on youth development. In particular, I examine the ubiquitous genre of photography one takes of oneself known as the "selfie" as a mechanism for creating and testing versions of oneself to present online. This practice of individuation and socialization occurs within the context of larger social imperatives that advocate self-branding as a creative act of authentic identity presentation to others and to the market. I argue that anxious debates concerning adolescents learning to individuate and socialize on online media platforms participate in the persistent history of how changing media ecologies demand renegotiation of preexisting social codes, since cultural discourses assign adolescents the cultural task of learning to individuate and socialize. Furthermore, I contend that the selfie, a common yet vilified practice associated closely with youth, upends preexisting conceptions of authenticity and artificiality in a world of self-branding. This in turn highlights the limit of recognizing the authentic self as a creative subject—as a site for creative work in its presentation to and socialization with others—particularly in how permissible identity performances, especially of racialized and minoritarian subjects, are policed by both peers and platforms in digitally mediated socialities.

The fourth and final chapter of this book interrogates discourses of design, which, I suggest, represents the most privileged form of work within the creative labor economy. Focusing particularly on the increasing popularity of speculative technological design practices, such as design fiction, science fiction prototyping, and value fiction, I unpack an ideology of design and the future pervasive in contemporary digital culture that values childlike imagination in laboring adults to imagine technological products through engagements with the genre of science fiction. I examine how design discourses throughout the twentieth and twenty-first centuries construct designers as the ideal laboring subjects of a creative economy. I argue that the discourses surrounding the specific practice of design fiction and other speculative technological design practices underscore how design generally, both as a postwar academic field of study as well as an omnipresent label for privileged forms of creative labor, is bound up in modern conceptions of futurity and practices of speculation. As such, I connect design to the field of futures studies as well as science fiction. I show how central to this cultural history of futurity and speculation are enduring attempts since the eighteenth century to cultivate while also regulating primarily white and middle-class children's imagination toward productive and inventive ends. Consequently, this chapter explores how the futures of contemporary digital culture are produced, proliferated, and foreclosed by designers who are expected to draw on their childlike imaginations as creative adult workers, asking how design and imaginative thinking might instead reimagine futures both that can exist beyond the consumer landscape that conventional industrial and commercial design takes for granted and that can include those historically excluded from participation.

Much is believed to be at stake at the intersection of youth, digital media, and creativity.

Rather than taking creative digital youth as a natural fact, however, *The Digital Is Kid Stuff* investigates how youth are instrumental to the creative economy not solely as the future labor force but as cultural sites for negotiating the political, economic, and ideological meanings of the creative economy itself. By critically attending to the ideological work that images of creative digital youth perform—often as symbolic figures of the promise of future innovation at perennial risk of improper development—this book examines how contemporary American digital culture makes sense of economic and political precarity under the guise of creative labor, creative industries, and the creative economy through figurations of creative digital youth. As much as images of creative digital youth task adults to shape youth in particular ways to contribute to the creative economy, such images compel adults to shape themselves in particular ways as well. This book is interested, then, in exploring what we are to make of creative digital youth.

CHAPTER 1

Minecraft and the Building Blocks of Creative Individuality

The digital game *Minecraft* has provided a focal point for discussions of creativity since its earliest developmental releases in 2009.[1] Created by Swedish programmer Markus "Notch" Persson and his game development company Mojang, the massively popular construction-based survival game enables players to explore, rearrange, and combine the various virtual blocks that constitute the virtual worlds it generates (see Figures 1, 2, 3, and 4). Responses by fans, educators, and academics to *Minecraft* often characterize it as both a tool for developing and showcasing creativity as well as a landmark in the history of digital gaming. As a platform for creative expression, for example, Greg Lastowka argues that "*Minecraft requires* players to be creative, even if that creativity is limited to designing a crude shelter or tunneling the layout of a mine."[2] Moreover, creation is central to *Minecraft* both during and after play as players not only create within the game but also outside of it, such as in the production of original artwork and instructional videos based on the game's content and player experiences. Regarding *Minecraft*'s place in gaming history, Logan Decker asserts that *Minecraft* represents "the future of gaming. You know, this collaboration, this emphasis on creativity, on freedom."[3]

Stemming from interest in the game's creative potential, educators have increasingly identified *Minecraft* as an adaptable technology well-suited for pedagogical use. For instance, in a video titled "Is Minecraft the Ultimate Educational Tool?" for PBS Idea Channel, host Mike Rugnetta argues that *Minecraft* as a customizable digital game allows teachers to cover diverse topics, including physics, mathematical probability, architecture, and drama.[4] While acknowledging the history of educational software preceding *Minecraft,* Rugnetta contends that most of that software has been limited in what can be taught. Example titles such as *Oregon Trail* (Minnesota Educational Computing Consortium,

FIGURE 1. *A player-created house and garden in* Minecraft. *(Source: Mojang,* Minecraft, *2011; screenshot by author.)*

FIGURE 2. *A player-created underground chicken farm in* Minecraft. *(Source: Mojang,* Minecraft, *2011; screenshot by author.)*

1971), *Reader Rabbit* (The Learning Company, 1983), and *Mavis Beacon* (The Software Toolworks, 1987) represent rigidly content-specific educational games. Against this, he contrasts *Minecraft* as a flexible educational platform amenable to a range of subjects. This adaptability that Rugnetta identifies results, in part, from *Minecraft*'s capacities for modding—user customization to alter and augment base technologies.

FIGURE 3. *A player-created underground library in* Minecraft. *(Source: Mojang,* Minecraft, *2011; screenshot by author.)*

FIGURE 4. *Several players together on a multiplayer* Minecraft *server beside a player-created portal. (Source: Mojang,* Minecraft, *2011; screenshot by author.)*

Writing for the Illinois Association for Gifted Children, Cathy Risberg describes *Minecraft* as "a highly effective classroom tool for personalizing the curriculum and promoting creativity, collaboration, and problem solving," emphasizing the game's ability to accommodate different curricular demands to encourage student development.[5] This is particularly important, Risberg suggests, as she characterizes children as "the inventors, creators, and leaders of tomorrow's world [who get] an early start in realizing their dreams by learning valuable skills in Minecraft."[6] Even Microsoft has taken notice of *Minecraft*'s popularity and educational potential, acquiring both the game title and Mojang for US$2.5 billion in the fall of 2014.[7]

While many identify *Minecraft* as a creative product and an incubator for creativity, in what follows I examine the ideological beliefs about creativity at play in and around the game, particularly within prevailing creative economy discourses. I trace *Minecraft*'s relationship to construction toys as well as fictional island narratives to investigate how creativity, commonly conceived as the capacity to create something new and original, functions as a privileged cultural concept that is understood as highly individual rather than social within the contemporary logics of creative labor in digital culture.[8] I begin by placing *Minecraft* and its virtual building blocks within a history of U.S. preoccupation with construction toys to unpack how discussions of toys, generally, and construction blocks, in particular, express cultural anxieties about cultivating creativity in children. Looking at a longer tradition of construction toys and linking this tradition to midcentury American psychological discourses about creativity, I then examine how contemporary conceptions of creativity negotiate tensions between the individual, understood as autonomous and original, and the social, associated with dependence and conformity.

To explore these tensions between the individual and the social further, I situate *Minecraft* in a genealogy of island fictions that narrate competing models of development for modern creative and inventive subjects. I argue that *Minecraft* as a digital game allows players to experiment with various sociopolitical and environmental conditions historically debated as necessary for shaping creative subjects and facilitating invention, rooted in island narratives that dramatize conflicts between the individual and the social, such as Francis Bacon's *New Atlantis* (1624) and Daniel Defoe's *Robinson Crusoe* (1719). *Minecraft* players become digitally inventive subjects by simulating a version of Crusoe's island and acquire proficiencies in code work through engagement with the game as software embedded in a network of players and media technologies. Finally, I examine the logics of modding as a central mode of creative invention embedded in the game of *Minecraft* and in the playing communities surrounding it to demonstrate how

Minecraft positions modders as the archetypal creative subjects of an increasingly digital modernity, individual subjects deeply tethered to their social ties despite cultural desires to believe otherwise.

Block by Block

Occupying a privileged position in contemporary American thought from Richard Florida's 2002 book describing a creative class to President Barack Obama's 2011 State of the Union address, creative economy discourses have situated creativity as the driving force for economic growth and national prosperity.[9] But while discourses since the mid-twentieth century often treat creativity as a natural human quality, it is only more recently that critical studies have sought to understand the ideologies that shape contemporary conceptions of creativity as a cultural construct.[10] In work examining midcentury consumer culture, for instance, Amy F. Ogata traces how the then-changing views of childhood alongside evolving cultural conceptions of creativity expressed anxieties over America's economic and political status in the postwar world.[11] I extend this body of critical scholarship to examine how *Minecraft* renders visible ways in which images of children and youth are mobilized in discourses about creativity in contemporary digital culture.[12]

Proponents of *Minecraft* assert that the digital game, although not initially designed for pedagogical use, is well-suited to support not only educational lessons but also individual creative development, highlighting specific cultural values at play.[13] Toys and the discourses surrounding them function as mediators connecting cultural conditions with underlying assumptions regarding children's education and, ultimately, beliefs about the adult world for which children are to prepare through the acquisition of desired skills and values.[14] As Mary Flanagan and Helen Nissenbaum argue, all social and material technologies are ladened with values—attitudes toward specific ideals, traits, and conditions.[15] In analyzing digital games, and by extension all toys, they assert that critics and designers must recognize how such technologies possess and express particular values at play.[16]

Going back several centuries, the educational and developmental potential housed in children's playthings—blocks in particular—has been of cultural interest since at least seventeenth-century philosopher

John Locke's suggestion for "Dice and Play-things, with the Letters on them, to teach Children the *Alphabet* by playing."[17] This focus of Locke's toy blocks on the alphabet, for example, underscored the sociocultural value attached to literacy, which late seventeenth-century readers in an increasingly literate public required in order to engage with Locke's own writings. As another example, Virginia Zimmerman's study of nineteenth-century scientific toys for children demonstrate not only the value placed on knowledge in natural history but also beliefs over how that knowledge should be taught through domesticating scientific concepts into recreational home life.[18] From learning foreign languages to improving running ability, recent interests in making educational, political, and fitness objectives more gamelike through processes of gamification similarly show how games privilege specific cultural values through play.[19]

Contemporary U.S. interests in and anxieties surrounding creativity are especially prominent in concerns regarding the role of proper education for children's development into creative adults, particularly toward the future of scientific and technological innovation via training in science, technology, engineering, and mathematics (STEM) fields. With respect to contemporary STEM fields, construction toys often anchor debates over children's education and play as they are imagined to affect creative development.[20] *Minecraft* fits into a popular American tradition of construction blocks and toys, since arguments for its use as a creative tool emphasize its sandbox nature, where players can build with virtual blocks of different materials and corresponding properties: wood, stone, sand, glass, iron, and so forth.[21] Emphasizing the block as the fundamental unit of the virtual world, the game's kinship with physical building toys, and the association between construction and creativity, the 2011 trailer for *Minecraft* declares, "Let's go to a place where everything is made of blocks, where the only limit is your imagination."[22] By articulating the limit of play as one's own imagination in an entire world fabricated by blocks at their disposal, the trailer suggests that the creative potential of *Minecraft* is both endless and highly individualized.

In his work on children and toy cultures in the United States, Gary Cross notes a distinctly American identification with construction toys beginning in the early twentieth century, which includes such playthings as electric train sets and Lincoln Logs.[23] Erector sets, for instance, were thought to shape boys' interests in science and engineering early in the twentieth century "when most adults had faith in a world of endless technological progress."[24] Continuing this affinity, postwar interest in construction toys—particularly abstract geometric blocks—coincided with then-contemporary psychological and political discussions of creativity, popularizations of child development theories, and expanding consumer culture.[25]

Current initiatives seeking to increase women's participation in STEM fields often similarly treat childhood as a key period of intervention in the historic gender disparity in STEM fields.[26] For instance, GoldieBlox, initially launched as a project on the online crowdfunding platform Kickstarter in 2012, sought to transform the genre of construction toys. According to founder and designer Debbie Sterling, construction toys had "for over a hundred years . . . been considered 'boys' toys."[27] Sterling developed GoldieBlox in order to "inspire the future generation of female engineers" by offering a construction toy suited to what she identified as girls' natural strengths and interests: "strong verbal skills" and "stories and characters."[28] While criticism of GoldieBlox argued that the toy series' pink and purple aesthetics and the discourses advertising it perpetuated conventional gender stereotypes and essentialized gender differences, GoldieBlox and responses to it not only indexed social anxieties around the presence of women in STEM fields (or lack thereof) but also reinforced specific conceptions of childhood development and gender identity tied to construction toys, which all presumed the inherent value of creativity and its relationship to STEM careers (see Figure 5).[29]

From Locke's alphabet dice to GoldieBlox, construction toys operate as sites not only of imagining what children can create with blocks but also what kinds of subjects such construction toys can create from those who encounter them. Similarly, discussions of playing *Minecraft* often focus on developing creativity through individual self-expression. In his introduction for Mojang at the 2011 Penny Arcade Expo, for example, Decker proclaimed that *Minecraft* "hands the creative keys over to the gamers," celebrating the freedom the game offers players to explore, construct, and express themselves.[30] Similarly, Common Sense Media, a nonprofit organization providing parental advice on digital games, television shows, and other media, describes *Minecraft* as "a sandbox-style game with open online play [fostering] creativity. . . . Players explore the

FIGURE 5. *Promotional image for the first GoldieBlox construction set, "GoldieBlox and the Spinning Machine," which featured a "girly" aesthetic in reimagining construction toys for girls. (Source: GoldieBlox, http://goldieblox.com/, 2013.)*

world and use the building blocks of the game to customize that world to create nearly anything they can imagine."[31] This description, in particular, highlights the virtual worlds created in *Minecraft* as ready material to shape, deploy, and craft at the discretion and pleasure of players. As a virtual construction toy, *Minecraft* and the discourses articulating its creative potential emphasize the centrality of individual autonomy and self-expression in contemporary conceptions of creativity.

Building Creative Individuality

Discussions of *Minecraft* and its virtual blocks emphasize how reception of construction toys have historically negotiated between the individual and the social, a tension central to modern conceptions of creativity that finds clear expression in concerns over the limits of creativity in construction toys themselves. This has been particularly the case with the history of the popular Danish construction toy brand LEGO. With its blocky graphics and construction-based gameplay, comparisons of

FIGURE 6. *Promotional image for the "The First Night" set as part of the popular* Minecraft-*themed LEGO line, capitalizing on comparisons between* Minecraft *and LEGO. (Source: LEGO, http://lego.com/, 2014.)*

Minecraft to LEGO abound.[32] In fact, the LEGO company has embraced this comparison by producing official *Minecraft* tie-in sets, such as "The First Night" (see Figure 6).[33]

Although fans since the 1960s have specifically celebrated the plastic construction toy for fostering creative play in children, discussions of LEGO have also expressed concerns over increasing constraints on the freedom to play, limitations on who can play, and a perceived loss of creativity.[34] One such concern centered on the deeply heteronormative gendering of the LEGO blocks themselves through the introduction of the LEGO Friends line of toys in the early 1980s, which was marketed specifically toward girls and has contained figures incompatible with the main line of LEGO products. This designated line for girls suggested that LEGO toys were and had been normally intended for boys all along, reinforcing historic associations of construction toys with boys at the exclusion of girls.[35]

Additional critiques often point to prescriptive kits and tie-ins to digital games, films, and other media franchises as evidence of increasing constraints on player freedom from the LEGO company. Renowned game designer Peter Molyneux, for instance, uses this perception of LEGO's loss of creativity to characterize *Minecraft* as a creative landmark in game design:

> LEGO used to be a creative toy, which I don't think it is so much anymore, because it's much more prescriptive. . . . It's buy the box, open the box, turn to the instruction sheet, make the model, stick it on the shelf, buy the next box. That's exactly like traditional game design, you know. Buy the game, go through the challenges, finish the challenges, stick it on the shelf, buy the next game. Where LEGO used to be just a big box of bricks, and you used to take the bricks, pour them on the carpet, and then make stuff. And that's exactly what *Minecraft* is.[36]

For Molyneux, LEGO's increasing prescriptiveness, which he analogizes to the automated process of consuming traditional game design, betrays its original creative potential through encroachment on individual expression. By contrast, *Minecraft* offers the individualized and unrestricted play that he considers creative.

In discussing creativity in *Minecraft,* however, Colin Fanning and Rebecca Mir argue that the attention to "limitless play and universal didactic value highlight the unspoken privileging of specific kinds of creativity in adult discourse."[37] The privileging of individually directed active construction and building as exemplary of individual creativity aligns with what Alfred Gell identifies as the dominant model of creativity in many Western cultures. Gell contends that the dominant Western conception of creativity is "activist"—intentional and directed—and, subsequently, forecloses the recognition of what he describes as "quietist" modes of creativity, such as found art practices in non-Western traditions.[38] Molyneux's own conception of creativity with respect to LEGO, for instance, assumes particular compliance by consumers with respect to instructions, ignoring that many earlier construction toys regarded as distinctly creative also came with detailed instructions. Moreover, instructions themselves do not enforce absolute compliance from consumers.[39] Yet Molyneux's position echoes the dominant conception of creativity as the negotiation of individual freedom as it encounters instruction, restriction, or other social pressures to conform.

This understanding of individual creativity and its opposition to social conformity, which fundamentally informs contemporary discourses of creativity and creative labor, is deeply influenced by mid-century psychologist Abraham H. Maslow and his theories of individual development, self-actualization, and creative expression. For instance, Teresa Amabile, Tom Peters, and other recognized organizational and management theorists have espoused models of idealized work and workers moored to Maslow's conception of creative individuals.[40] According to Maslow, creativity was the ultimate expression of an individual's most actualized and authentic self.[41] He defined creativity as unrestrained and unconventional inspiration and action, an innocence of perceiving and behaving "without a priori expectations."[42] Socialization, through what he termed "rubricization," was the obstacle to creativity, since rubricizing was "a form of not-cognizing, a quick, easy cataloguing whose function is to make unnecessary the effort required by more careful, idiographic perceiving and thinking."[43] Maslow linked self-actualization and creativity together, suggesting that to think creatively was to resist rubricization and the non-cognizing of existing social conventions by fostering individual agency.

Maslow advanced his definition of creativity through recurring images of children as presumably naturally innocent and creative beings who had yet to be rubricized by conventional thinking, drawing on the imagined naturalness attributed to children. As he argued, "Almost any child can perceive more freely, without a priori expectations about what ought to be there, what must be there, or what has always been there."[44] In identifying key characteristics of self-actualized individuals, Maslow noted that they were, among other traits, honest, ingenuous, and, in particular, childlike.[45] Elaborating on this, he wrote that "the creativeness of the self-actualized man seems rather to be kin to the naïve and universal creativeness of unspoiled children," since creativity was "what all babies are, in principle, born with."[46] Consequently, Maslow and those influenced by him rendered creative individuality as natural and the social its threatening enemy.

The logics of Maslovian creativity, however, required rubricization to define the conditions of creativity itself.[47] While Maslow articulated the social as a constraint to be overcome by the creative self-actualized individual, the social also existed to provide the requisite conditions for rubricization needed in order to demarcate creativity as the excesses beyond convention.[48] This conception of creativity necessarily defined it in relation to rubric, socialization, and instructions, such as those accompanying construction toys and model-building kits.

For the Maslovian model of psychological development, cultivating creativity was inextricable from actualizing the individual self.[49] Precarity rather than security developed creativity, since Maslow equated creativity with handling insecurity effectively. According to Maslow, "Creativeness is correlated with the ability to withstand the lack of structure, the lack of future, lack of predictability, of control, the tolerance for ambiguity, for planlessness."[50] Precarious conditions play a central role in Maslow's well-known model of psychological development structured on a hierarchy of needs, from base physiological survival concerns over food and shelter up toward social desires for acceptance until peaking in individual self-actualization and creativity.[51] Satisfaction of more pressing lower order survival needs allowed opportunity to address higher ones in individual development, since "the pursuit and gratification of the higher needs leads to greater, stronger, and truer individualism" and, thus, creativity.[52]

Application of Maslovian psychology in management theory rose in the 1960s, as Maslow began championing creativity beyond individual psychological development to occupy a central place in business and innovation.[53] He titled his contribution to management theory, *Eupsychian Management,* after his fantasy of Eupsychia, an imagined "culture that would be generated by 1,000 self-actualizing people on some sheltered island where they would not be interfered with."[54] Maslow's utopian civilization would support unobstructed self-actualization of psychologically healthy, autonomous, and creative individuals.[55] Maslow argued that previous utopian fictions were limited by their fixation on solving economic conflict. Eupsychia would instead meet the requirements for a psychologically healthy utopia constituted by self-actualized and creative individuals.[56] Eupsychia would exist beyond material concerns, being able to focus on the requirements for a psychologically healthy utopia constituted by self-actualized and creative individuals after having eliminated material conflict—shifting attention from what Maslow characterized as lower-order needs of survival to the highest-order need of individual psychological development.[57]

Maslow's Eupsychian fantasy, however, while imagining a utopian island populated by self-actualizing people, omitted how those individuals became self-actualizing. This oversight is particularly significant since Maslovian psychological development required social rubricization to define what constitutes creativity as well as conditions of insecurity for its growth and expression. Ultimately, Eupsychia, like other utopian fantasies, was organized around addressing the core tensions between the individual and the social in the development and constitution of creativity, what discourses around construction toys such as LEGO reveal, and what *Minecraft* itself inherits and modifies through its gameplay as players explore, mine, and build in the game's virtual worlds.

Two Modes, Many Islands

Minecraft participates in an enduring narrative tradition that deploys the island, or similarly isolated geography, as the experimental setting to negotiate tensions between the individual and the social in the development of creative subjects.[58] Ogata asserts that modern conceptions of creativity have "roots in the discourses around individuality and invention that flourished in the eighteenth and nineteenth centuries."[59] One of these roots, I contend, is found in the island narrative as the generic site for contesting the relationship between the individual and the social in order to establish the necessary conditions for creativity and invention.[60] As an insular geography, islands have historically provided what Richard H. Grove describes as a dominant setting for the "fundamental questioning of the nature of existence, societies and the self, and, consequently, for fictional or experimental constructions of new societies and analyses of old ones."[61]

Minecraft and its two primary playing modes, Creative Mode and Survival Mode, enable players to experiment with various environmental and sociopolitical conditions imagined in island narratives in the Western tradition.[62] In Survival Mode, players begin with only their hands as tools, are vulnerable to hostile creatures and other players, and must use what they gather to survive on the dangerous virtual island often described as a simulation of Robinson Crusoe's adventure.[63] In *Minecraft*'s other major mode, Creative Mode, players are invulnerable to hostile threats and have infinite access to every material resource offered by the game, akin to a more utopian island setting. Although both modes enable construction—as players build shelters to

survive or are free to build as an expression of individual creativity—
Survival Mode relies on scarcity and precarity, while Creative Mode
grants infinite abundance and physical immunity.[64]

Both *Minecraft* modes, I argue, correspond to different environmental and social conditions historically dramatized in the development of
creativity and invention and, in so doing, negotiate tensions between
individual autonomy and social dependence. I identify earlier island
narratives, such as *Utopia, New Atlantis,* and *Robinson Crusoe,* as providing narrative scripts that scaffold the production and reception of later
cultural artifacts, such as *Minecraft,* and inform contemporary discussions of creative development and invention.[65] As Colin Milburn argues,
island narratives have long been present in the cultural imagination of
modern scientific writing.[66] If "as early as Francis Bacon's *New Atlantis,*
itself borrowing from Thomas More's *Utopia,* the island becomes the
natural home of experimental science and the scientific society," then
the island also becomes the natural home of creativity and invention.[67]

The modern island narrative commonly follows the protagonists
shipwrecked on an island previously unknown to them. Fundamental
to island narratives is the juxtaposition of ideological constructions of
civilization and savagery with respect to the protagonists, typically as
stand-ins for readers. In this way, island narratives in the Western tradition contributed to long-standing cultural negotiations of race and
gender through discourses of civilization and savagery largely in favor
of securely coupling male dominance with white supremacy.[68] Readers
by way of the predominantly white and male protagonists encounter
fictional depictions of more advanced civilizations, resonant with the
imagined possible future trajectory of European and white American
development, or of ones constructed as primitive and savage, coded
through tropes of hostile indigenous Black and Brown bodies as well
as lawless pirate figures. Island narratives participated in the racialization that binds civilization with whiteness and savagery with nonwhite
others, which developed alongside European and, subsequently, U.S.
colonization of Asian, African, Oceanian, and American geographies.
Underlying many island narratives are the racial ideologies that advanced beliefs in the superiority of white cultures, including, for example, myths of the frontier and of Manifest Destiny in the United States
that justified the removal and genocide of Indigenous peoples.[69] Such

ideologies endure today, as seen in the prevalent racial logics of white and European colonization that inform contemporary digital games including *Minecraft*.[70]

I group island narratives describing conditions for producing new knowledge and inventions into two major traditions, which form a continuum of texts rather than sharply divided categories. In the social utopian tradition, after Thomas More's *Utopia* (1516), the protagonist arrives at an island inhabited by a peaceful and typically more "advanced" society that invents collectively through routinized processes in a world of infinite abundance and social concord. In the individual survivalist tradition—aligning with the Robinsonade genre following Daniel Defoe's *Robinson Crusoe* (1719)—privation pits the protagonist against the hostile "savage" inhabitants and the island itself demanding that they create in order to survive.[71] These two narrative traditions respond diametrically to tensions between individual autonomy and social dependence by outlining idealized sociopolitical and environmental conditions necessary for creative development and innovation, which find reimagination in the primary playing modes *Minecraft* offers.

In texts such as More's *Utopia* and Francis Bacon's *New Atlantis* (1624), which is centrally interested in technoscientific invention, the protagonist of the social utopian narrative encounters an island populated by a seemingly advanced civilization previously unknown to them that has eliminated strife, usually through abundant resources and enforced similitude. Similitude through uniform housing and attire, as *Utopia* depicts, fosters concord, while bureaucratic organization places inhabitants into specific positions to contribute to collective welfare.[72] In *New Atlantis,* for example, Salomon's House organizes collective efforts of impressive invention to produce

> prepared engines and instruments for all sorts of motions. There
> we imitate and practise to make swifter motions than any you have,
> either out of your muskets or any engine that you have, and to make
> them and multiply them more easily, and with small force, by wheels
> and other means: and to make them stronger, and more violent than
> yours are; exceeding your greatest cannons and basilisks.[73]

Through bureaucratic social organization, invention emerges from collective work that is functionally mechanical and unindividualized. An individual is not a creative genius but part of a larger social mechanism for generating novel output.

Although he described it as a utopian society, Maslow imagined creativity in Eupsychia as distinctly individual rather than social, stemming from self-actualized subjects rather than institutional processes. In fact, in defining models of creativity, Maslow argued that scientific methods were not creative. Admittedly cheeky, he wrote, "If I wanted to be mischievous about it, I could go so far as to define science as a technique whereby noncreative people can create. . . . Science is a technique, social and institutionalized, whereby even unintelligent people can be useful in the advance of knowledge."[74] He suggested that while science produces novelty, it only invents through uncreative processes. For Maslow, structured activity can render the uncreative individual capable of producing novelty but does not further the development of individual creativity.

Minecraft's Creative Mode draws on a version of the social utopian narrative by augmenting players' individual inventories with direct access to infinite resources without the labors (and dangers) of searching, mining, or crafting.[75] Unlike social utopias, however, no remarkably advanced or aspirational society exists in-game nor are there any distinct social or bureaucratic institutions present to regulate players' actions, though villagers do sparsely inhabit the world. Rather, the game's software ultimately serves to regulate players, since the code manifests the game's rules.[76] In addition to providing players with infinite resources, Creative Mode renders player avatars immune to hunger and all sources of damage, including other players, which functionally enforces pacifism among them. Although the game environment can no longer harm players, since normally hostile monsters become docile, players can still damage animals and monsters in-game as expressions of individual player agency.

As another distinction from social utopian narratives, *Minecraft's* Creative Mode allows individuated creation as opposed to the bureaucratically collective model found in social utopias. Critiques of utopian island narratives often argue that the challenge of suppressing individual desires undermines the utopian island's possibility to exist. In *The Island of Doctor Moreau* (1896), for example, H. G. Wells depicts the eponymous doctor's attempts to realize his own vision of utopia by creating new subjects from animals through horrific vivisection against their will. Similarly, Aldous Huxley's novel *Brave New World* (1932), alluding to the island of William Shakespeare's *The Tempest* (1623) and parodying Wells's *A Modern Utopia* (1905), explores the failures of the government of the World State in its denial of individual freedoms.

Opposing social utopian narratives, I conceive of the individual survivalist tradition as expressed in narratives that embrace the wants of individuals, testing their capabilities amid precarity. In these narratives, the protagonist is stranded on a hostile island and must repeatedly explore, gather, experiment, and build to tame the environment and produce increasingly hospitable conditions, depicted most influentially in Defoe's *The Life and Strange Surprizing Adventures of Robinson Crusoe*. As Crusoe recounts of the beginning of his ordeal on the island, for example, "My Thoughts were now wholly employ'd about securing my self against either Savages, if any should appear, or wild Beasts, if any were in the Island; and I had many Thoughts of the Method how to do this, and what kind of Dwelling to make."[77] But through years of gathering and building, Crusoe erects himself a fortified and stocked haven he dubs his "castle," a symbol of self-made security through acquiring knowledge and resources.[78]

Robinson Crusoe established a lasting cultural myth of the individual survivalist island as the dominant narrative template structuring modern Maslovian conceptions of creative individuality.[79] Despite the unmistakably hostile island conditions, the dramatization of individual self-actualization and economic success rendered *Robinson Crusoe* an ideal utopian fiction under the purview of capitalist economic theory.[80] In isolating Crusoe on the island, Defoe offered to modern capitalist economists an influential archetype that Michael McKeon identifies as "the self-possessed and enlightened capitalist entrepreneur of the modern age," becoming the model for *homo economicus*.[81] Like the ideal self-actualized subject of Maslovian psychology, Crusoe as *homo economicus* validates his creative capacities by testing his wants, judgments, and plans through his survival amid precarious conditions. Robinson Crusoe represents the idealized modern capitalist, an individual weaving the creative pursuit of knowledge and invention with successful self-actualization and economic success. Moreover, Robinson Crusoe as idealized modern capitalist is a figure constituted through fantasies of white (middle-class) masculinity, despite, as feminist and postcolonial readings of and responses to Defoe's novel have demonstrated, his deep reliance on and inseparability from the racialized and gendered labors of others, including the "uncivilized native" Friday.[82]

Beyond economic thought, eighteenth-century educational theorists such as Jean-Jacques Rousseau as well as Maria and Richard Lovell Edgeworth argued for the pedagogical value of having children read *Robinson Crusoe* to develop individual judgment.[83] Rousseau in his educational treatise *Emile; or, On Education* (1762), in particular, framed Crusoe on his desert island as a model social subject, since, for him, "the surest means of raising oneself above prejudices and ordering one's judgment about the true relations of things is to put oneself in the place of an isolated man and to judge everything as this man himself ought to judge of it with respect to his own utility."[84] Crusoe, for Rousseau, overcomes the constraints of the social in his isolation by organizing everything with respect to his individual self to see their "true relations," in recognizing their utility to him during survival. Rousseau's eighteenth-century thoughts on Crusoe echo in Maslow's twentieth-century theories of creative development and self-actualization and in contemporary discussions of individual identity.[85]

Following *Robinson Crusoe*'s publication and widespread success, several authors developed their own island survival narratives, often pressing the boundaries of individual autonomy associated with Defoe's protagonist.[86] Johann David Wyss's novel *The Swiss Family Robinson* (1812), for example, reimagines the individual subject of Crusoe through the individual social unit of the family that draws its name from Defoe's hero; where conflicts emerge among sons, father always knows best. And in R. M. Ballantyne's novel *The Coral Island: A Tale of the Pacific Ocean* (1858), three boys mature into young men as they learn to cooperate to survive on an island. However, in a direct attack on the heroic Robinsonade, generally, and Ballantyne's version, in particular, William Golding's novel *Lord of the Flies* (1954) depicts a group of British school boys marooned on an island.[87] Unable to cooperate to maintain either social order or a signal fire for rescue, the boys slowly turn against each other, revealing innate tensions between individual desire and social accountability that result in two gruesome deaths at their own hands. In dramatizing underlying violent tendencies in young British boys stranded on an island, *Lord of the Flies* suggests that the belief that supposedly civilized European subjects are above "savage" behaviors may be, ultimately, unfounded.

In spite of such critiques, *Minecraft*'s Survival Mode inherits the Robinsonade as the organizing narrative for the mode's primary objectives: construction and survival.[88] In an interview about *Minecraft,* for example, game journalist Chris Hecker suggests the digital game's kinship with survival narratives by noting that the moment of "gameplay that everyone talks about is just surviving the first night. You're not saving the world. You're just trying not to die."[89] To acquire food and shelter, players must perform iterative processes of exploring, gathering, and constructing—switching between safety and insecurity.[90] Although described as a fundamental experience to *Minecraft,* Survival Mode was not a part of the earliest versions of the game, now called *Minecraft* Classic, which only provided functionality for mining and crafting. Sean Duncan notes that "as a domain of creativity, *Minecraft* Classic was evocative and interesting, but it was lacking in impetus—there needed to be something more to drive the player's actions."[91] Introducing survival concerns established the initial drive to create in this mode of *Minecraft,* since, as Sara Grimes argues, *Minecraft*'s Survival Mode offers "'the elemental requirement for creativity—you need to build from scratch to survive your first night.'"[92] Concerns over survival produce the chaotic conditions necessary for individualist manipulation of the world by motivating players to secure safety.

From looting his island to potentially the globe, Crusoe learns to view his environment as ready material at his disposal. *Minecraft* as a digital game virtualizes this view of the entire world as standing reserve—*Bestand,* following Martin Heidegger—through the depiction of an entire world made of blocks to be shaped, gathered, and crafted into players' castles, suggested textually in *Robinson Crusoe* and the individual survivalist narrative tradition.[93] Although *Minecraft* participates in both the social utopian and the individual survivalist traditions as part of a genealogy of island narratives, its digital game form modifies the traditions in significant ways, particularly through its integration with the history of construction toys. While players initially set the mode of the virtual worlds they create in *Minecraft,* they can switch between the two modes at their discretion during gameplay, moving back and forth from Survival to Creative Mode—Robinsonade to utopia. By launching multiple instantiations of virtual worlds, modifying the game settings, and being able to change modes and settings while playing, *Minecraft* players experiment with different sociopolitical and environmental configurations of islands that have been historically debated for creation and invention.

Programmed for Modding and Hacking

From Crusoe and LEGO to *Minecraft,* creativity, even if viewed as individual, is always dependent on the social that offers it both materials for expression and the limits it must exceed. *Minecraft*'s game mechanics, which are organized around the logics of recombination, encourage players to create by working with preexisting forms. Peter Christiansen, for instance, argues that *Minecraft*'s gameplay directs players to learn to invent through modding, creating content that modifies an existing computing technology.[94] In this way, *Minecraft* participates in a history of programmable media, software that teaches players how to work with computers.[95] As an early example, Seymour Papert along with colleagues at the Massachusetts research firm Bolt Beranek and Newman (now BBN Technologies) developed Logo (1967) as a programming language designed for children to learn mathematics and coding by giving instructions to move a "turtle," a triangular cursor, to draw on the screen.[96] Programmable media, such as MIT Media Lab's visual programming environment Scratch (2003) and LEGO Mindstorms robotics kits, often mobilize literal and figurative blocks central to construction toys to provide users training in what Mizuko Ito calls hacker literacy, competencies in working and authoring with computers.[97] Through engagements with programmable media, users learn to operate like programmers, modders, and hackers.

Many commentators laud how *Minecraft* enables players to gain competencies in working with code and software despite the absence of that as an articulated objective of the game's original design.[98] Integrating programmable media with island fiction, *Minecraft* infuses virtual islands with the logics of construction, creativity, and individual self-actualization running from *Robinson Crusoe* up through Maslovian psychology. As Kurt Squire argues, "All creativity in *Minecraft* derives from and furthers the fiction presented by the game. To build something from wood blocks, one must first cut down trees. To build from

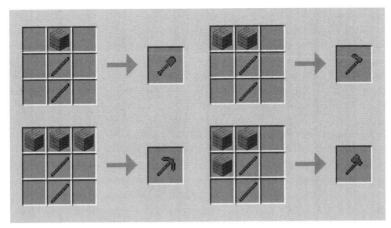

FIGURE 7. *Comparison of different crafting arrangements of wooden planks and sticks to produce different wooden tools in* Minecraft. *(Source: Mojang,* Minecraft, *2011; image from author screenshots.)*

stone, one must mine blocks from the ground. *Minecraft*'s creative tools are enmeshed with its simulated world."[99] Gathering resources, crafting tools, and building shelters provide goals for players to understand how the logics of creation in the virtual world operate, training them to become digital creators as they play. In *Minecraft,* most crafting materials, including resources to make tools, armor, food, textiles, and other resources, can be arranged in a crafting grid in different ways to produce different items. This recombination operates through predetermined crafting recipes that the game recognizes. Given wooden sticks and wooden planks, for example, different quantities and arrangements of these materials will yield a wooden hoe, shovel, ax, or pickax (see Figure 7). Players initially have access to a two-by-two crafting grid, but by creating a crafting table, players have access to a three-by-three grid for crafting. This suggests that creations can scaffold the production of other, more complex, creations (see Figure 8).

Minecraft offers no detailed instruction within the game itself on how to craft particular items, suggesting that players arrange materials experimentally to discover crafting recipes. According to LearningWorks for Kids' *Minecraft* Playbook, this "backward approach to item creation rewards intuitive and creative players with tools, weapons, furniture, items and dozens of other objects they can use in their world,"

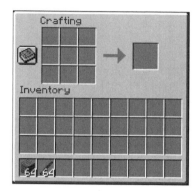

FIGURE 8. *Comparison of initial player crafting grid* (left) *and larger crafting grid enabled by crafting table* (right) *in* Minecraft. *(Source: Mojang,* Minecraft, *2011; image from author screenshots.)*

emphasizing the self-actualization the game offers to those who experiment in order to learn the game's crafting recipes.[100] Similarly, Crusoe develops confidence in his capacities to create in the world through his crafting successes. Based on his triumphs on the island, such as developing his own method of fashioning pottery, he asserts, "I improv'd my self in this time in all the mechanick Exercises which my Necessities put me upon applying my self to, and I believe cou'd, upon occasion, make a very good Carpenter."[101]

I contend that the crafting recipes coded into *Minecraft* constitute the game's rubric, the specifications for what is conventional that serve as the necessary constraints for players to recognize their work as creative. By first requiring players to build tools and materials necessary for survival within the game's crafting recipes, *Minecraft* trains players to build within conventional guidelines in preparation for them to build beyond them. For example, Christiansen notes that "whereas there is only one way to craft an iron pickaxe, there are limitless ways that a player could construct her home," since there is no singular and recognizable in-game home object.[102] Moreover, *Minecraft*'s structured model of crafting trains players to consider spatial arrangements in combining materials to create new entities first in the crafting grid and then in the virtual world organized spatially in blocks.

Creativity in *Minecraft* is formally and procedurally articulated as the process of arranging existing game blocks outside of the game's crafting recipes, emphasizing that constructing new things is always about modding, remixing, and hacking what already exists or is known. Consequently, creativity against *Minecraft*'s rubric occurs in the game when players place blocks into arrangements the game's code cannot recognize as a unified product, item, or resource. For example, while *Minecraft* supports dirt, stone, water, and explosive TNT blocks as recognized and labeled resources in the game, players can configure them into a functioning cannon that launches TNT, despite the fact that the game cannot internally identify the TNT cannon as a unified and named entity in its code (see Figure 9). Like arranging materials in crafting grids to create other materials, players must arrange blocks spatially in the game world in particular ways to create functioning assemblages that exceed what the game's coded rubric recognizes as a single item.

For Christiansen, this progression in *Minecraft* leads into modding the game itself, as the game "encourages players to investigate its world, tinker with it, and ultimately take the world apart to see how it works."[103] The game's crude visual aesthetic reinforces a desire to reduce the world down to functional pixels and blocks to be manipulated spatially and mixed together. Building with the pixelated blocks of *Minecraft* primes players to modify the game's existing code as they acquire hacker literacy, often by implementing new items and blocks.[104] Crusoe performs a similar process of modding when he creates a multi-musquet array by recombining known forms in a previously unexpected way. With seven musquets salvaged from the wrecked ship, Crusoe states, "[I] fitted them into Frames that held them like a Carriage, that so I could fire all the seven Guns in two Minutes Time."[105] As descendants of Crusoe recombining known elements into previously unknown forms, modders represent the archetypal creative individuals, and creative workers, of an increasingly digital modernity.

Among Wolves

Despite the emphasis on individuality in *Minecraft* and in dominant conceptions of creativity more broadly, *Minecraft*'s development and its success rely heavily on its player community and the creativity throughout it.[106] From involvement in influencing the game's direction to providing resources for new players, "community," as game journalist Geoff Keighly asserts, "is always going to be probably the most

FIGURE 9. *Player-created TNT cannon in* Minecraft. Top left, *cannon loaded with TNT;* top right, *cannon ignited and about to launch TNT;* bottom left, *cannon immediately after firing TNT;* bottom right, *cannon with launched TNT exploding in air. (Source: Mojang,* Minecraft, *2011; screenshot by author.)*

important thing when it comes to *Minecraft.*"[107] For instance, while *Minecraft's* lack of instructions might suggest that players must individually experiment to discover the game's crafting recipes, players are not isolated from the rest of the *Minecraft* community as if on an island. Players can mine the community and its knowledge base, such as the Official Minecraft Wiki, for assistance in playing the game.[108] Such user-created

references cover only a portion of what is identified as the *Minecraft* community's creativity, which also includes server builds, educational lessons, as well as podcasts and videos among the media that players create for each other.[109]

Making custom maps and mods for the game itself are prominent ways for players to create materials based on the game, often using the existing resources of *Minecraft*'s community. Christiansen, for example, notes that modders draw on "hundreds of resources online, including forums, tutorials, videos, and even custom software."[110] Modders mine existing code and references to craft their own mods, building on the collective knowledge already available. These player activities inside and outside of the game, as Scott Smith argues, "[use] other players' knowledge and creativity [as] both an adaptive survival tool and a form of social currency."[111]

While noting how players participate in the community to survive and accomplish their creative goals with the game, Smith's comment regarding social currency also suggests individual desires for celebrity, credit, and control. Like contemporary conceptions of individual creativity, tensions between the individual and the social reverberate through constructions of the modder as creative individual. For example, the popular *Minecraft* mod Better Than Wolves and its creator, under the handle FlowerChild, prompted debate in the *Minecraft* modding community over individual modder intentions, community desires, and the conditions of creativity and credit. After posting to the website Minecraft Forum in early 2011 about their belief that Notch would better spend his time adding other items, tools, and functions to *Minecraft* rather than the recently introduced wolves, FlowerChild began developing Better Than Wolves to implement such things as windmills, bellows, and hoppers, which were not part of the unmodded base or "vanilla" version of the game (see Figure 10).[112] FlowerChild was initially part of Minecraft Forge, a popular application programming interface (API) designed for modders to create their own content that would be compatible with other mods also using the API.[113] But after disagreements about the relationship between Better Than Wolves and Minecraft Forge, FlowerChild dropped affiliation to develop Better Than Wolves as a standalone mod by themself.[114]

Better Than Wolves, while popular, was also known for its incompatibility with other mods, requiring players to use FlowerChild's mod alone or not at all. Described as a "total conversion," the mod altered much of *Minecraft*'s core code beyond adding new items or resources.[115] As a direct response to FlowerChild's departure from Minecraft Forge and the desire to make features Better Than Wolves introduced compatible with other mods, the Minecraft Forge team began developing a parallel mod called Better with Forge. Following this, the ethics of modding, the definitions of software plagiarism, the intentions of mod

FIGURE 10. *Player-tamed wolves in* Minecraft. *(Source: Mojang,* Minecraft, *2011; screenshot by author.)*

creators, and the fundamental values of the modding community were debated across several *Minecraft*-related discussion boards.[116]

The conflict surrounding Better Than Wolves showcased enduring negotiations between individual autonomy and social dependence central to modern conceptions of creativity. While often recognizing Better Than Wolves as a creative mod, many players were quick to identify that FlowerChild's individual ego drove much of FlowerChild's comments and actions. For example, user Randomsteve wrote, "If [FlowerChild] really was just modding for [their] own enjoyment then I don't see any reason why [FlowerChild] couldn't take advantage of the forge team and have them add a few hooks to forge to make [their] mods base edits easier to do," noting a tension between individual recognition and community membership.[117] Others such as user AlukaMak, in contrast, asserted, "I can understand wanting to play other mods with Better Than Wolves. But do you not have any respect for the wishes of the Creator of BTW [Better Than Wolves]?"[118] AlukaMak's comment, in particular, expressed a belief that individual creators should dictate how their creations are received and used by the community.

In claiming creative individuality through the mod Better Than Wolves, FlowerChild illustrated what Gilles Deleuze and Félix Guattari articulate as becoming-wolf. For Deleuze and Guattari, becoming-wolf defines the struggle to occupy the periphery of a multiplicity, mass, or crowd as a strategy to maintain both one's individuality as well as one's social ties, a tense position to balance: "I would die if I let myself be drawn into the center of the fray, but just as certainly if I let go of the crowd."[119] Becoming-wolf suggests ongoing negotiations over one's social dependence and one's individual autonomy; the extreme of the former results in being fully consumed, while the extreme of the latter ends in isolation. Consequently, FlowerChild's negotiations resulted in their characterization as "an outsider in the modding community at large."[120]

FlowerChild, who had previously worked with Minecraft Forge, drew on resources from the modding community and Notch's game to produce their own mod. FlowerChild, however, attempted to render *Minecraft,* a digital game famous for modding, subsequently unmodifiable through their own creation. As FlowerChild described Better Than Wolves, it offered "a vision of what Mincraft [*sic*] could have been, designed by a very serious player, for other like minded [*sic*] individuals," suggesting that they improved Notch's game and do so out of reverence for it in a way that Notch himself could or would not.[121] But as user ShaRose commented: "[FlowerChild's] basically of the viewpoint where [they] just straight up [want their] own game," one derived from Notch's original.[122] In discussing "respect for the wishes of the Creator," AlukaMak inadvertently highlighted the irony of FlowerChild's development of Better Than Wolves as a direct critique of Notch's implementation of wolves in *Minecraft.* FlowerChild, rather than respecting Notch's own wishes to introduce wolves, explicitly created a mod, in function and in name, to be better—a provocation exemplifying online trolling behavior.[123]

The Better Than Wolves conflict and *Minecraft,* in general, reinforce a paradox central to modern conceptions of creative individuality, harkening back to *Robinson Crusoe.* As Ian Watt notes, *Robinson Crusoe's* publication participated in the emergence of the individualist era of eighteenth-century English culture that lingers today.[124] According to Watt, individualism "posits a whole society mainly governed by the idea of every individual's intrinsic independence both from other individuals and from that multifarious allegiance to past modes of thought and action denoted by the word 'tradition'—a force that is always social, not individual."[125] The rise of individualism and its celebration of autonomy, however, paradoxically underscored the ways in which individuals were inextricable from the very social relations and traditions they sought to eschew.

Crusoe's privileged position as ideal modern economic and self-actualized individual relies on his supposed isolation from the rest of modern society on the island, dramatizing a single subject thinking and acting without recourse to the wants and interferences of others.[126] During his early time on the island, Crusoe initially laments this isolation from society as his "affliction on one Hand" but fortunately "found no ravenous Beasts, no furious Wolves or Tygers" on the other.[127] Without the dangers of wolves and other beasts as well as the confines of society, Crusoe is believed to develop his creative and self-actualized individuality seemingly unimpeded. Crusoe, however, draws from the resources of the shipwreck and his previously acquired knowledge from English society to survive.[128] Moreover, Crusoe receives much assistance through the labors and local knowledge of Friday, the historically uncredited collaborator in securing Crusoe's successes as well as his individual identity. After finally escaping the island, Crusoe heads back to England with profits from his Brazilian plantation.[129] On his journey back, however, Crusoe encounters wolves, symbolizing threats to both his life and his personal wealth, but defeats them in another triumph that affirms his individuality amid insecurity, having fully matured into the self-possessed economic subject through his ordeals on the island as capitalist economics would believe.[130]

Discussions of *Minecraft* often provide a narrative of a lone hobbyist programmer creating something that offers players a space for their own creativity.[131] But this player creativity is only enabled through Notch's creation. Moreover, while discussions of the game continually frame Notch as a creative inventor, he is deeply indebted to the community that supported him and his work and to the resources of a larger computing community from which he drew expertise. Notch did not create *Minecraft* alone. *Minecraft* and its success are due to its community.[132] Modders, as contemporary models of individual creativity, continually interact with, draw from, and are produced by their social dependencies and ties to wolves and all.

As a prominent cultural artifact in contemporary digital culture and the creative economy, *Minecraft* shows that to be recognized as creative requires the capacity to be recognized, to recognize oneself first, as an individual subject rather than one encumbered by social ties and dependencies. But to define something as creative—that is, original— requires the establishment of convention, tradition, and rubric, which are all products of sociality. Furthermore, players of *Minecraft* rarely encounter the game in isolation, since they draw on a wide range of social resources to play, whether looking up instructional guides or interacting with other players on *Minecraft* servers, through message boards, or at fan conventions. *Minecraft* underscores that contemporary conceptions of creativity paradoxically desire to view creativity as individual and independent from social forces even while creative work is inextricable from the social conditions of its and its individual creator's production.

Interest in *Minecraft's* use as an educational tool with children, including Microsoft's acquisition of the game and its parent company Mojang, highlights several core beliefs regarding creativity and creative development in contemporary American discourses about its future workforce. Discussions of *Minecraft* as a digital construction toy emphasize the values at play not only of creativity as a socioeconomic imperative but also the kinds of education and play believed to matter for children to develop creativity in order to pursue innovations. Inheriting debates historically dramatized in island fictions, such as *Robinson Crusoe, Minecraft* reimagines the idealized sociopolitical and environmental conditions necessary for creative development and invention that negotiate tensions between individual autonomy and social dependence. Contemporary understandings of creativity and creative development derive primarily from narratives in the Robinsonade tradition, narratives akin to *Robinson Crusoe* that emphasize individual survival and economic success amid precarious conditions, routed through Maslovian models of individual creativity and psychological development.

Rather than reading Crusoe's influential developmental narrative, however, *Minecraft* as a digital game enables players to experiment with and simulate a range of socioeconomic and environmental conditions while acquiring computational proficiencies. By playing *Minecraft* and other programmable media, players acquire hacker literacies to become modders. *Minecraft* and the communities of practice surrounding the game encourage players to engage in processes of modding central to contemporary creative work through game mechanics that support crafting items, equipment, and other creations within the game that extend to creating outside of it. *Minecraft*'s crafting system, in particular, provides the contextual conditions for the legibility of creative work and invention by providing the limits that player creativity must exceed to be recognized as such. Ultimately, *Minecraft* is a digital game about modding a digitally modern world produced and populated by code.

In a 2015 *The Atlantic* article "Teaching in the Age of Minecraft," Alexandra Ossola profiled Joel Levin, also known as the Minecraft Teacher, a leading proponent for *Minecraft*'s educational use through his startup called TeacherGaming.[133] TeacherGaming developed a modified version of *Minecraft* for use in schools called MinecraftEdu.[134] For Levin, it was not simply a matter of generating lesson plans for *Minecraft*. He had to modify the base game to accommodate children, since Survival Mode allows players to harm each other, which posed a problem for collaborative use among young students. As Ossola wrote, "It's understandable that Levin wanted to restrict some of these capabilities to give his students a safe, age-appropriate experience. He modified the code so that kids weren't able to fight with one another in the game," constraining the simulation in favor of the pedagogical benefits of exploration and construction by enforcing pacifism among players while retaining environmental precarity and scarcity.[135] That Ossola remarks that this modification is understandable reveals an assumed view that children require regulation in their creative development and their social conduct else they will fight among themselves, a lurking potential to enact the destructive impulses dramatized in *Lord of the Flies*. These concerns over needing to modify *Minecraft* to become an appropriate tool for developing and expressing creativity suggests that children, while imagined as naturally creative beings developing into self-actualized individuals, also require proper training as creative workers in the making to become better than wolves.

CHAPTER 2
- - - - - - - - - - -

Make Magazine and the
Responsible Risks of
DIY Innovation

Contributors to *Make: Technology on Your Time,* a U.S. hybrid technology and parenting magazine, advocate do-it-yourself (DIY) engagements in making, an umbrella term they use to characterize crafting, hacking, and repairing technologies.[1] With O'Reilly Media, the Silicon Valley publisher known for programming language and computing guides, Dale Dougherty launched *Make* in 2005 to help hobbyists, families, and children become makers: individuals committed to the practices of making.[2] One of *Make*'s primary target audiences is parents interested in raising children under the banner of the "maker movement," which the magazine uses to encompass broad contemporary interests in making. The fifth volume of *Make,* for example, offers readers discussions of rockets and propulsion, along with instructions for making rockets at home. This includes a guide by William Gurstelle for building a jet engine from a jar. Addressing readers, Gurstelle asks, "Don't think you can build a jet engine at home? Here's a simple jet engine—a pulsejet—that you can make out of a jam jar in an afternoon."[3] Such a project, Gurstelle and *Make* suggest, demonstrates that rocket science does not, in fact, have to be rocket science.

Gurstelle's instructions provide information for building a pulsejet as well as historical background on Swiss engineer François Reynst, who "discovered this combustor as a pyromaniac child."[4] But while a pyromaniac with a combustor might cause alarm, Gurstelle focuses on how young Reynst harnessed his fiery interests when he "perforated the lid of a glass jar, put a small amount of alcohol inside, and lit the top. Flames shot out of the hole and then were sucked back into the bottle before being ejected again."[5] This account of Reynst's experiment deemphasizes dangerous risks in what Gurstelle describes as an "almost-magical process," characterizing Reynst as wondrous rather than destructive.[6] However, the specter of pyromania that this description offers—accompanied by photographs of the jam jar jet engine about to be lit, with its methanol fuel and its protruding copper wires—suggests a dangerous explosive as much as, and perhaps more than, a child-friendly afternoon project (see Figure 11).

The construction of young Reynst as both a potentially destructive child and an innovator in rocket science highlights tensions between risks and responsibility underlying amateur and DIY modes of technoscience. Operating outside professional institutions and regulations, amateur models of technoscience widen the population of participants by increasing access to information, equipment, and other resources. For example, *Make* magazine—through its articles, editorials, and instructional guides—asserts that anyone can innovate in technoscience without the expensive equipment and professional education that normally exclude the wider public from participation. *Make,* in fact, argues that such work is critical for everyone to perform. But if everyone is given Gurstelle's instructions to do-it-themselves, what prevents pyromaniacs from making explosive weapons instead of jet engines? Moreover, even with the best of intentions, what guarantees that amateurs could execute Gurstelle's instructions safely? Amateur and DIY models of technoscience, while encouraging more individuals to engage in experimentation and innovation, also increase the production of risks through such work and thereby an attendant demand for responsibility.

In this chapter, I examine recurring themes throughout *Make* to consider the magazine as a symptom of, and a response to, tensions between proliferating risks in the name of democratizing innovation and regulating risks in the name of responsibility. I situate the magazine within broader historic and contemporary interests in craft, hacking, and DIY before teasing out its differentiation of risks and responsibility as it envisions democratized amateur technoscience and innovation. I argue that *Make,* as a hybrid technology and parenting magazine, mobilizes constructions of creative children to naturalize responsible risk-taking as necessary for future innovation in order to address anxieties over risks produced through DIY technoscience. I show how *Make* transforms the regulation of amateur and DIY technoscience into a problem of private domestic politics by advocating for individually responsible risk-taking through its suggestion of child-rearing. The magazine's proposed model of child-rearing is constituted

9. VAPORIZE SOME OF THE FUEL

Prepare the jar by letting it sit in the freezer for two minutes. Hold your thumb over the opening in the lid. Vigorously swirl and shake the methanol inside the jar. Place the jam jar jet on a cookie sheet and place the cookie sheet on a secure surface, away from any flammable objects.

NOTE: When you remove your finger from the hole, you should notice a slight pressure release, and the jar should make a very faint "ptfft" sound. If you feel no slight pressure and hear no sound, shake the jar again. If there is still no pressure, there is a leak in the seal of the jar that you'll need to fix.

10. FIRE IT UP

Wearing safety glasses and gloves, hold a flame over the opening in the jar's lid.

The fuel will ignite, and for the next 5 to 15 seconds, the jam jar jet will cycle, pulse, and buzz, running at a low but audible frequency of about 20Hz, depending on conditions in the jar and in the surrounding air. With the lights down low, you'll enjoy a noisy, deep blue pulse of flame that grows and shrinks under the lid as the jar breathes fire. It's an amazing effect.

Pint-Sized Fireworks

During the air-intake part of the cycle, the bottom of the jam jar jet glows brightly. The photo on page 102 shows the blue flame you'll get from burning straight methanol, and this photo (at right) shows the yellow variant that comes from adding a little salt to the fuel. By adding salt or boric acid crystals, you can color your flames in a variety of attractive, retina-burning hues, as described on the next page.

FIGURE 11. *Final page of instructions for William Gurstelle's jam jar jet engine, including photograph of project about to be ignited. (Source: Make Community LLC,* Make *volume 5, 2006, p. 108.)*

through reimagining gendered, racialized, and classed crafts, domestic spaces, and conditions that tie political and state legitimacy to capacities in preparing subjects to innovate in a creative economy. In doing so, *Make* positions manual craftwork as a response to contemporary overreliance on mass-produced commodities and computing technologies while simultaneously reinforcing fundamental neoliberal logics of digital culture through figures of children as naturally creative subjects requiring proper education into innovative risk-taking and entrepreneurial adults capable of self-governance.

Making an Imagined Community of Makers

Make magazine represents one among many contemporary manifestations of interest in hands-on material engagements through activities spanning practices such as hacking, crafting, and do-it-yourself, which magazine contributors broadly call "making."[7] The magazine celebrates makers as subjects embodying the DIY or maker mindset, what Dougherty defines as a hands-on approach to technoscience, politics, and other aspects of daily life.[8] Although *Make* is based in the United States, which is reflected in much of its content, efforts characterized as "making" are not limited to the United States, do not necessarily adopt the label of "making," nor do they all abide by the tenets of *Make*.[9] In spite of the diversity of making, crafting, and DIY practices and communities, *Make* offers a particular disseminated vision of making that claims to be "leading the maker movement" globally.[10]

This particular vision of making informs the magazine's imagined community. Following Benedict Anderson, members of a larger imagined community such as a nation, in contrast to a smaller local community, participate in a fiction of deep sociality enabled through mass media communication with other members whom they may never directly encounter or know.[11] *Make*—as a print magazine also distributed digitally—constructs its imagined community through discussions of core values readers are expected to share regarding making as it affects technoscientific innovation, child-rearing, and politics.[12] The magazine's discursive construction of the maker as a valorized figure embodies grassroots innovation and ingenuity, a figure whom the magazine encourages readers to become.[13]

Emerging out of Silicon Valley culture, *Make* echoes the white middle-class masculinity underlying preceding technoscience publications including *Mondo 2000* and, most directly, *Wired*.[14] Many critics identify *Wired*, in particular, as a key artifact of the Californian ideology foundational to Silicon Valley politics. Richard Barbrook and Andy Cameron coined "the Californian ideology" to characterize the techno-utopian-infused libertarianism that integrated American neoliberal politics with the computing industry in California beginning in the late twentieth century.[15] Also described as techno-libertarianism or cyber-libertarianism, the political underpinnings of Silicon Valley culture harbor what Paulina Borsook characterizes as a "romance between libertarianism and high tech," which idealizes entrepreneurship, free markets, and individual liberties through the pursuit of technological innovations.[16] With philosophical roots in midcentury American counterculture and the Whole Earth Network, the maker as the celebrated figure of *Make*'s imagined community is informed by these histories of white middle-class masculinity.[17] Regarding gender and class, for instance, as of 2012, the latest publicly available report on magazine subscription statistics, the median annual income for *Make* subscribers was US$106,000, with eight in ten subscribers identifying as male and four in ten claiming to have children.[18]

Shaping the magazine's imagined community, *Make* mobilizes the titular term "making" as the privileged label for the constellation of related practices described by "hacking," "crafting," and "DIY." Although not comprehensive, my ensuing discussion of related and overlapping terms that "making" characterizes emphasizes how they are not wholly interchangeable, since each manifests distinctive values in its historic emergence and usage. Moreover, *Make* contributors negotiate unevenly these different values as they attempt to bring these various terms under (and sometimes to exclude from) "making," often in order to address the family-friendly mission of the magazine.

For instance, "hacking," originally popularized as a computing term in the mid-twentieth century for an inelegant but functional solution, has been framed in popular imagination as a rebellious, antiauthoritarian, and (potentially) illegal activity, such as breaching networked security systems.[19] Anxieties about the illicit connotations of hacking inform efforts in *Make*, as some contributors view hacking as antithetical to the family-friendly practices of the preferred term "making."[20] For example, the *Makerspace Playbook*, a *Make*-affiliated guide for establishing home resources to support making, asserts that "while many hackers consider themselves Makers and vice versa, hacker-spaces often have an adult atmosphere that's not always very welcoming to kids," thereby distinguishing between hacking and making based on appropriateness for children.[21] This understanding of hacking is not universally shared among *Make* contributors, however, particularly in light of increasing mainstream usage of the term to describe short cuts, such as in the rise of life hacking advice.[22]

My interest in *Make* and its contributors' use of "making" as an umbrella term for related practices in contemporary digital culture focuses on the historically persistent celebration of particular voluntary leisure activities, whether known as "making," "craft," or "DIY," as responses to perceptions of alienating and stupefying labor and consumption resulting from modern industrialization and capitalism.[23] For example, the Arts and Crafts Movement, which represents one such celebration of craft, began in England before spreading to affluent white Americans in the United States around the turn of the twentieth century. Supporters espoused the Arts and Crafts Movement as enacting socioeconomic reform to remedy a sense of alienation caused by industrial labor.[24]

As another term, "DIY" gained popularity in the United States during the mid-twentieth century to characterize hobbyist home maintenance, repair, and improvement practices primarily undertaken by white suburban middle-class men as a reprieve from their dissatisfaction with office work.[25] In the historic presumption of such activities as voluntary, the leisure histories of making, craft, and DIY often elide similar practices undertaken by disabled subjects, poor subjects, rural subjects, and others who must modify, salvage, improve, and rebuild the materials around them out of economic and physical necessity in order to survive, but who are often excluded from the privileged imagination of making, craft, and DIY understood as hobby.[26]

In addition to the participation of the label of "making" in the history of voluntary middle-class leisure, "making" also negotiates the gendering and valuation of particular types of craftwork, skills, and trades.[27] While attempting to cover a broad range of making skills to include accounts of both men and women as makers, *Make* magazine has reinforced traditional gendered conceptions of craft and DIY activities, having focused primarily on masculinized practices, such as electronics, woodworking, and welding. This is evident in the creation of *Craft* magazine, which *Make* spun off in 2006 in order to reach a larger readership via the creation of a second imagined community. *Make* described *Craft* explicitly as its "sister" magazine devoted to projects such as embroidering skateboards, programming LED tank tops, and felt-making iPod cozies to cover technological projects involving more traditionally feminized practices, including textile and fiber arts (see Figure 12).[28]

The magazine's titular adoption of the term "make" and the subsequent creation of *Craft* specifically to offer content historically relegated to women under the feminized and comparatively devalued label of "craft" underscores that *Make* and making is primarily for (or presumes) men.[29] That broadening the coverage of making practices to include those historically associated with women resulted in a separate and secondary magazine (and a separate and secondary imagined community of readers) perpetuated the historic gendering of particular craft practices. This gendered division of craft and making is reinforced in sorting projects into categories of "soft" feminine projects and "hard" masculine projects—such as "bookbinding, rubber stamping, and silicone molds" as opposed to "a rocket with a miniature videocamera, a headphone amp in a mint tin, and a wind-powered wi-fi hotspot," respectively.[30]

O'Reilly Media ceased printing *Craft* in 2009, however, claiming there were issues with production costs, and converted the title to a web-based resource with promises to include *Craft* content in future issues of *Make*.[31] In a subsequent letter printed in *Make,* reader Adrian Miller urges the magazine not to renege on its promise to support the practices *Craft* represented, encouraging "a stronger emphasis on female makers and writers, to affirm their presence in the creative community," which expresses concerns over the visibility of women makers in the magazine's imagined community.[32] Following the end of *Craft, Make*'s explicit attempts to expand the imagination and inclusion of who participates in its vision of maker culture—such as in highlighting the presence of, or the continued need to include, those historically excluded from the traditions that making draws on—further emphasizes the underlying perspective of *Make*'s imagined community that centers men. For instance, articles about specifically encouraging girls

FIGURE 12. *Announcement of the then-upcoming publication of* Craft *magazine in* Make, *suggesting distinctions between content across the two magazines. (Source: Make Community LLC,* Make *volume 7, 2006, p. 11.)*

to make, addressing issues regarding the lack of women in maker workshops, as well as celebrating the notable participation of Arab girls and women at international Maker Faires mark women's participation in making as particularly burgeoning, threatened, or remarkable, in contrast to the assumed and stable presence of men as makers.[33] Moreover, efforts to increase making's availability explicitly to poorer communities as well as Black and Latino communities highlight the magazine's outlook from the white middle class.[34] The dominant construction of the maker subject throughout *Make*, the celebrated hero leading its vision of the maker movement for its imagined community, is the idealized white middle-class male subject of Silicon Valley.

Making the Future for Self-Reliant Makers

The justification for the maker as aspirational subject demonstrates how *Make* magazine participates in broader cultural interests in making, crafting, and other forms of hands-on material engagements as an expression of resistance to modes of labor, production, and consumption in contemporary digital culture.[35] Bernard Stiegler, for example, laments "hyperindustrial, service societies that lead to consumers not being in charge of their very existence," since he argues that individuals become uncritical and over-reliant on new media technologies.[36] To remedy this, Stiegler advocates for consumers to acquire knowledges rooted in conscious skills and abilities, including "how to cook, drive one's car, know how to orient yourself in a landscape without having a GPS system, know how to bring up your children, to knit, to bake your bread."[37] Such diverse practices, from navigating space to raising children, he suggests, develop the critical intelligence and self-reliance necessary for the future.

Similarly, contributors to *Make* express anxieties over people's relationship to technology and labor. For example, Cory Doctorow warns of a bleak future where society "treats humans as objects to be scanned, managed, and regimented" resulting from uncritical technological consumption.[38] Tim O'Reilly cautions readers of the vision provided by "E. M. Forster in 'The Machine Stops,' in which people cocooned in their high-tech homes are helpless when their technological assistants go silent," because people depend completely on technology.[39] *Make* contributors, then, champion practices of making in order to develop deeper engagements with technoscience, capabilities for resisting the blind consumption of and ignorant over-reliance on mass-produced technologies.[40]

Contemporary advocacy of making, craft, and DIY continues a history of cultural responses since the late eighteenth century addressing perceived socioeconomic, environmental, and moral problems attributed to industrial capitalism by advocating handicraft and manual expertise as idealized work.[41] From the Arts and Crafts Movement to American DIY, the various historic responses have been motivated by and committed to different values concerning their relationship to capitalism itself as well as to individualism.[42] For example, the Oneida Community in the mid-nineteenth century, the counterculture in the 1960s, and other communally oriented groups throughout U.S. history have practiced craftwork as part of collective living in rejection of modern industrial capitalism and its perceived detrimental effects.[43]

This distinction between individualist and capitalist values on the one hand and more communal and anti-capitalist movements on the other is particularly visible in the U.S. Arts and Crafts Movement of the late nineteenth and early twentieth centuries. The American manifestation of the Arts and Crafts Movement departed significantly in ideological commitments from its anti-capitalist English origins, which were influenced primarily by socialist William Morris. As T. J. Jackson Lears demonstrates, U.S. Arts and Crafts leaders held an unquestioned acceptance of capitalism as well as subscription to American individualist ideologies.[44] Participants in the movement were mainly affluent white Americans who turned to Arts and Crafts ideology out of class and racial anxieties, motivated by the perceived threat of socialists and immigrants.[45] U.S. Arts and Crafts enabled these affluent participants to blame poor and nonwhite subjects within capitalism as who was harming society rather than blaming capitalism itself.[46] Moreover, U.S. Arts and Crafts ideology drew heavily on moral frameworks from Puritanism, including the moral value of hard work, and from perfectionism, believing that individual moral betterment rather than communal efforts would improve social conditions.[47]

U.S. Arts and Crafts ideology, which focused on individualistic work ethic and tacit acceptance of modern capitalism, provided an important antecedent to *Make*'s imagined community of makers, since *Make* similarly presents itself as a means to reform the problems of current industrial capitalist production through individual and self-reliant making practices rather than seeking to reject it completely. Articles throughout *Make* encourage readers to remedy the failures they identify with contemporary production through the entrepreneurial ingenuity of innovative makers equipped with digital tools.[48] The presence of pages of ads, advice for establishing a corporation, and the sale of Maker SHED products—official commercially produced *Make* project kits—underscores the magazine's willingness to revise rather than reject contemporary conditions of capitalist production. Dougherty, for example, celebrates that "we're seeing some makers . . . making kits, developing products, providing services, or marketing their expertise."[49]

Moreover, as visible throughout its magazine issues, advertisements and sponsorships from Microsoft, Nokia, General Electric, and other electronics and digital technology corporations reinforce *Make*'s commitments to renovating current modes of production with support from corporate allies. Chris Anderson—prominent maker figure and former editor-in-chief of *Wired*—contends that contemporary makers are the driving force for a new industrial revolution that is informed by traditions of craft and advances in computing technologies and is expected to transcend the pitfalls of conventional industrial production through individual entrepreneurship.[50] This revolution of production, situated within the context of the creative economy, is imagined to rely on innovative makers to create goods that will remake the current systems of mass production and, ultimately, society itself. Consequently, *Make* joins other mainstream efforts in making, craft, and DIY in digital culture, participating in the imagination of a predominantly white creative class, including virtual marketplaces like Etsy.[51] Such platforms similarly traffic in handmade commodities through rhetoric positioning the products, the creators, and the platforms against mass industrial production, while maintaining the continuation of commodity capitalism.[52]

Make also positions making as necessary even beyond market intervention. As Dougherty argues, "Our future security lies in knowing what we're capable of creating."[53] This is particularly evident, if also (unintentionally) exaggerated, in the magazine column titled "MakeShift," which places readers into various emergency, survival, and apocalyptic scenarios to underscore the broad utility of making, such as building a water filter in the wilderness, treating a leg injured by a tree branch, and being stranded in a snowy forest.[54] Through such features that echo the outdoorsy masculinity that informed the founding of the Boy Scouts of America, *Make* contends that resourceful and self-reliant making is fundamental to survival.[55]

In one particular scenario, readers are tasked with evacuating their wife and teenage children after an earthquake sets off impending rock slides and floods toward their rustic mountain home.[56] This scenario at once renders (heterosexual male) readers responsible to their nuclear family and references a desire to live off the grid, suggesting an urge to exist independent of governmental infrastructure and unnecessary social associations. Furthermore, a moral dilemma inserted into the scenario involves whether to save "your only neighbor, a single guy named Dave, [who] probably partied hard last night and slept through the quake. But his house will flood just as quickly as yours. . . . In a disaster like this, [is it] every man for himself?"[57] The scenario constructs whether to aid this neighbor—depicted as irresponsible and burdensome—as a question of individual personal responsibility and self-reliance in the face of disaster, suggesting that tenuous ties to others may interfere with protecting one's own self and family.

But while the underlying libertarian impulse seeks to live off the grid with one's own family through growing one's own food and generating one's own electricity, instructions for which *Make* provides, the magazine also prepares its readers to survive should the grid decompose during the apocalypse. Although early versions of the column described conceivably practical situations, such as needing to construct a water purifier, subsequent "MakeShift" features moved increasingly toward apocalyptic scenarios, including surviving a zombie infestation and weathering nuclear disaster.[58] Consequently, the magazine underscores how making is necessary, whether for the future of technological innovation in the creative economy or for autonomous living amid future catastrophe. In either case, the maker is the idealized self-reliant and entrepreneurial individual for the future whom readers should aspire to become.

Making Risks through the Mass Amateurization of Technoscience

For *Make* magazine, a significant element of making involves democratizing science, which entails broadening the range of participants in technoscientific work beyond those in professional laboratories. Arguing that "the future of science will come to those who make their own science," *Make* positions the maker as pivotal to coming technoscientific innovations.[59] Informed by the free and open source software movement, in particular, the makers represented in *Make* seek to share information and educate others in practices of making, encouraging the public to become knowledgeable amateur scientists and technologists in spite of a lack of professional training.[60]

Sharing much with this conception of making, amateur and DIY science has emerged as a popular mode for laypersons to participate in technoscientific research and innovation.[61] Scholarship on amateur and DIY science has examined the democratizing opportunities and limitations that opening up technoscience to non-traditional spaces, practices, and persons might afford, broadening the range of participants in technoscientific work through mass amateurization.[62] As Clay Shirky notes, professions such as the scientist exist to address particular social needs whose difficulties demand expertise not readily available to nonprofessionals or amateurs.[63] Where members of a profession were historically limited in number compared to the general population, various social and material changes enable renegotiation of such boundaries. Shirky, for example, describes how the rise of digital and internet publishing tools has resulted in the mass amateurization of media generation as a broader population of nonprofessional journalists, writers, and photographers now produce content alongside traditional media professionals.

Similarly, articles throughout *Make* insist to readers that "real science is happening outside the hallowed halls of high-priced research facilities."[64] *Make* seeks to "[provide] amateur enthusiasts with the skills and tools to make useful contributions to the body of scientific knowledge without having a Ph.D. and millions of dollars in funding," barriers that have historically excluded the public from participating in professional work.[65] Such comments, in particular, rhetorically lower the threshold for engagement, suggesting that anyone can become an amateur scientist and technologist as a maker.[66] Supporting its vision of making as mass amateurization of technoscience, *Make* offers instructional content and project guides in order to proliferate amateur workshops as scientific spaces staffed by amateur scientific subjects, that is, makers.[67]

These amateur workshops emerge through what I call the "workshop-function," an extension of Hans-Jörg Rheinberger's concept of the laboratory-function. According to Rheinberger, the laboratory-function consists of the protocols and documents of a laboratory necessary for generating scientific subjects appropriate to that given scientific milieu.[68] While the laboratory-function characterizes how professional scientific spaces reproduce themselves, the workshop-function accounts for the material reproduction and circulation that creates alternative spaces of technoscience, such as workshops run in garages, kitchens, and backyards, all of which typically operate outside professional regulatory mechanisms. Whereas the laboratory-function hinges on textual reproduction and circulation within the confines of a bounded professional setting to socialize scientists, the workshop-function requires that the textual reproduction to instantiate new scientific spaces and subjects circulates through mass media, such as magazines, television programs, and internet sites. *Make*'s workshop-function, for example, relies on mass dissemination primarily through print and internet channels to situate workshop operation as a core issue for the magazine's imagined community.

Mass amateurization of technoscience, however, has raised concerns over the administration of risks, since individuals participating in amateur technoscience create potential hazards and dangers to themselves and to others, such as in the form of sharp edges, toxic chemicals, electrical currents, and so forth. Furthermore, these workshops are run by amateur, DIY, and other unconventional scientists who might not possess professional technoscientific education or credentialing. Andrew Keen laments the loss of such gatekeeping, a historically central function of professionals who regulate the boundaries of their professions through various socioeconomic, legal, and material structures. Against the impulse to equate all efforts described as democratization as desirable, Keen warns that "democratization, despite its lofty idealization, is undermining truth, souring civic discourse, and belittling expertise, experience, and talent."[69] Keen's comment counters "the noble amateur" that he argues draws a cultlike following in digital culture, a figure he contends opposes the quality of work offered by the trained professional.[70] This quality of work, in part, extends beyond the product to include the process of work itself and, in the case of DIY technoscience, questions of competency and safety of execution. Because amateurs are not regulated by the systems that have historically governed professional technoscience, the regulation and responsibility for such risks created through mass amateurization become central issues.

Anxieties over risks are particularly visible in the policing of DIY biology, especially amateur experimentation with the genetic materials of living agents.[71] Government authorities, such as the Federal Bureau of Investigation, for instance, have raided several DIY biology laboratories and events out of concern for risks to national security, despite explicit commitment to promoting safe scientific practices by these laboratory groups and event organizers.[72] Similar concerns emerge as *Make* champions the proliferation of home workshops for makers to participate in their own technoscientific innovations.

To address concerns around the mass amateurization of technoscientific work through its workshop-function, *Make* contributors mobilize particular constructions of risk as necessary for technoscientific innovation through the figure of the maker in order to negotiate the risks resulting from increasing nonprofessional participation in technoscience. Risk and risk-taking, as Gina Neff shows, have been central to discourses of contemporary internet and digital industry entrepreneurship, which suggests that taking risks is vital to technological innovation and economic success.[73] Extending Neff's examination of risk discourse in digital culture, I tease out how *Make* suggests two broad categories of risks present throughout its discussions of innovation and responsibility: physical risk and ideological risk. In addition to concerns over personal and material safety tied to dangers related to technoscientific innovation, which I categorize under physical risks, *Make* is also concerned with ideological risks, constructions of risk against the development of a desired social, epistemic, or ideological subject. Ideological risks identify tensions around interpellation, what Louis Althusser defines as the process of converting individuals into ideological subjects.[74] Ideological risks emphasize how risk discourses specify not only how different subjects are constructed as at risk but also how different subjects are constituted through varying exposure and responses to perceived risks.

Through its constructions of ideological and physical risks, *Make* attempts to quell concerns over the risks engendered by mass amateurization of technoscience by arguing that risks and innovation are inseparable, that amateurs are necessary for technoscientific innovation, and that amateurs are capable of mass distribution of responsibility for the risks that mass amateurization of technoscientific work produces. Central to this rhetorical work is distinguishing physical risks from ideological risks, constructing the former as necessary for innovation and the latter as a more serious concern to avoid. *Make* contributors suggest that overemphasis on avoiding physical risks associated with making at the expense of avoiding ideological risks to individuals to become makers is graver than any of the possible physical risks themselves, as it interferes with both the subject formation of makers and future technoscientific innovation. Consequently, the maker represents a desired ideological subject, one that can responsibly handle the physical risks associated with innovative making in their own amateur workshop.

Make's workshop-function highlights a core tension between the mass amateurization of innovation through risk-taking while requiring subjects to be responsible for the risks involved as they operate outside professional regulatory mechanisms. In *Make*'s construction and assessment of risk, makers are educated to self-govern their engagements with physical risks necessary for DIY technoscience and making as a means of preventing the more serious threat posed by the ideological risks that ensue from preventing individuals from making altogether. For example, a *Make* article profiling synthetic biologist Drew Endy argues that educating the public in responsible garage biotechnology will only improve security. Acknowledging the presence of risks, the article explains that "the best course of action is to . . . provide free access to [DIY biology] and educate as many amateurs and professionals as possible in the ways of using it and spotting trouble."[75] Publicly accessible DIY biology creates specific risks, but rather than police these potential dangers, Endy advocates widespread education as the guarantor of responsible self-governance of biologists, amateur or professional, in the name of democratized innovation. DIY technoscientific innovation, consequently, requires that individuals take on the mass amateurization of responsibility to handle the ensuing mass amateurization of risks.

Making Parents Responsible for Children at Risk

Make magazine mobilizes physical and ideological risks to advocate its model of social reproduction, which constructs parents and children through risks and responsibility in relation to innovation. Social reproduction describes, following Cindi Katz, processes of "acquiring and assimilating the shared knowledge, values, and practices of the group to which one belongs by birth or choice."[76] Social reproduction includes various systems, institutions, and labors that provide education, the socialization of risk, and other processes of subject formation.[77] While parenting books and magazines articulate idealized roles and relations between children and parents within a proposed model of social reproduction, they do not guarantee details of actual parental beliefs or practices.[78] Consequently, like other child-rearing literature, *Make* offers an aspirational and marketed program of social reproduction.

According to *Make*, raising children requires guiding them to become makers who take on individual responsibility for physical risks associated with amateur innovation, otherwise they are at ideological risk of failing to become self-reliant and entrepreneurial makers. In this way, *Make* demonstrates how expectations of risk and responsibility often serve to divide children from adults. Stiegler, for instance, identifies responsibility as the defining attribute of adulthood, elaborating that the primary responsibility of adulthood is responsibility for the young, who require guidance to mature into responsible adults themselves.[79] Whereas Stiegler focuses on responsibility to define adulthood, Stevi Jackson and Sue Scott show that contemporary childhood often becomes marked through risk anxieties.[80] While adults are expected to be responsible for the risks they take, children are not, as they may be incapable of being adequately responsible. Consequently, they argue that parenting involves weighing different risks against others as they affect children through making decisions on their behalf.[81] This distinction between childhood and adulthood, then, is conceived not in the elimination of risks but the ability to take risks voluntarily and accept responsibility for their consequences.

Images and discussions of children in *Make* function to cement the relationship between risks and innovation as natural and necessary. *Make* mobilizes constructions of children as naturally creative individuals, as many contributors contend that being childlike is a distinct advantage for innovative making.[82] For example, Saul Griffith depicts children as naturally creative by celebrating their imaginary inventions, such as "cars that run on water, a vending machine for any combination of soda flavors, an automatically loading marshmallow-making cannon, a single book that feels like paper and contains all the library books in the world."[83] These imagined inventions allow Griffith to show the innovations that children dream up that must be encouraged for the future, which reinforces what Rebecca Onion identifies as the historic linking together of children, technoscientific progress, and future innovation since the early twentieth century.[84]

In addition to idealizing children as creative subjects, *Make* also argues that children are at risk, since their development into makers requires guided exposure to making so that they can become responsible risk-takers themselves. Constructions of ideological risks to the development of naturally creative children into makers renders physical risks in pursuit of innovation natural, while framing ideological risks as a graver problem than hazardous encounters with fire, electricity, or chemicals. The magazine argues that parents must be responsible for developing their children's naturally creative instincts into responsible risk-taking. Consequently, *Make* not only operates as a program of social reproduction for readers to become makers themselves but also assigns to readers the responsibility of social reproduction for raising children to become the next generation of makers contributing innovations to the creative economy. Responsibility and risk function as the organizing principles for subject formation, since parents are responsible for raising naturally creative children and this child-rearing must include education in responsible risk-taking for innovation. Failure to raise children to become responsible risk-takers signals a failure of parenting and adulthood and puts the future of technoscientific innovation at risk.

Toward this end, *Make* contributors often blame existing educational institutions for posing ideological risks to children, arguing that only by exposing children to hands-on experiences will they grow up properly into makers.[85] Dougherty, for example, describes making as a means of "learning more than any written test can measure," deriding an overemphasis on standardized education and examination practices at the expense of hands-on experience.[86] This construction of conventional school curricula champions making as "a practical and productive way to learn almost anything and a viable alternative to textbook learning."[87]

Furthermore, *Make* contributors blame a lack of making in schools and homes on a risk-adverse approach to raising children. AnnMarie Thomas, for example, writes, "Kids were once trusted with real, metal tools. . . . I understand the fear of injuries, and suspect it's one of the reasons behind the decline in kids gaining hands-on skills."[88] Similarly, Dougherty and Gever Tulley argue that because "American kids are raised in an overly cautious manner, out of fear that they might get hurt, [we] are limiting their ability to explore a wider range of experience."[89] These comments respond to a rise in overly cautious U.S. parenting attitudes since the 1960s and can be seen in contemporary trends motivated by concerns over physical risks, such as helicopter parenting and hyper-safe playgrounds.[90] This opposition between ideological and physical risks demonstrates how assessment of children's risks negotiate overprotection and safety.[91]

Make argues that the gravity of the ideological risks of keeping children from making must outweigh the physical risks that making produces. In an article regarding children's development and risk, for example, Dougherty and Tulley identify ideological risks of commercially produced toys that parents may purchase for their children, emphasizing the significance of parental choice in children's development into makers.[92] Supplementing the article, Dougherty and Tulley provide mock-ups of safety labels parodying conventional warnings to articulate ideological risks as more threatening to children than the physical risks such labels typically describe (see Figure 13). The "Caution: Reduction of Expanded Play Opportunities" label, for instance, warns parents that the concerns marked on packaging materials seek to keep children's attention on the toy, which might be less interesting than the packaging materials itself. Dougherty and Tulley take issue with this, since keeping children from encountering such raw materials keeps children from exploring creative ways to engage with them.

Expanding from this, Tulley, along with Julie Spiegler, contribute a column called "Danger!," which endorses deliberate and controlled encounters with physical risks in order to teach children how to manage risks responsibly. Encouraging children to put strange stuff in the microwave to learn about electromagnetic radiation, to lick a 9 V battery to experience electricity through the sense of taste, and to burn things with a magnifying glass to understand light refraction, Tulley and Spiegler suggest, will prevent ideological risks to their development into makers.[93] This persistent construction of physical and ideological risks as an issue of voluntariness, however, signals the presumed white middle-class suburban child as maker-to-be of the magazine's imagined

FIGURE 13. *Mock warning labels describing ideological risks parodying conventional warning labels for physical risks on children's toys. (Source: Make Community LLC, Make volume 7, 2006, p. 181.)*

community. Such assessments of choosing to engage in voluntary risk assume an otherwise overwhelmingly safe and risk-free childhood, which poorer and nonwhite children subjected to environmental injustice or increased policing and violence, for instance, do not experience.

Moreover, *Make*'s construction of physical risks in relation to children focuses primarily on those associated with licking a 9 V battery or playing with small-scale fire, often ignoring or minimizing more serious forms of physical risk. For instance, in a *Make* blog post announcing a chemistry gift guide, Phillip Torrone lists Robert Brent's 1960 children's chemistry guide *The Golden Book of Chemistry Experiments*, despite noting that "many of the experiments contained in the book are now considered highly dangerous for unsupervised children, and would not appear in a modern children's chemistry book."[94] Torrone details how the book, which had a reputation "that the experiments and information contained herein were too dangerous for the general public," influenced David Hahn, who as a teenager in the 1990s attempted to build a nuclear reactor in his family's backyard shed in pursuit of a Boy Scout Atomic Energy merit badge.[95] Torrone's description of Hahn, who has since been known as "The Radioactive Boy Scout," ends by mentioning his investigation by government authorities. The account, however, ignores the serious harm and consequences resulting from Hahn's young eagerness to engage in amateur science independently, as Torrone omits that the Environmental Protection Agency ultimately declared the area a dangerous federal Superfund site.[96] Torrone's selective depiction of Hahn attempts to minimize some of the potentially serious physical risks of making while celebrating the young maker engaging in amateur science. Additionally, the inclusion and characterization of *The Golden Book of Chemistry Experiments* as "too dangerous," while providing a link to a free digital copy of the entire book, simultaneously acknowledges the presence of risk while also increasing its risky allure by suggesting that it is a dangerous resource available only for the most daring of makers.

Regardless of the nature of the physical risks of making, *Make* encourages parents to raise self-assured children to take such risks responsibly. Thomas argues, for example, that when you combine "an eager child, real tools and materials, appropriate training, and supervision, . . . you'll see a young maker who is gaining a useful skill and confidence in her ability to bring ideas to life."[97] Thomas's comment echoes contemporary parenting advice concerned with raising children into independent and self-assured adults, such as the popular *Your Self-Confident Baby* by Magda Gerber and Allison Johnson (1997). This construction of a causal relationship of providing children guidance into becoming confident individuals relies on the developmental paradigm—a dominant contemporary assumption of childhood as a linear progression toward adulthood and the future.[98] The developmental paradigm tethers the future to and for children, as the child's development also stands in for the development of society as a whole.[99] For *Make*, caretaking of children as the primary responsibility of adulthood equates to caretaking of innovation and the future.

Make and affiliated projects reinforce this relationship between children and the future. O'Reilly, for instance, writes, "One of the best pieces of advice I ever received when my kids were young was this: 'Your job as a parent is to prepare your children for their future.' For their future, not the one that you grew into—that's their past."[100] For O'Reilly, parents are expected to raise children for the future to acquire the expertise that making provides, since *Make*'s projects and instructions "are not just hobbies but essential skills in a world growing ever more complex."[101] Similarly, the *Makerspace Playbook* argues that "it isn't enough to train current students for the world of today—we have to train them for tomorrow, a tomorrow that will require them to master technologies that don't yet exist. . . . We have no idea what the world will be like then."[102] Children require training for the future, even if unknown, and making is believed to be the only means of effectively providing that training.

Many discussions by magazine contributors reminiscing on their past experiences also ask readers to remember their own childhood memories that influenced their development into makers.[103] In one piece, Griffith reflects on his childhood to declare that "the adventures that stuck . . . were with homemade toys and homemade experiences."[104] Griffith closes the article by explicitly inviting readers to reflect on their own childhoods and share their own memories: "If this column helps you recall the triumphant toy inventions of your youth, I'd love to hear about what they were (and are)!"[105] Such invitations to participate in the magazine's imagined community encourage readers to view childhood exposure to making as necessary for adulthood as a responsible maker, suggesting that, as parents, readers of *Make* are responsible for similarly exposing their children to making.

Consequently, much of *Make* suggests privatizing children's education, moving what it believes to be the failed work of conventional schooling into domestic spaces. This shift reinforces the general trend in contemporary social reproduction toward privatization, such as the increasing reliance on familial wealth to meet the rising costs of higher education.[106] Griffith, for example, asserts that "until our school system is reformed, . . . the burden falls on parents, guardians, and friends to teach children the skills of life," arguing that the failures of schools to produce makers must be addressed through privatization rather than through attention to structural or systemic issues.[107] The home workshop, in particular, recurs throughout *Make* articles as a key site for acquiring these necessary experiences in making. For instance, Robyn Miller, co-designer of the wildly popular computer adventure game *Myst* (Cyan, 1993), writes that "[Grandpop's machine] shop was always a magical place for us kids."[108] In doing so, the magazine conflates issues of science politics, the democratization of access and participation in technoscientific work, with issues of domestic politics, the privatization of social reproduction and education.

Make frames the domestic workshop as a necessary part of social reproduction by tying the future of innovation to children's development into makers.[109] The establishing of specific domestic space for raising children has long been a feature of educational theories from Maria and Richard Lovell Edgeworth's *Practical Education* in 1798 through to present-day parenting literature.[110] This participation in social reproduction, however, is differentially expressed based on resources to perform this work, since social reproduction requires access to particular resources, labor, and time that are historically and culturally determined and unevenly distributed.[111] While professional-grade equipment to stock a workshop is often unaffordable to many households, *Make* contributors believe that that should not stop makers.[112] For instance, Griffith's article "The Ultimate Tool Buying Guide" outlines somewhat hyperbolically "a complete list of tools . . . to [outfit] yourself with the ultimate shop for launching your own space program" at what he defines as both a deluxe and a budget level (see Figure 14).[113] A household can opt for a $3,000 plasma cutter rather than the $20,000 version, if on a budget. The concession of accepting the $3,000 model, however, reinforces the economic resources necessary to participate in *Make*'s vision of democratized innovation and the middle-class position

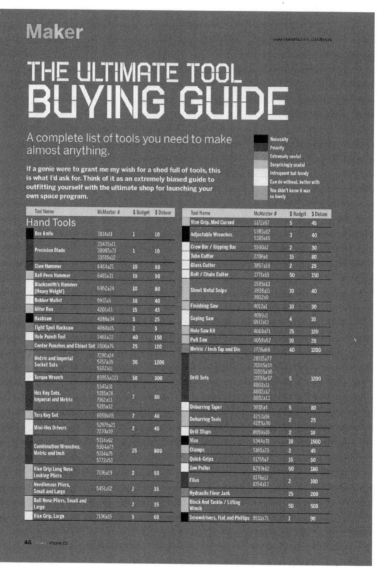

FIGURE 14. *First and second pages of the inventory list with costs for Saul Griffith's ideal workshop, which presumes substantial funds to acquire even at the "budget" level. (Source: Make Community LLC,* Make volume 3, 2005, pp. 46–47.)

of *Make*'s imagined community. Although Griffith frames performing technoscientific work at home as more accessible than imagined, his comments marginalize households without sufficient funds for or access to that equipment.

To address the tensions involving risk and responsibility in DIY technoscience, *Make* reimagines—by means of its standardized project instructions as well as advice for child-rearing and amateur scientific social reproduction—self-governing subjects capable of responsible risk-taking for innovation. *Make* mobilizes children to represent the future of innovation, children who must be raised appropriately in order to cultivate what is believed to be their natural creativity. Pyromania, like that of young Reynst, must be channeled into innovation rather than quashed due to fears of physical risks. By joining the future of technoscience with the future of children under the auspices of neoliberal privatization, *Make* conflates the work of technoscientific innovation with the social reproduction of amateur makers as responsible risk-takers, distributing this responsibility individually to parents capable of executing this workshop-function at home.

Making States and Citizens at Home

To ensure the responsible administration of self-governed making across millions of amateur workshops, *Make* magazine seeks to provide standards for creating, equipping, and operating such alternative technoscientific spaces without threats of ideological risks through the magazine's circulation and its attendant workshop-function. The home workshop operates not only as the site of amateur technoscientific innovation but also of the social reproduction of amateur technoscientific subjects. In this way, contributors to *Make* seek to realize a utopian world of makers raising makers, all of whom responsibly take risks to innovate, particularly to improve social conditions through making by "[imagining] a better country, a better world for our children . . . based on renewable energy, efficient transportation, and flexible, local alternatives for manufacturing and agriculture."[114] This desire to envision the future performs what Benedict Anderson suggests is the anticipatory and self-reflexive capabilities of an imagined community.[115] Through an integration of American individualism and techno-utopianism, *Make* magazine advocates its practices as capable of remaking industrial production, digital culture, technoscientific work, and the nation at large simply by remaking the home.[116]

Makers, the magazine suggests, are not only amateur and DIY scientists but also necessary civic subjects who must mobilize their entrepreneurial sensibilities to remake the entire nation through innovation. Dougherty, for example, urges *Make* readers to recognize that "it's time for us, individually and working together in business, to reconsider what it means to be productive, not just profitable. It's time for us to re-engage in how our government sets priorities for education, health care, housing, and transportation."[117] In this way, *Make* outlines a project of entrepreneurial citizenship, which, following Lilly Irani, "promises that citizens can construct markets, produce value, and do nation building all at the same time."[118] Whereas Charles Peters, journalist and founder of the *Washington Monthly,* had argued that "our hero is the risk-taking entrepreneur who creates new jobs and better products" in "A Neoliberal's Manifesto," *Make* infuses this risk-taking entrepreneur with the maker mindset as a nation-building project.[119]

The 2009 *Make* issue on "ReMake: America," for instance, encourages readers to view uncertainty as an opportunity to take risks for innovation, in pursuit of transforming the nation through transformation of private and individual lives (see Figure 15).[120] This issue of *Make,* in particular, seeks to reframe the 2008 global economic crisis as an opportunity to take risks, demonstrating its investment in the value of risk and its management for innovating material, social, and political infrastructures. As the preface to the special "ReMake: America" section reads:

> A global economic crisis isn't something anyone would wish for, but that doesn't mean it's all bad. These challenging times have presented us with a rare chance to try out new ways of doing things. The opportunities for makers are terrific—we can start at home to remake manufacturing, education, food production, transportation, and recreation.[121]

The characterization of a global economic crisis as not "all bad," however, underscores the economically secure position of *Make*'s imagined readers, who find opportunities ripe for innovating amid widespread conditions of economic uncertainty. Furthermore, *Make* participates in the enduring legacy of the 1990s and 2000s dot-com era, which framed taking economic risks as an active and individual exertion of control contrasted with the passivity associated with recognizing oneself as a victim of systemic economic precarity.[122]

FIGURE 15. *Title page for the "ReMake: America" special section of* Make, *volume 18, which presents a series of private home projects as steps toward remaking the nation. (Source: Make Community LLC,* Make *volume 18, 2009, p. 45.)*

Reimagining citizens as makers who can actively and responsibly take risks, contributors to *Make* often express anxieties over governmental and other restrictive agents, who interfere with the lives of makers, such as those interrupting the work of DIY bio.[123] Although describing remaking at the national scale, for example, the projects featured in "ReMake: America" present private opportunities to remake the nation at the site of the home, in line with the Silicon Valley ethos, and its antecedent countercultural beliefs from the mid-twentieth century, that large government operations should be scaled down to local levels.[124] This approach to governmental reform infused with the start-up mentality central to Silicon Valley, as Stephanie Ricker Schulte demonstrates, frames established government as stale and in need of the disruptive youthful potential of start-ups.[125] Similarly, *Make*'s application of making toward social change expresses what Christina Dunbar-Hester identifies as common to the contemporary hacker ethic, which is a desire to translate hands-on problem solving practices for technology to address community dynamics and politics.[126] However, DIY and hacker practices alone are inadequate in remedying structural social issues.[127] Instead, the magazine's instructions for building an off-the-grid laundry machine and other homesteading projects highlight the individualist and libertarian Silicon Valley politics underlying *Make*, championing individual private change rather than addressing structural or governmental reform.[128]

In considering possible state models that might prove suitable for governing makers, Gurstelle outlines two distinct options that fail to offer both the freedom to innovate and the social reproduction required for the responsible administration of physical risks that mass amateur innovation proliferates:

> In a "nanny state," somebody else—governments, insurance companies, education administrators—decides which projects makers may attempt and which they may not.... On the opposite end of the spectrum is the "night watchman state." Here, authorities try to keep thugs off the street, keep the electricity on, and that's about it. You're pretty much on your own.[129]

Invoking the overly restrictive and feminized nanny state, Gurstelle's nanny figure stifles all makers for fear of physical risks.[130] In contrast, the excessively permissive and masculinized night watchman figure provides insufficient education for novices to handle physical risks. Consequently, Gurstelle's comparison of personified state models draws on constructions of women as overbearing and hypercautious, more likely to enact ideological risks in fear of physical risks, as well as constructions of men as permissive but not nurturing, tacitly more preferable in the allowance of physical risks even without adequate guidance or support.

Instead of either option, however, Gurstelle proposes what he calls the "Maker State," a model organized around mass individual self-governance, where "everyone takes reasonable precautions and wears protective equipment" to innovate responsibly and without interference.[131] Dismissing centralized administration, neoliberal approaches to risk require that individuals take accountability for their own risk encounters.[132] In this way, *Make* contributors believe makers operate best by learning to follow guidelines to handle risks safely so that they can perform the amateur technoscientific work they choose to undertake.[133] For *Make*, it is up to readers individually to monitor and take the risks that are necessary for the future.

Citizens of such a Maker State would hold DIY citizenship. John Hartley initially proposed DIY citizenship as a form of citizenship based in "self-determination not state coercion right down to the details of identity and selfhood."[134] DIY citizens construct their conditions of political citizenship without pressure from paternalistic administration.[135] Responses to Hartley's articulation of DIY citizenship, however, note that he relies both on the fantasy of the autonomous individual deeply entrenched in Western liberalism and on the consumerist model of civic participation that privileges deliberate choice without regard to the constraints of late capitalism on the liberatory potential imagined in DIY citizenship.[136]

Acknowledging critiques of Hartley, however, Matt Ratto and Megan Boler argue that DIY citizenship still provides a productive framework for understanding how site-specific practices of critical making—politically transformative practices of creation—can reimagine social power arrangements.[137] *Make*, making, and DIY models of technoscientific innovation highlight these tensions through negotiations between professional gatekeeping and mass amateurization. Where professionals align historically with exclusionary politics that operate through gatekeeping, democratizing science through the mass amateurization of technoscientific work calls into question who is responsible for related risks, since constitutions of risks and conditions of responsibility operate inextricably.

Within the civic framework that *Make* contributors imagine, education is critical for individuals to become responsible makers. To cultivate the maker mindset, *Make* contributors give "readers instructions to build things themselves, . . . and [they] think everyone is smart enough to understand what [they're] writing about."[138] For *Make*, readers are intelligent and competent individuals who require education to engage in amateur technoscience safely.[139] The magazine constructs makers as educated subjects who take full responsibility for deciding which projects they choose and the risks they take. As the disclaimer asserts in the front matter of every issue of *Make*, "Your safety is your own responsibility, including proper use of equipment and safety gear, and determining whether you have adequate skill and experience. . . . Use of the instructions and suggestions in MAKE is at your own risk."[140] Makers must administer these unavoidable risks with appropriate precautions. Because a maker does so responsibly, regulatory agents who would interfere with making are unnecessary. Consequently, do-it-yourself science and do-it-yourself citizenship amount to do-it-yourself governance.

The DIY citizenship imagined of a Maker State, in its suggestion as predicated on a learned competency of self-governing and self-reliant making, is a distinctly neoliberal model of citizenship, one akin to Julie Passante Elman's critique of contemporary rehabilitative citizenship. According to Elman, rehabilitative citizenship characterizes the discursive confluence of adolescent development, self-improvement, and citizenship in the United States beginning in the 1970s, as "images of rehabilitation became inextricable from endless calls for personal responsibility to promote national health, a type of self-rehabilitation that formed the underpinnings of U.S. neoliberalism."[141] Under the heteronormative and able-bodied framework of rehabilitative citizenship, individuals must learn to exercise unending emotional and physical self-surveillance in order to overcome what is perceived as their individual failings preventing them from becoming healthy and (re)productive citizens, lest they remain deficient. This perpetual self-surveillance and rehabilitation toward ideal citizenship enacts Michel Foucault's model of governmentality, the diffusion of regulatory power across individuals in a population exercising self-governance rather than enforced by localized state institutions and actors, particularly in the context of risk management.[142] Similarly, the Maker State that *Make* imagines requires that makers as innovative entrepreneurs engaging in amateur technoscience learn to monitor themselves continuously to take risks responsibly as well as participate in the social reproduction of responsible risk-taking makers. Without proper guidance in self-governing risk responsibly, creative children with risky pyromaniac tendencies like young Reynst might develop into full-blown arsonists rather than innovative makers sporting valid DIY citizenship.

Gurstelle, however, after making a quick reference to individuals interested in intentional harm by invoking the distinctly racialized and classed figure of the thug, suggests that the menacing thug requires removal from the streets of the Maker State as neither a maker nor reader of the magazine themself.[143] The looming and often Black-coded thug as a threatening figure further signals the white suburban middle-class perspective of *Make*'s imagined community, presuming the presence of menacing danger as constitutive of the streets themselves. While the thug, for Gurstelle, is not described explicitly as the unfortunate outcome of insufficient exposure or access to responsible and risk-taking making, Gurstelle implies that thugs cannot be the outcome of raising children as makers. *Make* articles, after all, "assume the best in people, not the worst," conceiving of readers as both capable in making and good in intention, always able to be fashioned into makers with DIY citizenship.[144] *Make* argues that makers must raise children to become makers themselves to achieve DIY citizenship in the Maker State, rather than potentially becoming malicious thugs, bioterrorists, or pyromaniacs. As antithetical to the responsible risk-taking makers, the deviant figures of thugs, bioterrorists, and pyromaniacs represent the potential subjects that naturally risky children may become if not raised to take risks responsibly toward proper development into entrepreneurial and innovative makers.

Those who *Make* imagines participating in its vision for the future do so in differing ways, based on varying capacities to operate domestic workshops as well as on varying competencies in raising creative children into innovative makers, all of which warrant different levels of valuation while ignoring the historic and continued uneven distribution of resources and access to participate in making that privileges white middle-class masculinity. As *Make* suggests that expertise in DIY is differentially distributed and differentially valued, it similarly suggests that specific individuals are differentially legitimated as DIY citizens in the envisioned Maker State and the future of innovation. One's DIY citizenship is based not only on one's capacities to make, to take risks responsibly toward innovation, but also on one's capacities to make makers, to participate in the magazine's workshop-function and the social reproduction of maker subjects capable of contributing future innovations to the creative economy.

Democratization of technoscientific innovation through mass amateurization entails processes for managing responsibility for the mass proliferation of risks that ensues. *Make* magazine offers one response to address this tension, one tied closely to desires to minimize the bearing of state and social forces on individual autonomy and entrepreneurship in favor of creative production and innovation. *Make* contributors situate the magazine as essential to good parenting by offering a technology-focused child-rearing resource that couples the material and textual reproduction of the workshop and the social reproduction of the epistemic subjects who are to operate them through its workshop-function. Informed by a techno-utopian libertarianism representative of Silicon Valley computing culture, *Make* suggests that individuals, rather than states, become responsible for the risks that innovation entails, rendering states unnecessary in this regard. In his instructions for building a jam jar jet engine at home, for example, Gurstelle warns, "I've never had any problems with this design, but no one—not me, not this magazine—can guarantee your safety."[145] This disclaimer is a reminder that readers must voluntarily take responsibility for the risks involved with this, or any other, project, since the magazine argues that individuals are, and should be, the only ones responsible for their own actions.

While constructing them as naturally creative, *Make* argues that children require particular domestic arrangements if their creativity is to develop into responsible and entrepreneurial risk-taking capable of future technoscientific innovation. Discussions throughout the magazine render this desire for self-governance of risks into a responsibility of social reproduction through the coupling of children with innovation that seeks to naturalize risk-taking itself. Description of young

Reynst as an innovative experimental subject, for instance, reinforces constructions of children as naturally creative. Reference to Reynst's pyromania, however, also suggests the latent potential for children to become dangerous subjects that must instead be shaped into responsible risk-taking. Through proper instruction, such as suggestions for variations on the jam jar jet engine that Gurstelle labels under the playful subheading "Flambé Recipes," parents can harness potentially risky pyromania into the productive making practice of cooking.[146] Even if they were not themselves raised in the ways that *Make* champions, readers participating in this paternalistic mode can demonstrate their own creativity by successfully raising children to be creative makers. Needing to raise children with a range of skills, both digital and nondigital, and with creative inclinations for an unknown future, however, suggests anxieties from Silicon Valley computing culture about the future directions of a digital world.

In addition to framing readers who are capable of raising a young Reynst into a rocket scientist as good parents, the ability to transform pyromania into cooking suggests that naturally risky behavior is not only domesticable but also productive. Figures of creative children serve both to naturalize risk-taking and to reimagine daily life at social scales ranging from the domestic to the national through privatized action, in support of self-governing risk-taking toward technoscientific innovation. In its aims to raise creative children to become entrepreneurial makers, *Make* emphasizes that technoscientific work privileges privatized middle-class and white material infrastructures and resources of social reproduction to create its desired subjects, favoring primarily masculinized practices in the process. To contribute to the future of technoscientific innovation in the creative economy, *Make* suggests that raising naturally creative children into innovative makers may not be rocket science, but it nonetheless requires competent DIY citizenship to self-govern one's own risks responsibly.

CHAPTER 3

Instagram and the Creative Filtering of Authentic Selves

In a November 2017 Twitter post, socialite Paris Hilton shared some photographs she had taken of herself with pop singer Britney Spears in 2006. The post claimed that eleven years ago the two young celebrity women had invented the selfie, a genre of self-photography that has become pervasive in and largely associated with contemporary digital youth culture. In response to Hilton's claims to the origin of the selfie, however, many online articles and social media posts were quick to discredit her.[1] As someone characterized as "famous for being famous," Hilton is often framed as vacuous, shallow, and undeserving of the attention she receives. This is particularly the case with regards to the various ways that Hilton herself is recognized as culturally notable: as born into a hotel empire, as a troubled young woman who parties excessively, as someone with an infamous sex tape, and as one of the leads along with fellow young celebrity Nicole Richie on the reality television show *The Simple Life* (Fox, 2003–5, E! 2006–7). Her claims to the origins of the selfie, regardless of their veracity, reinforce dominant associations of selfies with digital youth—young women and adolescent girls in particular—as well as superficiality, frivolousness, and narcissism. Ultimately, Hilton's claim to the selfie's invention and the many responses to her assertion highlight the intersections of creativity, self-promotion, youth culture, and questions of authenticity at the forefront of contemporary digital media.

This chapter investigates these issues through an examination of both selfies and Instagram, a popular social media platform that has become nearly synonymous with selfies. Famous for offering a range of filters—different visual alteration effects users can apply to images before sharing online—Instagram rose rapidly in popularity since its initial launch in October 2010, and the selfie has been a landmark feature of its user base.[2] Informed by a common desire to "bring out the creativity in all of us," Kevin Systrom and Mike Krieger designed Instagram as an online platform for users to create and share photographs in order to connect with others.[3] In what follows, I explore discourses of creativity about Instagram and the iconic selfie alongside contemporary anxieties around social media technologies as they are believed to impact negatively the individuation and socialization of digital youth. Popular and political discourses bemoaning screen addiction, online narcissism, and internet deception often construct youth, and adolescent girls in particular, as at risk for impoverished social skills, poor self-esteem, and dangerous predation. I examine how such constructions of at-risk adolescents reveal anxieties over shifts in acceptable socialization as they correspond to shifts in media ecologies. I argue that popular discourses surrounding adolescence and social media express concern regarding how new users of social media platforms must learn to individuate and socialize on them broadly. These anxieties manifest through intersecting constructions of adolescents as imagined subjects culturally tasked with the responsibility of learning how to individuate and socialize as they mature into adulthood.

Extending studies of adolescents as subjects amid cultural processes of individuation and socialization, I suggest that new users of social media platforms must similarly learn to individuate and socialize on them, rendering them analogous subjects to adolescents as they work toward acquiring the accepted competencies to engage others on and through different social media platforms. A particular focus for my analysis is the imperative of self-branding as a celebrated framework for understanding processes of individuation and socialization in contemporary digital culture and the creative economy. Self-branding discourses advocate for deliberate self-determination and self-presentation, drawing on commercial and promotional logics of advertising, such that individuals stand out in precarious and unstable creative labor markets by presenting distinctive employable identities. Self-branding culture, I suggest, renders everyone perpetually adolescent as they are expected to revise their identity and self-presentation continuously as economic and cultural conditions fluctuate under the continual deferral of stable (read: adult) identity and success.

Moreover, self-branding is paradoxically conceived as both a process of self-discovery as well as a practice of deliberate self-presentation.

Consequently, self-branding engenders anxieties over deceptive self-presentation of identity. Focusing primarily on selfies and Instagram, as prominent sites of self-branding in digital culture, I argue that discourses denigrating the selfie exemplify anxieties around the acceptable limits of self-presentation as a creative act on social media platforms and in daily life more generally in the era of self-branding. The selfie precipitates concerns over identities as potentially artificial at their core in acknowledging that self-presentation, as it is expected to correspond with an original and authentic identity, can be intentional—and potentially intentionally misleading—products of creative acts of self-branding. That is, the acknowledgment that the self can and should be created via self-branding suggests the potential for the self to be entirely artificial, the self as a con. The selfie, then, questions the limits of the authentic creative self, not only the self that creates but also the self that is created.

Adolescent Social Media

Since launching in the fall of 2010, Instagram has received much public attention, including the iPhone App of the Year award in 2011, acquisition by the social networking site Facebook in April 2012, and reaching a reported eight hundred million users in November 2017.[4] Acknowledging the importance of its users in its popularity as a creative social media platform, the Instagram blog argues that "Instagram, as a tool to inspire and connect, is only as powerful as the community it is made of."[5] From Friendster to LinkedIn, Facebook to Twitter, social media platforms like Instagram foreground user connectivity as a primary organizing principle, whether to send messages, create and share content, or make new contacts.[6] For Instagram, creating digital photographs to share enables users to connect with people all over the world, regardless of whether they have met in person.[7] As stated in Instagram's Google Play Store description, "See the world through somebody else's eyes by following not only the people [they] know, but inspirational Instagrammers, photographers, athletes, celebrities and fashion icons," suggesting connectivity through vicarious experience of others' lives online without requiring offline contact.[8]

This vision of a world of people digitally connected together is one of the many versions of techno-utopianism surrounding social media platforms like Instagram and Twitter, typically championing the potential that these technologies are believed to offer for improving contemporary social conditions. Many have asserted that web technologies enable increased democratic forms of media production as well as economic and political participation.[9] For example, many often argue that the in-person and online protests of the Arab Spring, Occupy Wall Street, #blacklivesmatter, and #metoo were not only made possible by social media platforms but also represent the future of collective action for social change.[10] This optimistic futuring concerning emerging social media often finds anchor in the perceived potential of youth to change the world. Clay Shirky, for instance, contends that youth subjects are often early adopters of new technologies and, as such, serve as indicators of the capacities that those emerging technologies possess to alter social conditions through innovative usage.[11]

Alongside these optimistic positions, however, more pessimistic views question the liberatory or democratic potential that digital technologies supposedly offer, with some characterizing the societal transformations that social media platforms cause as distinctly detrimental.[12] Sherry Turkle, for example, argues that the proliferation of digital communication technologies has minimized the role of face-to-face and, thus, according to her, more intimate forms of interpersonal interaction in favor of mediated and more disconnected relationships that isolate individuals.[13] From concerns of intense narcissism to anxieties over stilted emotional, social, and ethical development, these adult discourses—alongside those guided by optimism—mobilize constructions of youth, and adolescents in particular, to debate the perceived value and threat of emerging media technologies as they potentially unsettle existing social interactions.

Both utopian and dystopian visions of the future connected to emerging social media platforms and their purported effects on youth reinforce constructions of youth culture as paradoxically markers for both a society already in decline on the one hand and a society with a promising future ahead on the other.[14] While adult discourses about adolescents and emerging media often express moral panic over how new technologies increase exposure to inappropriate content, risks of predation, and pathological development, underlying anxieties found in such discussions often prove to be less about the technologies themselves and more about longstanding concerns over regulating the so-cialization of adolescents more broadly.[15]

My interest in the image of the adolescent subject of digital media fo-cuses on how public debates over adolescent behavior negotiate values surrounding processes of individuation and socialization within digital culture more broadly. While adolescence often coincides roughly with the physiological developmental stage of puberty, I treat adolescence less as a biological period of physiological maturation and more as a socially constructed period of designated identity and interpersonal development that youth undergo toward becoming imagined socialized and mature adult subjects. This period of development, in particular, is one anchored in acquiring competencies in individuation and social-ization, recognizing oneself as an individual in relationship with and among other individuals in society.

Discussions of adolescents and teenagers, in particular, provide key discursive battlegrounds over beliefs regarding the social constitution of the adult world, since adolescents operate as limit cases for expecta-tions of maturity, at the boundary between conceptions of childhood and adulthood.[16] Psychological and sociological studies often identify ado-lescence as a period of social development concerned primarily around intentional and reflective identity work in order to socialize into adults.[17] In his taxonomy of adolescent uses of media, for example, psychologist Jeffrey Jensen Arnett articulates identity formation as "one of the most important developmental challenges of adolescence," which is embed-ded in a larger trajectory of socialization with others.[18] Consequently, throughout this chapter, I describe both subjects and platforms as ado-lescent in order to signal tensions around shifting and unsettled prac-tices of individuation and socialization by both users of social media platforms and the platforms themselves, whether involving users at-tempting to figure out how to participate on social media or emerging social media platforms trying to fit into existing media ecologies.

Fundamentally, I suggest that while much of the literature on indi-viduation and socialization focuses on adolescents, all users new to any particular social media platform, whether teenaged or adult, undergo processes of learning to individuate and socialize as they acquire com-petencies for each social media platform they encounter in ways akin to the cultural developmental phase of adolescence. Each social media technology requires that all those who encounter them must learn processes of individuation and socialization enabled and constrained by those particular social media platforms, both their technical features and their normalized social conventions of use, as well as the ever-changing media ecologies they constitute. Examples of parents and grandparents transgressing nominally accepted boundaries of publicity and privacy or instructions prescribing how parents should interact with their children online, for instance, demonstrate how individuation and socialization are ongoing processes on social media platforms, even for those not conventionally identified as adolescent but are in the process of learning the acceptable uses of a communication technology in a given social domain.[19]

In addition to mobilizing adolescence to describe processes of individuation and socialization by users participating on social media platforms, I also characterize as adolescent how social media platforms themselves must negotiate adoption and standardization of use into particular social groups and contexts.[20] Determining their fit into existing media ecologies, whether social groups ultimately use them or not, and their socially acceptable conventions of participation are all constitutive elements of the adolescent character of emerging social media platforms. This is particularly the case as the companies developing them adapt the technologies in the hopes of achieving successful adoption into specific social milieus and their practices of individuation and socialization. In contemporary digital culture, adolescents are closely identified with social media use, though social media users include both youth and adult subjects alike.

Since the increasing availability of digital technologies beginning in the last quarter of the twentieth century, computing devices have been identified as increasingly important agents in processes of adolescent individuation and socialization, joining other forces such as family and various authority figures, preexisting media sources like television, and geographies of socialization like schools.[21] For instance, danah boyd argues that digital social media is already a part of everyday life for many American teenagers, "akin to watching television and using the phone."[22] boyd's use of television and the phone as familiar and accepted technologies in daily life for comparison represents media technologies that after their mass domestication during the twentieth century became closely identified with U.S. teenagers.

If, as boyd argues, "teens are modeling identity through social network profiles so that they can write themselves and their community into being," all users learning to model their identities through social media platforms are similarly learning how to write themselves and their communities into existence through co-constituted practices of individuation and socialization.[23] Trans, gender-fluid, and gender-nonconforming social media users, for example, demonstrate how individual exploration, experimentation, and self-presentation of gender identities online is done in tandem with creating and participating in communities of users who deconstruct and reimagine gender itself.[24] In so doing, users develop familiarity with practices of using social media technologies in order to participate as members of communities constituted, at least in part, through those technologies. Like other social media and communications technologies, Instagram requires specific adolescent processes of creating oneself individually while socializing with others through mechanisms enabled by the platform, which itself is negotiating its place in the lives of its users.

Filtering Selves and Selfies

From photographs celebrities take of themselves in the morning to Kyle Chayka and Marina Galperina's curated exhibition of contemporary artists' works in the *National #Selfie Portrait Gallery,* the selfie is one of the most recognizable, genres of photographs on social media platforms like Instagram.[25] Typically, selfies describe photographs people take of themselves often using mobile cameras and intended for digital network distribution. While acknowledging the inheritance of the tradition of self-portraiture, however, many scholars argue that the selfie is not simply the digital update of the artist's self-portrait.[26] The selfie requires specific technological and social arrangements that allow real-time or immediate feedback of photographs taken, such as digital front-facing cameras on mobile phones, which enable an iterative and recursive process of self-performance and self-presentation.[27] This is particularly exemplified in Carlos Sáez's contribution featured in the *National #Selfie Portrait Gallery,* which emphasizes the dynamic and recursive feedback of selfie creation via digital technologies through the recursive capture of his face (see Figure 16). Selfies express long-standing cultural desires to construct depictions of the self for others, a desire that intertwines

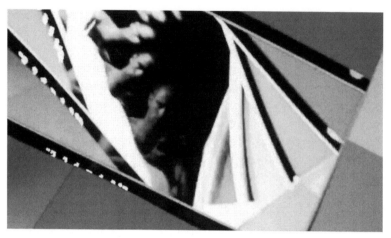

FIGURE 16. *Carlos Sáez's recursive selfie video art piece "Selfie" presented at the* National #Selfie Portrait Gallery. *(Source: Carlos Sáez, "Selfie," available at Kyle Chayka, Vimeo, 2013; screenshot by author.)*

individuation and socialization reimagined through digital networked technologies.[28]

Rather than conceive of selfies merely as images of the self, I examine selfies as a set of pervasive practices of communication in order to unpack how selfies operate in and negotiate technological and social dynamics of self-presentation in contemporary digital culture, particularly in the context of creative economy discourses.[29] Commonly associated with adolescents, and particularly "stereotypical young girls making duck faces in their bathrooms," the selfie is a frequently vilified feature of social media.[30] Anxieties about selfies, for instance, often express concern over the perceived pathological callousness, narcissism, and other psychological harm believed to be plaguing the youth who take them.[31] The premise of the short-lived television show *Selfie* (ABC, 2014), for example, dramatizes the life of Eliza Dooley, a reference to playwright George Bernard Shaw's *Pygmalion* (1912), as a social media–obsessed young woman who realizes that online fame cannot fulfill her need for intimate personal relationships. This concern over absent intimacy expresses what Turkle argues happens as users increasingly confuse "intimacy and solitude" through their digital interactions with each other.[32] Turkle's negative account of digital interactions, however, relies on preexisting conceptions of intimacy and solitude, which privilege face-to-face and pre-digital modes of communication. The selfie, when described as a narcissistic and isolating act, reinforces such assumptions.

What Turkle and others lament as a loss of intimacy resulting from emerging digital media usage represents a shift engendered through emerging digital media in the conditions of what constitute those very social values.[33] Castigation of selfie practices as an affront to existing social conventions of conduct ignores or resists that definitions of intimacy are in revision due to changing media ecologies, as adolescent social media platforms mature into integrated components of social life. Much of the public criticism of the now-defunct tumblr blog *Selfies at Funerals*, for example, bemoaned selfie-taking at sites of mourning as disrespectful, and often identified adolescents as the primary culprits of such acts.[34]

Running counter to disparaging accounts of the selfie, however, others praise—or at least take seriously—the selfie as a contemporary practice of communication, acknowledging its relationship to existing and emerging modes of individuation and socialization.[35] Against the construction of adolescents as callous or self-centered for taking selfies at funerals, for example, James Meese and his collaborators argue that the selfies featured on *Selfies at Funerals* represent a new model of mourning in a world saturated with digital networked technologies.[36] The negative criticisms reveal an inability or unwillingness to recognize new forms of socialization scaffolded by digital technologies, such as shifting interpersonal encounters of mourning from immediate physical interactions to online engagements with distributed communities.[37]

For Karen ann Donnachie, selfies offer "an ideal medium for experimentation of personality for both kids and kidults (adults who continue to enjoy childlike activities)."[38] In her comment, Donnachie attempts to defend selfie practices by drawing on existing conceptions of adolescence, or in her terms "pubertal society," as a period of acceptable identity experimentation. As a consequence, she frames those inclined to treat the selfie as a site for experimenting with self-presentation as children or childlike themselves, reinforcing the association of youth and adolescence with negotiating processes of individuation. Along this line of thinking, the creators of Instagram drew on images of youth in the creation of the platform. Systrom and Krieger attributed their passion for experimenting with cameras as children themselves as what informed the photography-oriented nature of the Instagram platform, arguing that photographs allow users to share moments in their individual lives.[39] Systrom and Krieger framed Instagram, then, as rooted in associations of childhood experiences with photography as experiences for experimenting with creative expression and autobiographic documentation.

Noting limitations in the quality of photographs that mobile phone cameras were capable of producing when launching the app, however, Instagram developed filters as a central feature of its platform, arguing that the "awesome looking filters [can] transform your photos into professional-looking snapshots" (see Figure 17).[40] The iconic filters of Instagram function as shortcuts to alter, enhance, and stylize photographs by tinkering with color saturation, hue, contrast, and sharpness as well as adding effects including halos and stylized edges. Taking photographs and applying filters represents the central creative process of Instagram. Instagram traffics in the amateur and mobile photography of its user base by providing a platform to "transform your everyday photos and videos into works of art and share them with your family and friends," a claim that attempts to elevate user photographs as highly creative products.[41]

While filtering on Instagram typically refers to a pivotal step in the process of editing photographs before uploading them to a user's account, I draw on Brooke Erin Duffy's conception of filtering to describe the many processes of selection required to fabricate the online self from a user's offline life. For Duffy, filtering manifests in "vigilant self-monitoring on social media" that involves a range of different practices, including deciding whom users friend, what they post, what they share, how they share it, as well as whom they ignore and what they omit.[42] Instagram users, if they are to create and circulate photographs to construct presentations of themselves online, must select discrete moments from their continuously unfolding offline lives to share with the Instagram community. This process of selecting and sharing moments from offline life—as well as how those moments are framed, edited, and presented—constitutes the filtering of the self for the social media platform. Performing autobiographic work, users filter to fashion themselves on Instagram through the series of photographs presented, whether taken in the kitchen, at the gym, or out hiking.[43] Filtering describes the creative processes of not only user content generation but of

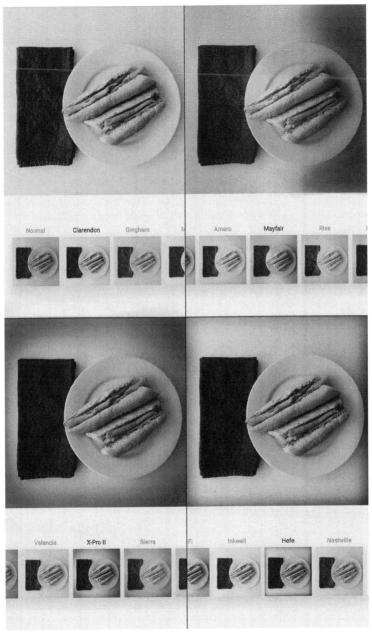

FIGURE 17. *Demonstration of different Instagram filters altering image qualities on the same source photograph, including color saturation, hue, contrast, and sharpness, as well as adding effects including halos and stylized edges. (Source: Instagram; image from author screenshots.)*

individuation and socialization on Instagram, specifically, and on social media platforms, more broadly.

As the descriptions on both the iTunes App Store and the Google Play Store claim, Instagram was designed for "creative people across the globe."[44] These "creative people" who take selfies and post them to their Instagram accounts are filtering photographs as part of the process of filtering their offline lives to construct presentation of their individual identities online.[45] Selfies, then, serve a role in identity creation and experimentation. How users filter these various elements is what is recognized as creative in their self-presentations. Understanding creativity with respect to selfies requires first understanding established social conventions and trends.[46] Creativity in this context functions in how users negotiate how to present themselves legibly to others as distinctive but acceptable individuals.[47] Consequently, creative experimentation with the filtering of photographs results in creative experimentation with the filtering of the offline self for online self-presentation as it engages with social expectations for the self via the selfie.

Self-Branding as Identity Work

The first act of the 27 November 2015 episode of the National Public Radio show *This American Life* (1995–present) examined the complex social negotiations that selfies demand of their creators, both online and offline.[48] Although speaking with three adolescent girls named Julia, Jane, and Ella as representatives of selfie culture reinforced associations of adolescent girls with selfies, host Ira Glass's investigation into how they post selfies revealed intricate logics regulating their conduct on and around Instagram. The adolescent girls, in particular, articulated to Glass the many "unspoken rules" that govern their selfie practices. Their conversation emphasized the thoughtful deliberations that go into posting selfies with the goal of successful online self-presentation through processes including peer review with friends before uploading photographs. Glass suggested this as similar to a "job," a comparison with which the girls enthusiastically agreed before likening it to directing a brand aiming to remain "relevant." Relevance, Jane explained, describes how much "people care about what you're posting on Instagram," to which Julia added that it is about people "[caring] about you."

The framing of people caring about you through caring about what you post, what the guests described as "relevance," traffics in contemporary economic and lifestyle advice on self-branding.[49] As Alice E. Marwick explains, imperatives for self-branding advocate strategic construction and presentation of the self to others and the market by drawing on commercial branding practices as the ideal mechanism for personal growth and success.[50] The rise of self-branding discourses in contemporary digital culture underscores how branding is not simply a business practice or perspective but "is now both reliant on, and reflective of, our most basic social and cultural relations" in a range of domains.[51] Nation branding, for example, arose in recent years as governmental practices to promote the nation in a globalized world wherein traditional views of geopolitical identities have changed.[52] The United Kingdom's "Cool Britannia" and Japan's "Cool Japan" initiatives represent examples of such government-directed projects to brand particular identities for themselves and their economies to others globally.[53]

Branding culture extends from the rise of promotional culture in the mid to late twentieth century, as techniques for marketing aimed to amplify and supplement the appeal of commodities.[54] The most recognized champion of self-branding is marketing consultant Tom Peters, who, in an influential 1997 *Fast Company* magazine article titled "The Brand Called You," argued that "it's time for me—and you—to take a lesson from the big brands, a lesson that's true for anyone who's interested in what it takes to stand out and prosper in the new world of work."[55] Amid contemporary economic precarity, self-branding has provided a self-regulating mechanism for the neoliberal subject.[56] In advocating for self-branding, for instance, Peters links self-branding with recognizing one's own power, a practice of individual self-actualization: "If you want to grow your brand, you've got to come to terms with power—your own."[57] Peters's comment deploys empowerment and self-discovery rhetoric to disguise this self-regulation "in the new world of work," one organized around "projects," a term that signals the conditions of the contemporary creative and precarious gig economy that leaves many workers without long-term employment security.[58]

Consequently, I conceive of this conflation of identity work and employability via self-branding as a form of cruel optimism. According to Lauren Berlant, cruel optimism names deep attachments to promissory ideals that both animate but also ultimately inhibit a subject's flourishing.[59] As a celebrated neoliberal framework of approaching the self and the market, self-branding promises to reward individuals with both self-knowledge and financial success if they can adapt continually under precarity, obfuscating the structural economic conditions that constitute the conditions of insecurity itself. Peters, for example, reimagines a person's career not as a long-term vocational commitment or trajectory but as "a portfolio of projects that teach you new skills, gain you new expertise, develop new capabilities, grow your colleague set, and constantly reinvent you as a brand."[60]

Rather than aspirational consumption, which was a previously dominant mode of self-expression manifest through consumptive choices commonly tied to brand recognition, self-branding tethers individual identity and self-expression to aspirational labor, how "self-expression is articulated through a patterned set of highly individualized, value-generating productive activities."[61] Aspirational labor results in the deferred compensation and achievement that aspiring creative laborers experience as they continue to undertake undercompensated or uncompensated work in the hopes of future recognition and security in the work they believe to find desirable, fulfilling, and actualizing of their individual characters.[62] Subsequently, a career now represents unending reconstruction of oneself as a brand, a deliberately and strategically unending deferral of matured adulthood and stable employment in a precarious creative economy. Self-branding's cruel optimism lies in this mobilization of aspirational labor.

Self-branding practices rely on contemporary web technologies, since effective construction and presentation of the self by many requires ubiquitous communication and information infrastructure.[63] Aspiring creative laborers use social media to improve their employability given the reduction of previously available options for acquiring work.[64] According to Marwick, software technologies like Facebook, LinkedIn, Twitter, and other social media sites, what comprise the platforms of Web 2.0, "[teach] their users to be good corporate citizens in the postindustrial, post-union world by harnessing marketing techniques to boost attention and visibility" in order for users to reinvent themselves to remain "relevant" in ever-changing and insecure conditions.[65] Contemporary social media platforms encourage users to construct and reconstruct presentations of themselves consciously and continuously for others as conditions change.

Like YouTube, DeviantArt, and many other social media platforms, Instagram relies on active user participation in creating and disseminating user-generated content. Such web platforms, rather than primarily producing content themselves, provide tools for users to create and share their own content, including personal profiles, images, music, and videos. Web 2.0's emphasis on user-generated content fundamentally relies on user creativity and labor, as the various platforms require continual supply of user creations for circulation. Users generate value for themselves and for social media platforms through the content they create and share, which platforms can monetize through strategies such as ad placement and subscription costs. Many studies of web 2.0 and social media platforms demonstrate that despite rhetoric about enabling users new modes of creation and socialization, however, such technologies continue to favor existing corporate interests by exploiting users as free, or underpaid, creative laborers.[66] Moreover, beyond the labor of creating content, users must also often fulfill demands for "emotional labor, self-branding labor, and an always-on mode of entrepreneurial labor" in order to be successful or achieve and maintain "relevance" on these platforms.[67]

The process of consciously producing what Marwick calls the "edited self," deliberate and ongoing construction and presentation of an identity, appears in similar accounts of contemporary identity formation work, particularly in relation to media technologies.[68] For instance, John Hartley's concept of DIY citizenship characterizes "the practice of putting together an identity from the available choices, patterns and opportunities on offer in the semiosphere and the mediasphere."[69] While describing everyday citizen identity in this model based largely in television culture, Hartley's conception of identity formation and presentation via DIY citizenship characterizes the idealized mode of individual self-presentation online under the logic of self-branding. Similarly, Sandra Weber and Claudia Mitchell propose describing ongoing youth practices of reconstructing online self-presentations as "identities-in-action" in order to emphasize that processes of identity formation and presentation are "multifaceted and in flux."[70] Weber and Mitchell, in particular, argue that "the creative construction that is involved in digital production permits the manipulation of gendered, raced, and sexualized identities, both online and offline."[71] This focus on deliberate self-fashioning as a model of identity work that values both individual autonomy and self-determination resonant with neoliberal ideals is seen as determined by individuals themselves rather than inherited from or coerced by social forces, including histories or cultural contexts.

In describing adolescent identity work, particularly with digital technologies, Weber and Mitchell invoke the tradition of construction toys to highlight what they regard as the "playful yet more or less deliberate creative 'assembling' involved—whether it be of the virtual components of websites or the constructing and deconstructing of gender as part of on- and offline role play."[72] Weber and Mitchell's comments link the tinkering of technological and digital parts with the tinkering of identity parts, recombined by internet users as they construct and present themselves to others as they wish.[73] Instagram as well as other social media platforms similarly suggest that the creation of the content posted online, and by extension the identities presented through these images, is deliberate construction work.

Identity work, largely attributed to adolescence, undergoes what Sarah Banet-Weiser suggests is a fundamental reorientation, since answering the question of "Who am I?" becomes that of "How do I sell myself?" in a world of self-branding.[74] If self-branding in the creative economy requires everyone to ask themselves continually "How do I sell myself?"—reconfiguring themselves to adapt to the uncertainties of the market as a form of cruel optimism—then self-branding culture, by virtue of associating self-branding as mechanisms for self-discovery, self-determination, and self-actualization, renders everyone adolescent in the continual interrogation of "Who am I?" As Duffy contends, "Aspirational labourers understand self-branding practices as imperative to their creative projects as they endeavour to market themselves to (current and potential) audiences and advertisers, while forging a consistent brand identity across social media platforms."[75] Self-branding as a never-ending project of identity work amid precarity defers the arrival of the fantasy of fully actualized and stable self-knowledge associated with an elusive adulthood alongside aspirational labor's deferral of idealized but elusive social and economic compensation.

Permissible Selves

Despite self-branding discourses framing online self-presentation as an ideal mechanism for self-discovery, what one is allowed to present about oneself and how—and by extension what one is allowed to learn about oneself—is socially and technologically policed, varying across different contextual negotiations of bodily and social differences, including race, gender, ability, sexuality, and the like. In exploring the permissibility of selfies themselves in this regard, I consider not only the permissibility of particular selfies (which selfies are or are not allowed) but also the permissibility of selfies in toto (whether selfies as a whole are acceptable or not) as limits to creative self-presentation. Selfies, in spite of their ubiquity on social media, are commonly reviled elements of digital culture, as evinced in discourses that frame selfie-taking as inane or pathological behavior. Such negative criticism of selfies also often operates to denigrate and discipline youth, and adolescent girls in particular, who are most closely associated with the practice.[76] Associating selfies with adolescent girls, which genders selfies as a feminine practice, also functions to dismiss the social value or legitimacy of selfies themselves as a cultural practice, since that which the adolescent girl loves is often the target of social ire.

Negative criticisms of selfies as an emerging media practice, and one linked to adolescent girls, draw on enduring histories of anxieties regarding new media technologies and youth that often characterize girls as haplessly at risk and unable to respond critically and deliberately to the media content and technologies they encounter.[77] Studies of girlhood and media practices, however—whether focused on online personal websites, chatting and messaging services, or handmade zines—demonstrate how deliberately and consciously young and adolescent girls can engage in critical media consumption and production practices to fashion themselves, experiment with their identities and sexualities, construct their social groups, and negotiate mainstream cultural productions.[78] Contemporary girl media engagements participate in existing and evolving practices of girls and young women producing cultural media about and for themselves, drawing on and transforming the—sometimes oppressive—cultural materials available to them in order to shape their identities, as individuals and as groups.[79] Similarly, selfie practices serve as important sites for constructing and exploring the gendered and racialized self, adolescent girl or otherwise, though not without contending with the constraints of social and technological forces.

Selfie-takers must negotiate permissible constructions of race and gender, among other dimensions of identity, highlighting how racialized and gendered corporeal bodies remain central to the production of digital content.[80] What might be otherwise conceived as disembodied or immaterial creative labor, social media self-presentation involves constraints to the creative freedom imagined as part of online self-branding and resonant models of identity such as Hartley's DIY citizenship. As Lisa Nakamura emphasizes, racial embodiment and experiences offline are among the many forces that persist to impact racial performances online, in spite of 1990s web discourses imagining post-racial internet participation.[81]

For example, by comparing and contrasting social media user attitudes toward permissible selfie practices—poses, backgrounds, posting frequency—Apryl A. Williams and Beatriz Aldana Marquez explore how selfies may operate differently for white men compared to Black men and Latino men. Selfies, as a practice dominantly gendered feminine, were broadly stigmatized by the white men in their study.[82] In contrast, Williams and Aldana Marquez explain that "the contested acceptance of selfies among Black and Latino men demonstrates that these images play an important role in the representation of masculinity. . . . Macho men are required to be confident and selfie taking allows them to blatantly construct that confidence."[83] Such practices demonstrate ways that bodies presented through selfies negotiate dynamics of race and gender as well as prevailing attitudes and conventions surrounding selfies themselves.

Exploring how images for online self-presentation can be mobilized to contest existing racial formations, Minh-Ha T. Pham examines Asian style bloggers working with their racialized and gendered bodies in order to present their senses of style in fashion photographs.[84] These bloggers use fashion photographs and their bodily poses to participate as style leaders in the Western fashion world, which has historically excluded Asians by relegating Asian subjects to the peripheral imagination of sweatshop factory laborers and counterfeiters.[85] Selfies, deployed as a form of fashion photography in this context, allow historically marginalized subjects to stake claim in the creative economy and in the fashion world. They do so, however, by working against, around, and through existing constructions of their gendered and racialized identities.[86]

Selfie-takers must not only negotiate existing social conventions to be successful among community members, whether to be permissible or to reimagine prevailing expectations; they must also contend with the policies and technical features of the social media platform itself as well as its ownership. As Tarleton Gillespie argues, while web 2.0 discourses often focus on social media platforms as enabling user-generation of content as the primary service, "content moderation is the essential offer platforms make" since the often invisible work of content moderation is necessary to regulate and provide user-generated content that is acceptable and appealing to the community at-large.[87] This regulation of content functions not only to protect users from each other, often by having predominantly workers of color outside the United States contend with and remove violent, graphic, and traumatizing content, but also to control the overall brand identity of the social media platform itself for a range of stakeholders from users and advertisers to the general public.[88] Content moderation, whether enacted by other users, platform workers, or coded algorithms, is the very business of social media sites and serves as a limiting force to online self-presentation and identity construction.

During the spring of 2015, controversy around the hashtag #curvy and its associated online movement demonstrated how social media platforms themselves, both the technologies as well as the administrative personnel that own and moderate them, police acceptable online self-presentation in relation to the bodies of content creators. Begun as a declaration of body positivity by a range of women seeking to celebrate their corporealities of varied shapes, proportions, and constitutions, the Instagram platform banned photographs bearing the hashtag #curvy, citing them as "pornographic" and, thus, in violation of the terms of service.[89] Users such as @mayah.camara protested the ban of #curvy by deploying other hashtags as replacements to circumvent Instagram's technological mechanism for banning their body positive images, often still gesturing to the original hashtag, such as with #curvee or #curvyban (see Figure 18). Instagram eventually lifted the ban on #curvy in July 2015.

Instagram's decision to enforce through the technical platform itself the banning of photographs of women linked to a hashtag meant to celebrate their bodies against conventionally narrow standards of beauty participates in long-standing anxieties over adolescent girls

FIGURE 18. *Instagram post from @mayah.camara using #curvee as a strategy to protest Instagram's ban on #curvy. (Source: @mayah.camara, Instagram, 2015; screenshot by author, December 2020.)*

and young woman who use online tools for exploration and expression of themselves as gendered, sexual, and fleshy individuals.[90] Through the #curvy hashtag, Instagram users attempted to present their corporeal bodies to the social networking community as a declaration of acceptance and pride in their offline selves. This celebration foregrounded many kinds of bodies that may otherwise be considered undesirable or viewed as in need of creative construction before becoming normatively suitable for online circulation, such as through fad exercise and diet regimes, "miracle" products, or Photoshopping. In this situation, however, Instagram policed women, treating them as if they were adolescent girls "inappropriately" sexualizing themselves. The hashtag #curvy exemplifies the limits of creative online self-presentation as it negotiates the corporealities of the gendered and racialized bodies of social media users and their selfies within the constraints of social and technological permissibility. Consequently, attending to how peers and platforms constrain creative experimentation with identity and self-presentation underscores how untenable the neoliberal fantasy of complete individual self-fashioning is at the core of self-branding.

FIGURE 19. *Young women taking a selfie in the Chainsmokers' music video "#Selfie," representing stereotypical superficial social media users. (Source: The Chainsmokers, "#Selfie," 2014; screenshot by author.)*

Authenticity and Artificiality

The 2014 hit song "#Selfie" by the Chainsmokers parodies many assumptions about selfie-takers.[91] Over the electronic dance track, a vapid-sounding young woman in a nightclub bathroom shares with her friend some thoughts on a rival's outfit, interactions with a love interest named Jason, and her quantity of online "likes" (see Figure 19). In parodying the imagined thought processes of a young woman posting selfies, an extension of the stereotypical social media–obsessed adolescent girl, however, the track, perhaps inadvertently, highlights many thoughtful decisions that go into posting what might be regarded as a successful selfie. From writing a clever caption to interpreting the approval it receives based on the "likes," the speaker consults her online and offline social networks for approval of her decisions regarding behavior both online and offline. This includes how to respond to the attention from Jason on whom she has been fixated all evening. The final comments from the song express validation that she "took a good selfie" based on the approval she receives from Jason not through him publicly "liking" her selfie online but through privately sending her a text message—a more intimate mode of communication in this media ecology.

Remarking on another young woman at the nightclub, however, the speaker of "#Selfie" dismisses her as "such a fake model" who "definitely bought all her Instagram followers." These disparaging comments rely on particular logics of authenticity and artificiality to discount the other young woman as competition. Accusations of being a "fake" rather than "real" model and of having purchased followers rather than having voluntary ones denigrate what is perceived as inauthentic in order to discredit the other young woman. Ironically, the song's speaker is unreflective about her own inauthentic self-presentation online, such as choosing a filter to "appear tan" in her selfie. While the song dramatizes how concerns around authenticity and artificiality function in assessments of self-presentation online, the different responses to purchasing followers compared to using a filter to appear tan demonstrate that different elements of self-presentation operate using varied logics of authenticity and artificiality.

Underlying these assessments of authenticity and artificiality is the perceived relationship between the online self-presentation and the corresponding offline identity of the user, with a commonplace preference for what is perceived to be authentic. Verisimilitude between both online and offline conventionally suggests greater authenticity, while excessive promotion or creative presentation of the self is performed at the expense of the authentic self. However, in recognizing the online production of selfies and other elements of a self-brand as deliberate creative work, I suggest that concerns about the authenticity or artificiality of selfies and online self-presentations correlate to concerns about the authenticity or artificiality of offline identities. That an online presentation of self as a malleable online presentation of identity might not correspond fully to an original authentic offline identity suggests that any and all offline identities may, ultimately, also be artificial.

I contend that celebrating deliberate decision-making about self-presentation online as creative in the logic of self-branding within creative economy discourses, then, is inextricably yoked to anxieties about deliberate decision-making that creates what is viewed as artificial and misleading representations of the self. This paradoxical binding of self-promotion and authenticity is a prominent element of American individualism, which finds particular salience in discourses of self-branding. Such discourses seek to justify self-branding as authentic self-determination and self-actualization by glossing over how the practice contradictorily entails calculated manufacturing of a seemingly authentic self for promotion to others.[92]

Moreover, there are various conceptions of authenticity in circulation—from honesty and transparency in motives to private and intimate disclosure of content.[93] For self-branding to be understood as authentic, following Banet-Weiser, self-branding must not be seen "as imposition of a concept or product by corporate culture but rather as the individual taking on the project herself as a way to access her 'true' self," wherein she chooses rather than is coerced into becoming part of corporate and commercial culture, supposedly on her own terms.[94] Discourses of authenticity in social media self-branding, as well as entangled discourses of ordinariness and relatability, however, often work to obscure privileges that improve aspirational laborers' capacities for success by focusing on the self as an unmediated entrepreneur rather than users' differential access to economic and social capital, such as financial resources for wardrobe and travel or advantageous personal connections.[95]

Despite this, self-branding as authenticity is imagined as a process of reflective identity work. Identity work as creative work in this model of self as self-brand, as a fantasy of identity as continually and intentionally reconfigurable through such models as DIY citizenship, however, suggests in its extreme a possible absence of an original authentic self that holds the presentation of online identity accountable to accurate correspondence. By providing platforms for constructing and revising the self and self-brand, social media platforms amplify anxieties regarding the authenticity of individual identities by highlighting self-presentation, as it is linked to offline identity, as artificially performed online without constraint. Turkle bemoans this as the desire to treat the "self as avatar," which she argues blurs distinctions between "performances of identity" and "identity itself."[96] Turkle's claim, however, suggests that the two can be completely divisible, with performance of identity, as artificial and thus bad, and identity itself, as authentic and thus good. Fears of the "self as avatar" suggest that acknowledgment of online self-presentation as an ongoing creative act that may be partially artificial risks becoming perceived as wholly inauthentic.

In terms of selfies and social media profiles, online self-presentation expects a significant, though not necessarily total, correspondence between online presentation and offline self.[97] The history of photography that informs selfie culture, in particular, relies on a logic of expressive authenticity, what Marcus Banks explains occurs when people believe that specific representations of "things are true to their own nature."[98] Conceptions of the authenticity of the selfie, particularly on Instagram, emerge, in part, from imagined immediate production and circulation, drawing on existing views of the immediate and authentic character imagined of Polaroid photography and in contrast to the artifice commonly associated with airbrushing and Photoshop.[99]

However, magazine and internet guides on "how to take a selfie" underscore the selfie as a creative act, one rife with decisions and opportunities for experimentation even without image manipulation technologies.[100] While general attitudes toward obvious alterations of visual effects on images typically render them outside labels of authentic, in certain subcultures of selfies, particular kinds of visible visual editing are accepted and even expected. For instance, Katrin Tiidenberg's analysis of specific body positive selfie practices in some communities on tumblr identifies that a set of distinctive image distortions and effects are conventionally used and accepted among the community members even if they would otherwise meet suspicion from mainstream audiences.[101]

Concerns around authenticity on social media suggest that knowing someone authentically is a precondition for knowing them intimately within a world constituted by digital technologies.[102] The importance of this authenticity and intimacy came under scrutiny through revisions made to the popular Instagram profile of Essena O'Neill at the end of 2015.[103] O'Neill, a young Australian woman, was a popular online celebrity and model across multiple social media platforms including Instagram, where she had nearly six hundred thousand followers at the time. Citing personal feelings of discontentment with her online fame, however, O'Neill revised the captions of many of her popular Instagram photographs to describe the time and resources as well as the physical and affective work that went into making her popular images.[104] Such descriptions of taking "countless photos," for example, directly opposed the imagined authenticity to which Instagram's claim to instant photography alludes (see Figure 20).

By revealing the calculated labors that went into her popular Instagram account, O'Neill revealed the constructed nature of perceived expressive authenticity. While some responded positively to O'Neill's unveiling of the work that went into her profile, others attacked her and framed her as inauthentic—both in regards to what was otherwise believed to be her previously authentic Instagram as well as to her own

FIGURE 20. *Instagram post by Essena O'Neill, with caption explaining the resources, labor, and time involved in taking the seemingly "instant" photograph. (Source: @essenaoneill, Instagram; via Thomas Gorton, "An Instagram Model Is Calling Bullshit on Her Fake Reality," http://dazeddigital.com/, 2015.)*

claims of wanting to be honest as to why she demystified her online self-presentation at all. Such criticism attempted to reestablish acceptable and familiar conditions for maintaining the conception of authenticity that O'Neill complicated. O'Neill's massive popularity coupled with her airing details that contradicted the perceived immediacy of her photographs undermined established social conceptions of authenticity on Instagram. To many of her followers, O'Neill revealed herself to them as a con artist or scammer, which, following Turkle, represents a figure whose "charm in fictional presentation . . . is more reviled for . . . duplicity and exploitiveness."[105] O'Neill's reveal suggested that her followers were incapable of assessing the difference between authenticity and artificiality as conventionally understood. If a user perceived to be inauthentic, like O'Neill, can amass widespread popularity by deceiving hundreds of thousands of users online, then it suggested both that any and all users may similarly be inauthentic and that any and all users may also be susceptible to such scams.

Similarly, popular Instagrammer Caroline Calloway became the center of controversy as a scammer following revelations that her autobiographic account cataloging her misadventures as an American college student studying at Cambridge University was not authored by her, or at least not by her alone. Calloway had approximately 850,000 followers when Natalie Beach, ex-friend and former Cambridge classmate, revealed in a 2019 *The Cut* article titled "I Was Caroline Calloway" that she had ghostwritten the lengthy captions on Calloway's Instagram posts, which were a primary draw for her audience.[106] Furthermore, Beach's article clarified the history of Calloway's growing Instagram popularity, including how Calloway's presentation of authenticity was fabricated through a collaboration with Beach, how Calloway had initially bought followers to grow her account, and how both Calloway's initial book deal and "Creativity Workshop" tour failed. Following Beach's article, several responses from journalists recounted Calloway's story through the language of the "scam." Subsequently, Calloway herself sought to capitalize on the ensuing controversy and attention. With her first book, titled *Scammer* and available for preorder as of the summer of 2021, selling tickets to workshops titled "The Scam," and a revised Instagram bio that explicitly identifies her as a scam, Calloway demonstrated that, despite anxieties surrounding authenticity and artificiality in the era of self-branding, even scamming itself can be incorporated into one's own identity and brand (see Figure 21).[107]

Suspicions of artificial online self-presentation find particularly strong expression in fears over catfishing, a more recent term describing intentionally deceptive and predatory online misrepresentations of self usually in the context of dating.[108] As the reality television show *Catfish: The TV Show* (MTV, 2012–present) depicts, catfishing users present themselves online as someone else for a range of reasons, including a desire for attention or a desire to explore different sexual identities, in addition to more conventionally assumed malicious intentions.[109] From inaccurate or out-of-date photographs of users on dating profiles to completely fabricated fictitious identities, worries around the perceived authenticity of online self-presentation negotiate the limits of celebrating online identity determination, experimentation, and expression on social media as a deliberate creative act—as a form of construction play. Significantly, *Catfish* often presents Black and poor victims as those duped by catfish, reinforcing racial and classed constructions of a digital divide or lack of digital media literacies regarding online interaction for those groups of users.

Online platforms as technologies mediating communication enable forms of self-representation and activity that afford anonymity and

FIGURE 21. *Instagram profile header for Caroline Calloway explicitly describing herself as "The other scam. The one you love" in her bio. (Source: @carolinecalloway, Instagram; screenshot by author, December 2020.)*

fabrication, which undermine the desire for accountable and authentic self-presentation. Questions surrounding O'Neill and Calloway as scammers, con artists, or deceptive catfish amplify pervasive concerns regarding accountable correspondence between offline and online bodies and behaviors. This is not unique to online social media sites, however, since suspicions of deception have accompanied the historic emergences of various communication technologies. For instance, Carolyn Marvin recounts telegraph operators' anxieties over deceitful reporting and hoaxes from pranksters during the nineteenth century, seen as a threat to public welfare.[110]

Internet technologies participate in this history of users exploring and exploiting the deceptive affordances of new media technologies, rooted in the difficult effort required to hold any and all users accountable to their potentially anonymized behaviors online. This is particularly prevalent in practices of cyberbullying, forms of bullying mediated through computational technologies and often using features that enable bullies to enact harm while remaining anonymous and at a distance.[111] Although discourses often construct cyberbullying almost exclusively as a troubling albeit supposedly "natural" behavior of adolescent girls, adults, including men, also participate in (anonymous) harassment and cyberbullying practices, as evidenced in the toxicity and misogyny of #gamergate.[112]

Anxieties about artificial self-presentation online emphasize that discourses of authenticity function to regulate how individuals individuate and socialize, negotiating the forms of anonymity that internet technologies themselves may afford. Discourses of authenticity have informed and been used to justify policies and practices that social media platforms like Twitter and Instagram implement in the desire to hold accountable and verifiable online and offline selves, which include verified accounts, real name policies, and submitting proof of legal identificatory documentation. Real name policies on social media platforms such as Facebook require that users display and use names online that correspond to what they use offline, which Facebook justifies as in the interest of protecting users from predatory scams, deceitful interactions, and fake accounts through logics of authentic and accountable self-presentation.

However, real name policies, which vary widely in constitution across different social media platforms, inconsistently enforce what counts a real name and, by extension, authentic self-presentation.[113] As one example, Facebook's real name policy requires a construction of authenticity that largely favors normative and mainstream identities and experiences, which disproportionately results in the deactivation of accounts for users with fluid, vulnerable, and marginalized identities. Primarily negatively impacting gender-fluid users, transfolk, Indigenous Americans, abuse survivors, sex workers, and drag performers, among others, Facebook's real name policy denies these users the ability to articulate their own authentic online self-representations and social interactions. Such regulation particularly affects these users, who already must negotiate tensions between the ability to access information, rehearse self-presentation, and participate in communities online while potentially being surveilled and subject to online harassment as a result, often in order to compensate for the comparatively insufficient resources and opportunities for support and self-presentation available to them in their (potentially hostile) local environments offline.[114]

Ultimately, authenticity in selfies, as in other contexts, is always a constructed quality; the difference between what is considered authentic and what is considered (acceptably) artificial is determined by social conventions.[115] Although concerns about the selfie being artificial operate as one anxiety around the correspondence of online self-presentation to offline identity, Aaron Hess notes an opposite tension when the selfie is seen as too authentic, or improperly filtered and inadequately artificial.[116] Hess, for instance, describes the genre of the "too authentic failed selfie," which "includes those instances where the user has included something too personal, such as the selfie taken in the bathroom with embarrassing products present and the night-out-at-the-bars selfie that accidentally features someone vomiting in the background."[117] The designation of "failed" suggests that the users uploading them lacked appropriate self-awareness and competencies in successfully filtering and constructing selfies and self-presentations online in socially accepted ways. Moreover, "too authentic" suggests a limit to the permissible amount of authenticity of the selfie, one that must, in part, demonstrate some requisite artifice in its crafting—even if simply filtering out those elements deemed inappropriately "too authentic."

As a photographic genre of digital culture, the selfie communicates particular stylistic and compositional elements to signal appropriate authenticity via elements that are socially accepted sites of disclosure.[118] For example, making particular aspects of the construction of the selfie legible—such as having only one arm visible to suggest that the other is extended to hold the camera—operates to frame the selfie and the self as more authentic.[119] Similarly, recognition that images are expected to be altered in specific ways, such as through cropping and filtering, suggests an acceptance for some but not all kinds of alterations to the initial photograph taken as they are believed to authenticate the photograph in their legible artificiality.[120]

The practice of users creating both rinsta ("real" Instagram) and finsta ("fake" Instagram) accounts further highlights the constructed nature of authenticity as a principle of self-presentation.[121] For users that maintain both kinds of accounts, rinstas refer to the wider public-facing Instagram account, which most likely abides by normative and mainstream Instagram conventions of self-presentation coherent with self-branding culture. Finstas are treated as secondary accounts that are more private, typically accessed by a much smaller and vetted audience, where content may be more emotionally dark, lower quality, vulnerable, unattractive, and experimental. Together, rinstas and finstas undermine and complicate Instagram's claims to authenticity in online self-presentation, since rinstas as the "real" Instagram accounts are treated as artificially positive presentations of self. Contrasting rinstas, finstas as the "fake" Instagram accounts are approached as containing supposedly more honest, sincere, and authentic content. That users with both rinsta and finsta accounts perceive their real Instagram accounts, and thus the dominant culture of Instagram, as populated with artifice, however, does not mean that finstas are inherently any more real or authentic, since normative conventions for finstas also impact how users create content for and construct their self-presentations on these accounts.[122]

Perceptions of authenticity online and offline rely on the capacity for representations to communicate claims to their authenticity through particular conventions including accepted signals for artificiality, regardless of whether they are ultimately regarded as truthful. O'Neill became the subject of scrutiny for exposing the constructions of her Instagram profile in a process that functionally sought to rebrand herself as more authentic by revealing her account's previous artifice. The backlash arose from her violating particular conventions that complicated perception by the social network of her images as appropriately authentic and appropriately artificial, questioning the capability of the entire social network to assess authenticity in the process. She violated social conventions by revealing too much of the "wrong" elements of her online self-presentation as constructed, questioning the existing models by which users filtered authentic from artificial photographs, profiles, and persons. In contrast, Calloway sought to rebrand herself as a scammer following her exposure by Beach that her popular Instagram account was itself a scam—less authentic than previously believed. In so doing, Calloway dispensed with claims to authenticity and instead opted to market a self-brand of artifice, of the scam. Consequently, the promise of continual and deliberate self-presentation in a culture of self-branding, when acknowledged as a creative act, is also the threat (or promise) of the con, the catfish, the scammer.

Anxieties over the supposedly negative effects of selfies and social media on adolescent individuation and socialization suggest concerns over the creative self, not the self that creates novelty but the self that creates its own presentation to others as part of self-branding culture. These conflicting tensions between self-branding as strategic self-construction for market value and self-branding as a mechanism for self-actualization, self-discovery, and self-empowerment in creative economy discourses negotiates competing expectations of artificiality and authenticity, respectively. Perceptions of authenticity regarding creative online self-presentation, like conceptions of authenticity in other contexts, require particular social conventions regarding expressing and interpreting authenticity and its limits, including what is considered artificial, what is considered too authentic, and what can and cannot be disclosed. To close, I turn to two different artificial virtual doll Instagram phenomena fraying the edges of authenticity.

The recent emergence and subsequent popularity of several computer-generated image (CGI) Instagram users embrace an online presentation of a fully artificial and manipulable subject that is fabricated at its core without traceable authenticity to a corresponding offline human—Turkle's biggest fears of individuals treating the "self as avatar." Miquela Sousa, better known as "Lil Miquela," for example, is a popular racially ambiguous CGI who has promoted luxury fashion lines including Proenza Schouler and Balenciaga on the account @lilmiquela.[123] Lil Miquela first appeared on Instagram in 2016 before her account confirmed her status as an artificial construct in April 2018. The delay in Lil Miquela's reveal parallels Essena O'Neill's own reveal regarding her account. However, where Essena O'Neill revealed the labor and resources that went into her seemingly effortless posts, Lil Miquela, or rather those managing the Instagram account, revealed that her very constitution was artificial and without an original corresponding offline identity. Consequently, @lilmiquela and other CGI Instagram accounts prompt persistent questions regarding authenticity and artificiality, such as over the need for transparency and disclosure over their existence as CGI rather than humans. This is particularly relevant for the negotiation of permissible artifice, since CGIs that strive toward passing as human in online appearance and behavior operate alongside the negotiation of permissible uses of Photoshop and plastic surgery for human Instagram users. What dictates the boundary between authenticity and artificiality—including the permissible amount of either—comes into question through the identification of such convincing cons.

While Lil Miquela and other CGI Instagram users represent virtual dolls that strive toward convincing human presentation—even if acknowledged at some point as artificial—the popular but now-defunct Instagram account @socalitybarbie used a physical Barbie doll to parody many of the conventional trends, features, and expectations associated

FIGURE 22. *Instagram post from @socalitybarbie featuring coffee and a spiritual quote as a parody of white middle-class mainstream Instagram culture. (Source: @socalitybarbie, Instagram, 2015; screenshot by author, December 2020.)*

with selfies and online youth culture (see Figure 22). As an account of the life of an obviously fictional young woman from Southern California, a region of the United States often regarded as superficial and fake, the use of a Barbie doll as the representation of the account's owner by user Darby, a young woman herself, emphasized conceptions of Instagram users as constructed and artificial. The account perpetuated anxious associations of social media–obsessed pathologies with young and adolescent girls through the use of Barbie, the iconic girl's doll, reinforcing selfie-takers as young and adolescent girls. Although @socalitybarbie lampoons the selfie-taker as a doll playing dress-up—immature, fake, and superficial—the use of the iconic Mattel brand Barbie to do so gestures to the contemporary influence of branding and imperatives of self-branding in identity construction and presentation. In particular, using mainstream conceptions of Barbie to perform the calculating desire to appear more serious, intelligent, and deep commonly associated with a white middle-class hipster culture amplifies the artificiality perceived in these practices.

Yet, self-branding and cons as two related creative practices enabled by contemporary digital media imagined as authentic and artificial, respectively, underscore how presenting oneself to others goes hand in hand with evaluating the presentation of others, which is always constituted contextually through particular arrangements of shifting media technologies and social conventions. Imperatives of self-branding within the precarious creative labor economy subject individuals to perpetual adolescence, requiring them to reimagine continually who they are as well as how they individuate and socialize in order to market themselves to others and to evaluate others similarly.

CHAPTER 4

Design Fiction and the Imagination of Technological Futures

The Creative Science Foundation (CSF) was founded in 2011 as a nonprofit educational organization "dedicated to the exploration and promotion of creative methods for supporting science, engineering, business and sociopolitical *innovation*."[1] The organization began as a collaboration among Brian David Johnson, a prominent futurist in the United States with industry experience at Intel, Michael Gardner, a technologist with an extensive career at British Telecommunications, and Victor Callaghan, a computer scientist at Essex University. Although centered in the United Kingdom, the organization has offered events, workshops, and services committed to joining "creative arts" with science, engineering, and business all around the world, including in Amsterdam, Kuala Lumpur, and Orlando.[2] Through such efforts, the CSF encourages the creation of speculative science fiction narratives "as a formal tool to advance science and engineering" and that are "grounded in existing knowledge."[3]

The CSF refers to these narratives as "science fiction prototypes," a term made famous by Johnson, and advocates for their utility in actively shaping futures to come. As the organization contends, "Fiction has the power to enthrall people of all ages, especially children who love stories, movies and games. Science-fiction is such a medium that has given rise to numerous books, films and games enjoyed by children. Moreover, as science-fiction is set in the future it connects with children's dreams for the future."[4] This description of the power of fiction, and science fiction in particular, invokes images of children and links them to the future. Subsequently, the CSF collaborates with educational organizations and schools to establish programs in order to foster the development of children's creativity, which it regards as necessary for science fiction prototyping, specifically, and future innovation, generally.[5] The organization's expressed mission, after all, is to "capture the imagine of children, showing how science is important for their future, and how it is both creative and fun."[6]

Science fiction prototyping represents one of many contemporary speculative technological design practices deployed to imagine and innovate for the future.[7] For instance, design fiction describes "a genre of hardware-literacy" meant to explore future possibilities through storytelling using imagined technological objects, which was first outlined by science fiction writer Bruce Sterling.[8] Similarly, Anthony Dunne and Fiona Raby developed value fiction as an experimental design methodology offering "critique of the present through the material embodiment of function derived from alternative value systems," that is, designed objects for fictional worlds.[9] Acknowledging the differences among science fiction prototyping, design fiction, value fiction, and similar speculative technological design practices coming to prominence, what is common to them all is the rhetorical emphasis on the imagination and its ability to produce accounts of the future through design.

This chapter investigates this interest in design informed by and generative of speculative narratives as a form of idealized work that adults are expected to perform in contemporary creative labor economies, work that should tap into their imaginations developed during childhood. In so doing, I explore the contours of an ideology of design and the future pervasive in contemporary digital culture, focusing on how design discourses in the mid to late twentieth and early twenty-first centuries construct designers as the ideal laboring subjects of a creative economy.[10] I argue that understandings of design—both as a postwar academic field of study as well as a pervasive label for privileged forms of creative labor—are bound up in modern conceptions of futurity and practices of speculation, intersecting the field of futures studies as well as science fiction literature.[11] Furthermore, I show how central to this cultural history of futurity and speculation are enduring attempts since the eighteenth century to regulate and render productive children's imagination, an imagination primarily granted to white childhood. In exploring how designers are expected to draw on their childlike imaginations as creative laboring adults for the future, this chapter also examines how the processes of extracting labor and value from youth and youthful imagination exclude subjects denied childhood from participating in shaping and inhabiting that future entirely.

Futures by Choice

Contemporary advocacy of design fiction and similar speculative technological design practices relies on a mid-twentieth-century shift in conceptions of futurity, which I trace through the emergence of two institutionalized academic fields invested in the future: futures studies and design. Though the histories and figures of both fields differ, the fundamental theoretical commonalities shared across futures studies and design demonstrate how dominant ideas about the future change over time. As Lawrence R. Samuel notes, "The future is not a fixed idea but a highly variable one that reflects the values of those who are imagining it."[12] Contextualizing speculative technological design practices within the histories of both futures studies and design, and the beliefs that underlie their conceptions of the future, demonstrates how the future has come to operate within the contemporary neoliberal values of a creative economy that privilege choice and individual responsibility in pursuit of innovation.

Central to design fiction—and to futures studies and design—is the premise that the future is something scrutable and malleable rather than unknowable or predetermined as had been previously thought. Regarding contemporary speculative design, for example, Johnson argued that "the future is not an accident. The future is not some fixed point on the horizon that we are all running toward, helpless to do anything about. The future is built every day by the actions of people."[13] Johnson's comment emphasizes that people actively, though not necessarily deliberately, construct the future.

Futures studies as a field, largely coalescing in the 1960s and 1970s in its U.S. and British variant, articulated the future as something its methods could both study and shape through futures workshops, forecasting and backcasting techniques, and other related practices.[14] While futures studies did meet criticism from skeptics, what was initially a marginal field of inquiry garnered increasing legitimacy through the championing of scientifically framed work that imagined futures coming into being, predicated on the belief that the future could be directed. For instance, Edward Cornish, who founded the World Future Society in 1966 and *The Futurist* magazine in 1967, asserted that futurism represented a departure from previous conceptions of the future by conceiving of it as undetermined.[15] According to Cornish's *The Study of the Future,* considered the premier guide for predicting the future upon publication in 1977, "The future world is plastic: Human beings are not moving toward a predetermined future world, but instead are active participants in the creation of the future world."[16] For futures studies, that the future is undetermined suggests that people can and should shape it. By extension, futurist Wendell Bell emphasized that the future is "influenced by individual and collective action," suggesting responsibility for how it comes into being.[17]

Emphasis on agency underscored the importance of choice in counteracting the previous fatalistic models of the predetermined or entirely chaotic future that futures studies rejected. Highlighting this, Cornish insisted that "to tell John Jones that he will get married next year is, for a futurist, not only impossible but insulting, for it denies Mr. Jones the freedom to determine his own future."[18] This deployment of the hypothetical Mr. Jones foregrounds futures studies' emphasis on self-determination of one's future, one that is not constrained by the predictions of others. Moreover, it also suggests that the primary objective of futures studies is not to predict the future with certainty but rather to account for possible futures that can inform present-day choices toward desirable outcomes.

The future conceived as the consequence of choices made suggested not only that people are responsible for their own futures but that they too are already responsible for their own present conditions: the futures of their past decisions. For instance, Cornish sought to minimize the role that luck or fate—representative of forces outside individual control—had in explanations for unfolding events by asserting that "if we recognize that choices really count in determining our future, we must also recognize that we ourselves are largely responsible for our own futures."[19] That individuals are perceived as ultimately responsible for their current and future conditions primarily based on the choices they are believed to have made represented a shift in conceptions of the future that reinforced the neoliberal value of totalizing individual responsibility, which suggests that moral character can be assessed with regard to one's present situation since one deserves the condition in which one finds oneself.[20]

While futures studies was founded expressly to study and direct the future, the academic field of design acquired increasingly explicit orientation toward questions of futurity throughout its development. Design as a professional academic field of study and practice largely emerged in the mid-twentieth century, though it has a longer industrial and commercial history often identified as beginning with British author, artist, and activist William Morris in the nineteenth century.[21] Despite the modern concept of design dating back to the nineteenth century—and having been associated with such terms as "industrial art," "decorative art," and "applied art" while commonly distinguished from "fine art"—"design" now serves as an omnipresent label describing a range of labor privileged in contemporary creative economies. As Kjetil Fallan argues, "Design has become such a buzzword lately, especially in marketing and media, that it seems to have taken on a positive value in itself, transforming ordinary products, as if by magic, into exclusive, stylish objects."[22] Moreover, "design thinking" has emerged as a celebrated term describing how designers approach problems, which, as Daniela K. Rosner notes, "[positions] the work as addressing challenges in ways that look less like craftwork than statecraft."[23]

My interest here is in accounting for a cultural history of design in relation to other speculative discourses and practices within the context of the creative economy.[24] As Fallan argues, a cultural history of design situates "design as 'any other cultural phenomenon'—that is not giving privilege to the artefacts, actors, institutions and structures studied."[25] Consequently, my approach to design focuses on discourses of what design is, of what it is imagined to do, and of who can participate in it as a privileged form of labor in the creative economy.

The rise and expansion of design industries in the West is linked to the rise and expansion of the market for cultural goods, particular commodities that offer culturally specific icons, knowledges, and styles for consumption.[26] Such commodities, including books, films, music, software titles, decorative crafts, and fashion garments, are the principal products of creative labor and the creative industries, which increasingly embrace short-term working conditions and project-oriented contract employment. Moreover, as Guy Julier explains, "the emphasis in the creative industries—particularly observable in design—on flexible working conditions, project-based employment structuring, multiskilling, entrepreneurship and individualism fits the labour regimes of neoliberalism since the 1980s."[27] Consequently, what is labeled "design" not only characterizes privileged work amid the precarious conditions of creative economies but also the idealized commodities that it circulates, since they manifest "the neoliberal pressures of marketisation and differentiation," often at the exclusion of other labor deemed "uncreative" or less profitable and less prestigious.[28]

Although "design" commonly describes both planned and deliberate action (to design) as well as the product of such planning (a design), definitions often articulate design expansively to encapsulate myriad activities and subjects.[29] For instance, Herbert A. Simon asserted that "everyone designs who devises courses of action aimed at changing existing situations into preferred ones."[30] Simon's capacious definition constructs design as naturally human to suggest that everyone is already a designer. Moreover, this definition frames design as a means of improvement, an intentional practice toward achieving preferable conditions, which is reinforced by subsequent design theorists including Gerald Nadler, Ezio Manzini, Victor Margolin, and Tony Fry.[31] This attention to improving current conditions expresses design's interest in futurity.

Discourses about the future are central to how contemporary designers often characterize their work.[32] Margolin, for example, argued that "[design occupies] a dialectical space between the world that is and the world that could be ... oriented towards the future."[33] Similarly, Anne Balsamo described design as "the process whereby the future is brought forth out of the present."[34] While these two conceptions of design articulate different relationships between the present and the future—either bridging between them or fashioning the latter from the former, respectively—they suggest that the future is constructed rather than received and that design is a mechanism for shaping that future. Rejecting predetermination of the future as did practitioners of futures studies, designers, as Fry suggested, believe "that the future is not a vast void, but a time and place constituted by directional forces of design, set in train in the past and the present, and which flow into the future."[35]

As critical studies of design demonstrate, however, recognizing design as a practice oriented toward shaping the future also requires interrogating the underlying beliefs informing designers and their desired futures. For instance, Christina Cogdell illustrates how the rise of streamline design in the 1930s was linked to then-contemporary eugenic ideology throughout U.S. culture. Streamline design sought to improve efficiency and hygiene through product design choices toward future ideal human perfection, influenced by the diffusion of eugenic thinking including in the work of Norman Bel Geddes, prominent champion of streamline design who was himself interested in eugenics.[36] In this way, streamline design's approach to product design mirrored eugenic practices seeking to direct the evolution of human bodies informed by the scientific racism and white supremacy motivating eugenicists' anxieties concerning poor and nonwhite persons.[37] As another example, Ronald Mace's coining of "universal design," as an explicit approach to increasing the accessibility of designed products, structures, and environments beginning in the 1980s, highlighted how bodies that did not meet presumptions of normative able-bodiedness have historically been and continue to be excluded or harmed in conventional design.[38] As Aimi Hamraie suggests, designers' choices have "implications [for] how we imagine the figure of the user, justify design for particular users, and tell stories about the value of such design for broader questions of difference and belonging."[39]

While design's popularity has consistently increased since its emergence, futures studies experienced a decline throughout the 1990s and early 2000s, demonstrated in the closing of university futures studies departments.[40] Yet despite such decline in futures studies as an academic field, the future remains a broad preoccupation within the United States. More recently, the increasing visibility of popular futurists—including Johnson and Sterling, along with Stewart Brand, Julian Bleecker, Stuart Candy, and Jane McGonigal—suggests a transformation of twentieth-century futurism into one entangled more intimately with contemporary digital culture.

Many such figures, in particular, positioned speculative technological design practices within this mode of futurism. Sterling, for instance, argued in 2012 that design fiction is "really a new set of tools that [is] giving futurism a second wind in some ways. Instead of talking about grand, overarching things like futurism in the 1960s—we need a new consciousness—it suits the tenor of our own period."[41] Sterling's comment, while connecting to midcentury futurism, dismisses earlier futurist work by characterizing it as suspiciously overblown in order to legitimate further the speculative practice of design fiction as a cutting-edge method for more consequential engagements of futurism attuned to contemporary conditions. Design as a field and practice for imagining the future and our relationship to it, then, revitalizes midcentury futurism by grounding speculative technological design practices, such as design fiction, within a conceived framework of deliberate planning via design and design thinking believed to make choices for desirable and, ideally, creative futures.

Imaginative Boundary Work

Throughout both futures studies and design, the intellectual influences for design fiction and similar speculative technological design practices, advocates have performed boundary work seeking to legitimate their respective fields by distinguishing science from a range of counterparts. According to Thomas Gieryn, when epistemic authority—the ability to pronounce truths about reality—is in question, boundary work represents maneuvers to construct "unique properties or accomplishments of science [that] make it a distinctly superior way of knowing."[42] Boundary work depends on conventional cultural perceptions of science as equivalent to nature, fact, and objectivity.[43] Consequently, what is constructed as not scientific, whether religion, the arts and humanities, or politics, often becomes associated with fantasy, fiction, or bias. Because both fields are centrally concerned with imagining the future, advocates of futures studies and of design have performed boundary work to negotiate tensions between broad conceptions of what is factual, real, and true on one hand and what is fantastic, speculative, and imaginary on the other.

For both design and futures studies, "science" consistently describes knowledge associated with rationality, reliability, and fact, while the counterparts to science—ranging from folk practices, the arts and humanities, and fiction—represent qualities as diverse as superstition, creativity, imagination, emotion, and speculation in different contexts. As a result, the attitudes toward science vary depending on which counterparts are positioned against it. Cornish, for instance, connected futures studies closely with scientific rationality by distancing the futurism he advocated away from earlier practices of predicting the future: "futurists use rational or scientific means to study the future possibilities rather than tea leaves, tarot cards, and other mystical mumbo-jumbo."[44] Aligning futures studies with science and distancing the field away from folk practices performs boundary work to establish the field of futures studies as a legitimate domain of knowledge about the future, reinforcing views that earlier practices claiming to know the future were dubious. For Cornish, the practices of futures studies are not unverified superstitions or pseudoscience—kinds of "mumbo-jumbo"—but are rigorous scientific methods.

Bell, however, identified a different pattern of boundary work recurring in futures studies, one concerned with the field's relation to science and to art. As Bell noted, debates over whether futures studies is a science or an art often relied on "inaccurate beliefs about the differences between art and science."[45] In his account, Bell cataloged several persistent assumptions about science—"technical and rigorous, mechanical, codified, standardized, and objective"—and assumptions about art— "intuitive, creative, imaginative, insightful, ingenious, subjective, fortuitous, and beautiful"—across different futurists' articulations of the field.[46] He argued that this oversimplification of science and art grossly misrepresents them as they each possess aspects more conventionally associated with the other and that were central to futures studies.

This debate in futures studies participates in a longer history of the two cultures problem: a large-scale disciplinary divide in Western education. Although similar debates predate him, chemist and novelist C. P. Snow famously characterized a chasm he perceived between the culture of science and the culture of the arts—inclusive of the humanities—in his influential 1959 lecture, *The Two Cultures*.[47] A similar division between science and literature, emblematic of the humanities and arts more broadly, anchored nineteenth-century debates over British education between biologist T. H. Huxley and poet Matthew Arnold as an earlier example of this boundary work.[48]

Like debates over whether futures studies is an art or a science, attempts to define design reveal assumptions about what science and the humanities are believed to be. Many designers have articulated design as a third culture of human life rather than trying to situate design within one of the two cultures at the exclusion of the other. For example, Bruce Archer defined design as a third culture that has largely been overshadowed by the prominence of science and the humanities.[49] Archer, in particular, defined science as "the attainment of understanding based upon observation, measurement, the formulation of theory and the testing of theory by further observation or experiment" and the humanities as "concerned with human values and the expression of the spirit of man."[50] From this, Archer articulated design as "the area of human experience, skill and understanding that reflects man's concern with the appreciation and adaption of his surroundings in the light of his material and spiritual needs."[51] The emphasis on adaptation to satisfy needs, for Archer, frames design as the third domain of knowledge that seeks to address "material and spiritual needs" through both science—observation and method—and the humanities—values and spirit.[52]

This interest in integrating what are conceived of as distinct, even antithetical, fields of knowledge finds particular manifestation in contemporary speculative technological design practices. The CSF, for example, aims to create conditions "where scientists, engineers, researchers, business professionals, politicians, sociologists, writers, artists, and the general public come together and use science-fiction as a common language to explore the futures they want to build."[53] In treating science fiction as a "common language" across a wide range of subjects, the organization participates in a history linking science fiction as a genre of technological speculation to thinking about the future.

Although practitioners both in futures studies and in design have engaged in rhetorical boundary work to situate their respective fields in relation to science and various nonscientific counterparts, debates in both fields over science fiction, as an established literary genre of speculation about futures hinging on technoscience, foreground persistent anxieties about credible speculation of the future with respect to the authority perceived of science. Genre debates, as a kind of boundary work—over what is and is not science fiction, the differences between "hard" and "soft" science fiction, and how acceptably accurate or incorrect a science fictional work can be, for instance—all signal how "science fiction" as a category invokes both the use of "science" to mark the content of what is represented as well as "science" to mark the accuracy of what is represented.[54] Negotiations of science fiction as simultaneously factual and fictional in discourses about imagining the future reveal enduring assumptions about fact and fiction, science and nonscience, and their contested boundaries.

Futures studies, for example, maintains a complicated relationship with science fiction in order to mobilize the imaginative aspects of the literary genre while affirming scientific rigor, most prominently demonstrated through the production of scenarios as a core activity of the field. As Bell explained, "The end product of all the methods of futures research is basically the same: a scenario, a story about the future."[55] This speculative story about the future resembles a kind of science fiction, an imagined narrative about a possible world assessed on its plausibility. Furthermore, for Cornish, the value of scenarios lies in the introduction of "imagination and creativity into the tool-box of futuristics," since imagination and creativity are believed to enable futurists to use current facts to speculate on future conditions.[56]

The origins of scenarios in futures studies similarly demonstrate underlying negotiations with fiction. Trained as a physicist, Herman Kahn worked for the RAND Corporation during the 1950s before publishing *Thinking about the Unthinkable: Scenarios and Metaphors* (1962), a primer establishing scenario-building as a central method of futures studies. As Kahn explained, "A scenario results from an attempt to describe in more or less detail some hypothetical sequence of events."[57] Kahn elaborated on the importance of reason, rationality, and factuality in producing and evaluating scenarios: "If a scenario is plausible, it must, of course, relate at the outset to some reasonable version of the present."[58] Kahn, then, advocated for the importance of balancing both fact and fiction by explaining how scenarios and other futurist methods "make the analysis less icily rational, to give it explicitly color, emotion, accident, irrationality, and so forth."[59] This reinforces historic associations of science, rationality, and facticity against arts, emotion, and fictionality while valuing the latter as a supplement to the former for imagining futures.

Since Kahn, futurists have advocated for the value of science fiction as both a source of inspiration for envisioning the future and a means of developing imaginative thinking necessary to address it.[60] Alvin Toffler, for example, argued that students should take science fiction courses to best prepare against "future shock"—a term he coined to describe a paralyzing response to rapid change in his 1970 bestseller of the same name.[61] Designers, too, have advocated for the importance of science fiction in their work. Charles Eames, for instance, strongly supported education in science fiction, arguing that "it is one of the few areas today in which the art of speculation is practiced."[62] Balsamo, likewise, emphasized that "science fiction has long served as a narrative lens through which we can read how the future is produced first in our imaginations, well before it is produced in the laboratories of scientists and engineers, the design studios, or the kitchens and the garages of everyday people."[63] Balsamo's comments, in particular, draw a trajectory for the future beginning in the imagination and passing through science fiction. Moreover, like futures studies, design has come to rely on scenarios as a central method of the field, indicative of design's orientation toward the future and its engagement with speculative narratives, including science fiction.[64]

In imagining worlds different from the present one while still grounded in what is currently known, design fiction similarly negotiates established conceptions of and tensions between science fact and science fiction. For example, despite being a renowned science fiction author himself, Sterling articulated a division between science fiction and science fact that characterizes the traits of science fiction as undesirable in order to propose design fiction as an important speculative practice. Sterling argued that

> the core distinction is that design [and, subsequently, design fiction] makes more sense on the page than science fiction does. Science fiction wants to invoke the grandeur and credibility of science for its own hand-waving hocus-pocus, but design fiction can be more practical, more hands-on. It sacrifices some sense of the miraculous, but it moves much closer to the glowing heat of technosocial conflict.[65]

Sterling's description of science fiction reinforces a pervasive anxiety about labels of "science fiction" in discussing the future, arguing that design fiction is more logical—implying scientific and realistic—than the popular speculative genre for which he is known. His comment seeks to increase design fiction's proximity to contemporary technoscientific concerns by dismissing science fiction as unrealistic fantasy. Furthermore, describing science fiction as "hand-waving hocus-pocus" equates science fiction with magic, a historically dismissed counterpart to science. In an attempt to position design, and thus design fiction, more closely to fact, distancing fiction, and science fiction, further away, Sterling also defined design fiction as "not a kind of fiction. It's a kind of design."[66]

While Sterling often distanced design fiction from science fiction, Julian Bleecker has consistently emphasized their convergence.[67] Bleecker defined design fiction as "a conflation of design, science fact, and science fiction. . . . It is a way of materializing ideas and speculations without the pragmatic curtailing that often happens when dead weights are fastened to the imagination."[68] By framing science fact as the necessary but potentially limiting component of design fiction, Bleecker suggested that design fiction must acknowledge science fiction as its core impulse that defends against the excessive constraints from science fact. Johnson, too, emphatically embraced science fiction as vital to his work as a futurist, describing his design work as an application of science fiction: "The tool is called science fiction prototyping, and I've been using it my entire career to help me explore different visions of tomorrow."[69]

Practices within futures studies and design, including design fiction, refract the boundary work of the two cultures problem into a problem of negotiating what is perceived to be realistic and presently verifiable (science) and what is perceived to be speculative, conditional, and imaginative (art, literature, and the humanities). A corresponding form of rhetorical boundary work negotiates the genre contours surrounding science fiction. Underlying this genre negotiation are persistent assumptions about science fiction and its relationship to both science and to fiction as advocates of design fiction, as with design and futures studies, seek to legitimate the imaginative practice as simultaneously both speculative and realistic. Since the future cannot immediately be verified as fact, legitimating cultural practices of imagining futures requires attending to the perceptions, methods, and materials that have historically been separated into the realm of science and the realm of art—fact and fiction, respectively.

Disciplining Childhood Imagination

Proponents of speculative technological design practices commonly link the act of speculation with the imagination, often articulated as a creative capacity to conceptualize possibilities beyond what is factual or presently known. Moreover, the increasing championing of science fiction in contemporary design, broadly, and in design fiction, specifically, embraces the historically marginalized genre by rendering it and its speculative work necessary for the future. Balsamo, for instance, argued that "the Future begins in the imagination. In this sense, science fiction authors are celebrated architects of the future."[70] In particular, describing science fiction authors as "architects" frames their speculative work as calculated and crafted imagination. Similarly, Dunne and Raby suggested that "speculating is based on imagination, the ability to literally imagine other worlds and alternatives."[71] Futures studies also foregrounds the significance of imagination. Cornish, for example, asserted that "we need to use our imagination and special idea-generating techniques to develop concepts for what might happen to make the future different from what the current trend suggests."[72]

While imagination is widely conceived as a generative ability to conceptualize the new or the otherwise, it is also framed as requiring discipline. For example, Sterling argued that "science fiction is not about the freedom of imagination. It's about the free imagination pinched and howling in a vise that other people call real life."[73] According to Sterling, imagination, while the engine for speculation, requires constraints within which to operate, such as conventions of realism. Forty years earlier, Kahn similarly argued that "imagination has always been one of the principal means for dealing in various ways with the future, and the scenario is simply one of many devices useful in stimulating and disciplining the imagination."[74] Like Sterling, Kahn suggested that the imagination needs both encouragement and constraint: stimulation and discipline.

I argue that this negotiation between fostering and restraining the imagination is a recoding of negotiations between fantasy and fiction on the one hand and realism and fact on the other. Moreover, this desire to balance wild speculation with strict restraint has served as an enduring problem in shifting attitudes toward children's imagination since at least the eighteenth century. As Brian Sutton-Smith contends, "The history of the imagination in childhood is a history of ever greater suppression and rationalization of the irrational," which is associated with the nonscientific and the impractical.[75] This cultural history of the imagination, and the desire to rationalize it through discourses that construct children as naturally creative subjects requiring proper education to regulate their imaginations demonstrates how the imagination is simultaneously conceived as generative and irrational with respect to the imbrication of rationality, factuality, and functionality resulting from modern ideologies of science, morality, and (economic) productivity rooted in the Enlightenment.

Cultural beliefs regarding the relationship between children and imagination, especially how to cultivate imagination in children, have historically presumed a normative white childhood. As Robin Bernstein demonstrates, associations of children with playfulness and imagination in the United States have relied on conceptions of natural childhood innocence that were fundamentally racialized through whiteness in negation of the childhood innocence of Black youth.[76] In particular, denying Black children the capacity for natural innocence reinforced the treatment of them as property through institutional slavery and systemic anti-Black racism. Unpacking a cultural history of childhood imagination, then, reveals, as Hannah Dyer suggests, how normative constructions of childhood themselves impact not only what children should or should not do but also what children are imagined to be capable or incapable of entirely.[77]

Particular conceptions of childhood imagination and prescriptions for its development, like other parenting advice, advance particular attitudes and practices that adults should adopt. Drawing on the educational theories of Enlightenment thinkers, including John Locke and Jean Jacques-Rousseau, Maria and Richard Lovell Edgeworth—daughter and father—published *Practical Education* in 1798 as a guide for raising rational and scientifically minded children into productive adults.[78] The Edgeworths proposed child-rearing practices that involved specific books, instruments, and spaces in order to direct children to exercise specific cognitive abilities, such as judgment, reasoning, and invention. Alongside cultivation of these mental faculties, the Edgeworths cautioned parents against allowing children to develop unproductive habits, particularly concerning the imagination.

For the Edgeworths, imagination described the power to form images, where image "extends to objects of all the senses."[79] But the imagination served as a tricky problem for the Edgeworths, since it was necessary for important activities like invention yet risked becoming distracting if improperly indulged:

> The most difficult exercises of the mind, such as invention, or strict reasoning, are those alone which are sufficient to subjugate and chain down the imagination of some active spirits. To such laborious exercises they should be excited by the encouraging voice of praise and affection. Imaginative children will be more disposed to invent than to reason, but they cannot perfect any invention without reasoning.[80]

Imagination needed to be encouraged but also constrained by reason and judgment, directed toward productive ends. While invention, experimentation, and discovery were the positive outcomes of a healthy imagination tempered by reason, the Edgeworths were especially concerned with a purposeless imagination that fostered the habit of reverie: "in reverie we are so intent upon a particular train of ideas, that we are unconscious of all external objects, and we exert but little voluntary power."[81] To prevent reverie, the Edgeworths recommended keeping children mentally and physically occupied, such as with tools to conduct scientific experiments.[82]

Contemporary with and yet counter to the rational and scientific child of the Edgeworths, the Romantic child was exalted as a manifestation of natural innocence and morality best left to grow according to their own instinctual course.[83] Romantic literature, visual arts, and philosophy established a cult of the child, conceived as the embodiment of imagination and emotion and in close kinship with nature, much of what the Enlightenment deemed irrational.[84] Of the Romantics, poet William Wordsworth notably celebrated children and childhood in his works. In the 1802 poem "My Heart Leaps Up When I Behold," for example, Wordsworth reflected that whenever he saw a rainbow he was filled with joy, proclaiming that "the Child is father of the Man," retaining a childlike sense of wonder as an adult at the natural world.[85] In this, Wordsworth suggested a potential loss that children might experience as they mature into adults, which he lamented in his 1807 poem "Ode on Intimations of Immortality from Recollections of Early Childhood."[86]

While Romantics created a cult of the child, Victorian culture developed interest in child psychology and behavior, with, as Sally Shuttleworth notes, "the second half of the nineteenth century [witnessing] the growth of a more permissive attitude towards the figure of the child, and the boundaries between lying and imagination."[87] In 1849's *Household Education,* for instance, Harriet Martineau argued for fostering imagination while maintaining truthfulness. Martineau regarded imagination as "the highest of human faculties," since "those in whom it is suppressed can never be capable of heroic acts, of lofty wisdom, of the purest happiness."[88] Nonetheless, "the child should, from the beginning, believe that truthfulness is a duty" in order to temper unruly imaginations that tended toward lying.[89]

By the early twentieth century, child-rearing experts such as Beatrix

Tudor-Hart, Patty Smith Hill, and Ethel Kawin began distinguishing between good and bad expressions of imagination and play. Gary Cross argues that such experts sought "to teach parents to distinguish between productive imagination and commercial fantasy, between 'constructive' and 'escapist' play."[90] Good uses of the imagination contributed productively to the world, while bad uses of the imagination became a diversion from it—a withdrawal from reality echoing the Edgeworths' concerns regarding reverie. Part of this anxiety around escapist play resulted from increasing commercial sale of toys that indulged fantasies—such as superhero and monster figurines—rather than prepared children for adult life, which had been the previous standard convention for toys. While more forms of play became increasingly permissible, such new toys encouraged children to inhabit imaginative worlds into which adults increasingly found difficult entry, troubling established expectations for parents to participate in and monitor children's recreation.[91]

This growing production of children's imaginative worlds that largely precluded adults signaled a deviation from the cute, innocent, and wondrous Romantic child first articulated at the turn of the nineteenth century toward the emergence of the cool—a marketed desire for rebellious autonomy from parents—manifest, for example, in the 1930s onward through the popularity of science fiction with youth, particularly adolescent boys.[92] As Cross notes, for example, the popularity of Philip Francis Nowlan's science fiction character Buck Rogers, a twentieth-century man transported to the twenty-fifth century who becomes a hero against the tyrant Killer Kane, "appealed to the escapist moods of working-class Americans and became cool to youth of all classes."[93] Science fiction and other literary genres associated with imagination and speculation, however, largely held marginal status within the mainstream domains of literature and culture, owing to their wide popularity and accessibility in pulp books and magazines, comics, and other supposedly "low culture" media.

The popularity of science fiction among older boys in the 1930s, in particular, would participate in the increasing gendering and racializaton of science fiction as an imaginative genre predominantly associated with white boys rather than girls and nonwhite youth. The genre of science fiction would predominantly assume and appeal to a largely heterosexual male readership.[94] This contributed to what Balsamo argues is the gendering of the technological imagination, the capacity to think with and through technologies, which has historically privileged men's participation in and imagination of technology largely at the exclusion or omission of women.[95] Addressing this, works by feminist and women science fiction writers, such as Joanna Russ, Ursula K. Le Guin, and Margaret Atwood, have intervened in the historic gendering of science fiction narrative.[96] Similarly, Black science fiction writers, including Octavia E. Butler, Samuel R. Delany, and Nnedi Okorafor, have complicated science fiction as a literary genre centered around whiteness, countering the historic exclusion of Black participation in the imagination of technology while also interrogating systems of social oppression affecting the African diaspora.[97] Consequently, the technological imagination was not only gendered but also racialized, privileging white men at the helm of the future of technology.

While anxieties about children and science fiction complicated imaginative play in the first half of the twentieth century, by midcentury, the modern creative child had been disseminated through a range of American discourses, including advertising materials, psychological studies, and educational reforms.[98] Unlike the worries expressed by the Edgeworths regarding unmonitored imagination's facilitation of reverie, however, midcentury parenting periodicals and children's texts, such as Crockett Johnson's children's book *Harold and the Purple Crayon* (1955), suggested that a creative child should explore the fantastic worlds of their own imagination, particularly if alone and bored.[99]

Such investment in childhood imagination at midcentury, especially with regard to technological innovation, is evident in the Experimental Prototype Community of Tomorrow (EPCOT), Walt Disney's imagined city of the future designed to be at the forefront of American industry and technology.[100] Although unrealized by his death in 1966, Disney's EPCOT design eventually influenced the development and opening of Epcot Center in 1982 (now just Epcot), which featured an iconic geodesic sphere known as Spaceship Earth, drawing on the work of architect and futurist Buckminster Fuller.[101] Joining Spaceship Earth in Future World, the area of Epcot devoted to technoscientific innovations, the attraction Journey into Imagination opened during Epcot's first year and provided visitors with scenes depicting how imagination was vital to self-actualization, technological progress, and the future. Journey into Imagination, and its subsequent iterations, would prove to be a popular mainstay of Epcot, advocating the power of imagination to adults and children alike. This desire to encourage children to develop their imaginations persists in contemporary discussions. In *21st Century Robot*, his primer on science fiction prototyping presented through his experiences building robots, for example, Brian David Johnson argued that "imagination is the most important skill needed to build your robot. In the twenty-first century, anyone can imagine, design, and build a robot," suggesting that the capacity to imagine is more critical than technical expertise necessary for construction.[102] Furthermore, Johnson emphasized the significance of imagination in *21st Century Robot* through discussions of children, including his experience working with youth in schools to imagine robots, his original design fiction narratives about robots, as well as anecdotes surrounding Jimmy—the childlike robot that is the product of Johnson's own imagination.

The modern history of imagination has largely sought to encourage the desirable potential of a carefully developed imagination for invention, discovery, and self-expression all while fending off its perversion into reverie, lying, and escapist fantasy. Throughout this history, while (primarily) white male children may be conceived as born with the potential for imagination, the mobilization of the child as a figure possessing natural imaginative potential but requiring particular conditions and discipline for development and application advanced particular attitudes regarding the role of adults in encouraging children's imagination toward invention, scientific work, and technological novelty. In the present day, these productive ends feed the creative economy that relies on the imagination to produce the innovations vital to its continued operation.

The Object of Design Fiction

Central to how practitioners often explain design fiction is the concept of the diegetic prototype, a fictional technology presented in an imagined world. David A. Kirby coined "diegetic prototype" to describe fictional technologies depicted as plausible and necessary in science fiction films, both within the narrative and to the audience watching.[103] Kirby contends that diegetic prototypes create hype for the depicted technology as a future product for potential consumers, such as for virtual reality and space travel.[104] Johnson, Bleecker, and Sterling have since mobilized Kirby's concept of the diegetic prototype in discussions of speculative technological design practices. While these advocates often describe design fiction as a critical practice, however, discussions of prominent examples of diegetic prototypes emphasize core tensions between commercial interests and critical investigation in applications of design fiction.

Perhaps the most discussed diegetic prototype is the gestural and touchless computing interface depicted in Steven Spielberg's *Minority Report*, the 2002 film adaptation of the 1956 Philip K. Dick science fiction story of the same name (see Figure 23). Bleecker, for instance, applauded the film as exemplary design fiction:

> There's a scene in the film *Minority Report*, which also happens to be a wonderful prototype of a ubiquitous computing future, in which Tom Cruise's character Inspector John Anderton manipulates a database of sound and images that are from the near future. Cruise's character makes orchestra conductor-like gestures, summoning and juxtaposing fuzzy snippets of what is almost about to happen.[105]

Bleecker elaborated that the film serves "as a point of conception, either explicitly or implicitly . . . for more and further explorations of the possibility for gesture interaction."[106] Similarly, Kirby identified this scene as a particularly effective use of diegetic prototyping. For Kirby, "*Minority Report* was a golden opportunity . . . to demonstrate to the public, and potential funders, not only that [the] gestural interface technology works, but also that the technology would appear as if it were 'natural' and intuitive for users."[107]

The focus on the diegetic prototype demonstrates how prospective futures in design, science fiction, and, by extension, design fiction, often hinge on imagined objects.[108] Sterling, for example, argued that design and science fiction's most significant "commonality is their fierce love of gadgetry. Design loves the glamorized object; while science fiction loves rayguns, robots, time machines, and rocketships—imaginary objects."[109] Moreover, Sterling argued that to read a diegetic prototype is to read through an imagined gadget in order to access a science fictional world, since designers believe that "objects do not merely have

FIGURE 23. *Influential depiction of a gestural and touchless computing interface in the film* Minority Report. *(Source: Steven Spielberg, dir.,* Minority Report, *2002; screenshot by author.)*

a designer's ideas embedded within them. To an attentive eye, objects have entire social relationships embedded within them."[110]

Consequently, design fiction requires a specific mode of interpretation, since creating design fiction is just part of the work of imagining possible futures. In this way, Sterling emphasized that "effective design fiction requires an ability to *read* hardware."[111] Bleecker, similarly, argued that engagement in "design fiction practice creates . . . stories about the kinds of experiences and social rituals that might surround the designed object," demanding an ability to read beyond the imagined prototype itself to access these stories.[112] This echoes Darko Suvin's definition of science fiction as a literary genre governed by the "hegemony of a fictional 'novum' (novelty, innovation)," a speculative or hypothetical entity that organizes the imagined narrative world around it in a believable manner to readers.[113]

Despite the centrality of the object in design and science fiction, advocates of design fiction often emphasize attending not to the object, the gadget, or the novum of a speculative scenario, but rather to the social world which that object inhabits. Bleecker's comments on the stories surrounding the designed object, for instance, suggest that the goal of design fiction is not primarily to imagine a new object but to investigate a world where the new object is folded into everyday life. Subsequently, speculative technological design practices negotiate the two key roles that Eugene Thacker identifies science fiction performing:

actualization and potentiality. Commonly in industry and commercial discourses, science fiction in the role of actualization contends that "scientific advancement and technological progress [are] the keys to a realization of the future."[114] In contrast, Thacker locates in potentiality the source of science fiction's critical function, since it "serves to signify futures that may exist, as well as futures that will not exist (or that should not exist)."[115] Rather than presenting inevitability as is the case with actualization, science fiction in the mode of potentiality investigates contingency and possibility.

Similarly, Dunne and Raby categorize design practices into two major domains based on a critical function that I argue aligns with Thacker's categorization of science fiction: affirmative design and critical design. As Dunne and Raby explain, affirmative design "reinforces how things are now, it conforms to cultural, social, technical and economic expectations," resonant with science fiction in the mode of actualization.[116] Opposing affirmative design, critical design, like science fiction in the mode of potentiality, "rejects how things are now as being the only possibility, it provides a critique of the prevailing situation through designs that embody alternative social, cultural, technical or economic values."[117] Design fiction when framed as an exploratory imaginative practice is often located under critical design.[118] Furthermore, design fiction and similar speculative technological design practices as critical design also operate as forms of critical fabulation, what Rosner describes as narrative practices that intervene in conventional design methods to generate possibilities for more just futures.[119]

Although advocates of design fiction often laud *Minority Report*, responses to the film demonstrate conflicting tensions between affirmative design and critical design, between science fiction as actualization and as potentiality, which questions the efficacy of design fiction's critical potential. While Kirby's concept of the diegetic prototype has been adopted by practitioners of speculative technological design practices, Kirby's original conception of the diegetic prototype describes "'pre-product placements' for technologies that do not yet exist" in order to create hype and widespread demand for them.[120] As such, Kirby's discussions of how design fiction films "[avoid] scenes that would undermine the technology or cast it as risky" to maximize interest for the development of the product emphasize the mobilization of the diegetic prototype and technological imagination for the ends of science fiction as actualization and of affirmative design.[121]

Bleecker asserts that "the *Minority Report* props are instruments that ultimately become expressions of human fallibility and hubris. They aren't primarily useful as design ideas for future technologies"—which, in contrast, demonstrates a desire to read the film as science fiction in the mode of potentiality and as critical design.[122] Bleecker described this iconic film scene as "a particularly rich context, a good story that involves people and their social practices rather than fetishizing the object and its imagined possibilities—this is what design fiction aspires to."[123] In claiming emphasis on the imagined context instead of fetishizing the gestural interface, then, Bleecker assumed a mode of interpretation reliant on an audience committed to science fiction in the mode of potentiality and to critical design:

> It's as if the story is sharing with the audience, who may be reasonably wondering—how do you edit and manipulate fragments of sound and images from the future? How does police evidence gathering work in the year 2054, when evidence is things that have not yet happened—but will? Do they travel into the future through some device and collect things that they bring back? Do detectives still use little baggies and tweezers to collect scraps of bone fragment, sending them to clever forensic scientists back at the lab? ... The audience wants to know what this thing is in the context of a story in which people—people in the year 2054—routinely (lets [*sic*] assume so) operate machines to do their work using gestures such as this.[124]

But while Bleecker seeks to focus on the futuring aspect of the dystopian scenario and not the interface itself, his celebration of *Minority Report* as exemplary design fiction ignores the dominant fetishizing of the gestural interface as a commodity to produce. This uncritical focus on the interface is demonstrated, for example, by the numerous interface designers who have aspired to develop the technology while ignoring the anticipatory surveillance police state that Bleecker suggested is supposed to be coupled tightly to the film's diegetic prototype.[125] Moreover, celebration of *Minority Report* as inspirational design fiction ignores not only the dystopian anticipatory surveillance state of the film but also the fact that the threat of such dystopia depicted is imagined precisely for white audiences, as heightened and preemptive policing has long been the lived reality for Brown and Black bodies.[126]

The widespread extraction of the imagined technology from *Minority Report* demonstrates that the diegetic prototypes of design fiction can similarly be extracted from their critical speculative contexts through modes of interpretation favoring the commodity over the context— through affirmative design or science fiction as actualization.[127] Consequently, design fiction commonly presupposes the existence of commodity capitalism in its articulation of the problems it seeks to explore while paradoxically excluding commodification as an alternate hardware literacy in engagements with design fiction, which reads the diegetic prototype as a ready-made commodity for the market.[128]

The coupling of diegetic prototype to context, which is vital to design fiction's critical function, is looser than Bleecker or Sterling articulate. As Matt Malpass notes, "In critical design, it is vital for the user to experience a dilemma and to carry something of a burden of interpretation," suggesting that the critical capacity is a function of analysis brought by those interpreting the design fiction rather than inherent to design fiction itself.[129] This is all the more evident given that practitioners describe design fiction as a way to read, a hermeneutic strategy, a kind of literacy. Since both science fiction and design routinely foreground objects as mechanisms for imagining future worlds, the critical potential of design fiction hinges not solely on the form of design fiction itself but also on the mode of interpretation brought to bear on it.

Ultimately, Bleecker's arguments that critical design fiction practitioners "don't design products, if such is taken to mean the product of manufacturing plants" assumes that the fictional commodity product form will not be extracted from their design fictions.[130] This expectation is untenable even if practitioners "design provocations that confront the assumptions about products, broadly," since the majority of design fiction relies on speculative objects as mechanisms to engender critique, an intended critique that also relies on interpretation of context rather than the extraction of a diegetic prototype as commodity.[131] The desire for analyzing a speculative narrative for the context instead of the diegetic prototype underscores the perspectival interpretations available in engagement with science fiction or design fiction, enacted by differently oriented audiences. One may attend to the world, as Sterling and Bleecker desire through their ideal informed audience but do not always follow through on themselves, or one may attend to the imagined object, as the machinations of the creative economy, and commodity capitalism more generally, are wont to do.

Extracting Youth

In 2016, Jennifer O'Connor, a CSF collaborator, ran a youth summer course on science fiction prototyping at the Centre of Talented Youth of Ireland. As the CSF explains regarding the course, "There is no doubt that children between the ages of eight and eleven harbour considerable imaginative skill," reinforcing the conception of children as imaginative as a natural fact.[132] In reflecting on the course's completion, the organization elaborates on this claim by asserting that "the benefits of teaching SFPs [science fiction prototypes] to children are vast and include the direct and obvious advantage of utilising a child's natural creative instincts," arguing for the value of their futurist methods by linking science fiction prototyping explicitly to children's innate imagination. Science fiction prototyping, the organization suggests, harnesses children's natural imagination to benefit society.[133] In identifying the significant elements of these speculative narratives and, by extension, of what children's imagination are to produce, however, the CSF highlights that "the benefits of these particular stories was the technology used to salvage the society."[134] This statement privileges not the narrative world or the context but the diegetic prototype itself, the imagined technology at the center of the imagined story.

Consequently, the description of this course to educate children in science fiction prototyping reinforces the gadget-centric tendencies of speculative technological design practices. In this way, I suggest that conceptions of youth as naturally imaginative as they are imbricated in speculative technological design practices express a logic of extracting youth for the creative economy.[135] Youth operate as a resource to extract within the creative economy along two dimensions. The first dimension posits that the value of youth subjects lies in the potential for them to imagine new commodities to produce. Second, youth as producers of these imagined commodities are also valued in as much as they are also consumers. Within creative economy discourses, then, extracting youth suggests that to educate youth is to teach them how to imagine products as creative workers in order to produce new commodities for themselves to consume.

Extracting youth for the creative economy, which hinges on youth imagination and consumption, however, is distinct from other forms of extracting value from youth. For instance, the extraction of labor power from Black slave children was justified through denying them childhood.[136] Extracting youth for chattel slavery in the United States demonstrates a context in which the extraction of labor power from Black children required denying entirely the category of youth from a whole group of children, denying Black children "access to childhood" while simultaneously affixing youth and attendant attributes such as innocence to white children.[137] The logics of extracting youth, then, are contextually defined through how children and youth subjects are constituted as valuable economic resources and agents.

In recent years, Arizona State University (ASU) has branded itself as a premier institution of higher education for cultivating student creativity for the future, expressing the logic of extracting youth for the creative economy. ASU's opening of the School for the Future of Innovation in Society (SFIS) in the fall of 2015 demonstrates one such commitment to this mission.[138] As noted in the 2016–17 SFIS annual report, founding director Dave Guston argued that "by examining the way we translate imagination into innovation—and how we blend technical and social concerns along the way—we learn to build a future for everyone."[139] Part of SFIS's project includes offering undergraduate degree programs in "Innovation in Society," which includes futurist-oriented courses such as "Welcome to the Future" and "Navigating Futures."[140] SFIS also appointed Johnson as their first futurist-in-residence in the spring of 2016, representing the school's commitment to industry and commercial partnerships. These efforts illustrate SFIS's mission of "[educating] new generations of informed citizens and skilled, productive workers as part of a larger social fabric—local, regional, national, global—that informs our wants and needs about the futures we will want to inhabit."[141]

Even before founding SFIS, ASU has hosted events to explore the future of technology with students, as youth subjects learning to shape futures to come. One flagship event was the inaugural Emerge: Artists + Scientists Redesign the Future, a gathering in 2012 that included design fiction workshops with Sterling, Bleecker, and others interested in producing "provocative and evocative stories, games, performances and objects from which a vision of the future develops."[142] This workshop, held 1–3 March 2012, produced a series of design fiction short films called *Corner Convenience* by Sterling, Bleecker, and several ASU students. Sterling proclaimed that these short films, which imagine potential products at the local convenience store, were "the crowning glory of the Emerge design-fiction workshops."[143] Regarding *Corner Convenience,* Bleecker explained that the aim was to consider how "the trajectory of all great innovations is to asymptotically trend towards the counter of your corner convenience store," by following different patrons—a drunk, a hoodie-clad youth, and a trucker—as they browse and purchase speculative goods.[144] For this Emerge project, the convenience store served as the setting to explore how speculative products can become mundane and widely available, treating the convenience store as emblematic of everyday consumerism now and in the future.

By doing so, however, the diegetic prototypes featured in the workshop's critical explorations stand as ready-made commodities for market production and consumption, as goods ready for extraction. In the short films, the various patrons browse portable video-playing cards for the collected works of Bruce Willis as well as lottery scratchers to win millions of Twitter followers (see Figures 24 and 25). Such fictional products, according to Bleecker, are supposed to be "evocative props, meant to activate the imagination rather than specify technology or make claims about what will or will not happen in the near future."[145] Sterling similarly argued that "by starting with the object, or the gadget, in some ways we quickly take the focus off of that object and place it more on populating the world around it, rather than creating a world in which our object of choice (whether it's a product or some irritant we hope to overcome) fits just so."[146] For both Bleecker and Sterling, while the diegetic prototypes serve to anchor the exploration of the speculative scenarios, the imagined products are not intended as the final purpose.

However, like Bleecker's reading of *Minority Report* and the gestural interface, this expectation of criticality requires an audience invested in focusing not on the objects but the narrative world, an audience engaged in critical rather than affirmative design or science fiction as potentiality rather than actualization. Yet the camera shots provide viewers the point of view of the various patrons through tight close-ups of

FIGURE 24. *Portable video-playing card for* The Collected Works of Bruce Willis *as a fictional product in* Corner Convenience. *(Source: Near Future Laboratory,* Corner Convenience, *available at Near Future Laboratory, Vimeo, 2012; screenshot by author.)*

the speculative objects themselves, reinforcing the diegetic prototypes as commodities and negating the critical distance design fiction requires of its imagined viewers to interrogate the speculative world they inhabit. In reflecting on the short films, Bleecker and Sterling do not address the fact that the diegetic prototypes they have created with their collaborators could be removed from their speculative context, especially since the very setting of *Corner Convenience* explicitly frames the diegetic prototypes as products for ubiquitous consumption.

In one segment called "The Hoodie," in particular, *Corner Convenience* presents an imagined surveillance system that charges patrons upon existing the store, portrayed to viewers through a shopper whose behavior is initially suggested as shoplifting. The titular hoodie-clad youth, after loitering outside, skulks around the store quietly before pocketing some items and exiting the store briskly without stopping by the register (see Figure 26, top row). With this suggestion of shoplifting established, it is only when the camera focuses on the unattended cash register screen that automatically rings the purchase up that *Corner Convenience* reveals the fictional interaction-less purchasing system (see Figure 26, bottom row).

But unlike the convenience store's purchasing system that charges

FIGURE 25. *Lottery scratcher card for Twitter followers as a fictional product in* Corner Convenience. *(Source: Near Future Laboratory,* Corner Convenience, *available at Near Future Laboratory, Vimeo, 2012; screenshot by author.)*

those who would otherwise appear as shoplifters for their lifted goods, design fiction has no apparatus to prevent audiences from pilfering diegetic prototypes and turning them into commodities devoid of their original critical purposes. Commodification, as another form of hardware literacy, transforms what design fiction authors create as critical provocations into actual products, since the means of producing provocation in design fiction is through imagined products and reliant on a particular mode of interpretation. As such, the films offer an allegory of the literal and figurative extractability of these imagined products from their imagined world. By extracting the diegetic prototype of design fiction, commodification renders moot the social world for the imagined object and the critical potential of design fiction. Like the hoodie-clad youth in *Corner Convenience,* commodity capitalism can literally remove, albeit at a minor price, the speculative product from its imagined diegetic context—from this imagined convenience store to sell at any actual shop. Ultimately, *Corner Convenience* dramatizes the double extraction of youthful imagination. The short films are the product of collaborations with ASU students as youth subjects in training to imagine a future of commodities; they also represent how youth are to extract these imagined products from the convenience store within the films as well as from the films themselves for consumption.

FIGURE 26. *Scenes from* Corner Convenience. Top left, *hoodie-clad white male youth loitering outside the convenience store.* Top right, *youth appearing suspicious in surveillance footage.* Bottom left, *youth leaving store without stopping by the register.* Bottom right, *youth automatically charged for purchases by an interaction-less payment system as a fictional technology. (Source: Near Future Laboratory,* Corner Convenience, *available at Near Future Laboratory, Vimeo, 2012; screenshot by author.)*

The figure of the hoodie-clad youth, in constructing but then inverting the suggestion of shoplifting, metaphorically gestures to this extraction as illicit theft of the diegetic prototype into a potentially real commodity. This invocation of the specter of shoplifting, however, em-

phasizes that not all youth subjects are equally viable under the logic of extracting youth for the creative economy. Not all youth subjects are able to participate evenly as contributors to thinking about the future. *Corner Convenience*'s use of the hoodie as a visual cue to suggest that the youth in question may be shoplifting relies on the hoodie's cultural associations with youth, delinquency, and crime. In particular, the hoodie conventionally operates as a marker of Blackness, a racialized and classed garment donned by the threatening "thug" figure roaming the urban landscape.[147]

Significantly, the hoodie-clad youth in *Corner Convenience* is a white-passing male. He is able to leave the corner convenience not only without harassment but also ultimately negating any suspicion of shoplifting.

In contrast, just four days before the start of the inaugural Emerge workshop in 2012 that created *Corner Convenience,* Trayvon Martin—a Black seventeen-year-old hoodie-clad youth—was shot and murdered by George Zimmerman, a white-passing Hispanic man and Neighborhood Watch volunteer. Zimmerman was suspicious of Martin, who was on a short trip to a convenience store to buy iced tea and Skittles during a visit to Sanford, Florida. Zimmerman's killing of Martin, trial, and subsequent acquittal for charges of second-degree murder sparked intensive coverage and debate over racial profiling, stand-your-ground self-defense laws, and the anti-Blackness of the justice system. The acquittal of Zimmerman in 2013, in particular, led to the establishing of the Black Lives Matter movement by Black activist and community organizers Alicia Garza, Patrisse Cullors, and Opal Tometi. In discussing this all in brief, I am admittedly doing great disservice to the complexities of the murder of Trayvon Martin, the longer preceding histories of anti-Black violence and injustice, and continuing anti-Black violence and injustice.[148]

My attention to Martin, here, is to emphasize that Martin was not seen as suspicious because he had shoplifted at the convenience store he visited. He had not shoplifted. Rather, as a Black male youth sporting a hoodie, he met particular visual cues that were suspect to Zimmerman, a surveilling force primed to look for what he deemed to be suspicious activity under white supremacy. Zimmerman demonstrated a manifestation of the dystopian policing imagined in *Minority Report* that is already present for Black and Brown bodies. Black youth are not only denied access to childhood metaphorically, as they are often imagined already as suspicious and threatening Black adults, but are under perpetual threat of being denied their childhood literally as victims of systematic anti-Black violence and injustice, through, for example, their capture into carceral systems or their untimely deaths at the hands of police or vigilante forces such as Zimmerman.

As a product of ASU students and metaphorized in the hoodie-clad white male figure, *Corner Convenience* demonstrates how extracting youth for the creative economy grants particular privileged youth subjects the ability, or, more accurately, the expectation, to imagine new commodities to create and consume. Other youths, however, are either ignored or forcefully excluded from participation. While *Corner Convenience* as design fiction gestures to critical exploration of surveillance through the diegetic prototype of the interaction-less purchasing system, its use of the hoodie-clad youth as a figure suggestive of shoplifting ignores the racial and class dynamics of who can and cannot contribute to and participate in the creative economy and, subsequently, the future. The ongoing denial of childhood to Black youth like Martin—in continuing the historic refusal to grant to Black children the same innocence and imagination granted to white childhood—also denies them not only their ability to shape their futures but even to have them at all. This denial, as Jacob Breslow suggests, links "the negation of black childhood and the negation of black citizenship."[149] Black youth like Trayvon Martin, in contrast to the white youth in *Corner Convenience,* may have no such future to imagine and to consume, no opportunity to develop and participate in creativity in any form, present or future whatsoever.

Design has not only become an idealized category of labor in the creative economy but is also believed to be instrumental in the deliberate shaping of futures to come. At the contemporary intersection of design and futurism, speculative technological design practices such as design fiction seek to shape futures through storytelling anchored to diegetic prototypes as imagined technologies. The capacity to think and shape the future, even to design it, has long been associated with the imagination, which is believed to require careful cultivation in childhood, negotiating between invention and reverie, fact and fiction, productivity and deceit. But as demonstrated through the shifting cultural history of imagination, one constituted primarily through conceptions of white childhood, to be productive under the logic of extracting youth for the creative economy, youthful imaginations, both of children as well as of adults, should be directed toward imagining future technologies, innovations, and commodities. As depicted in the narrative diegesis of *Corner Convenience,* youthful imaginations must also recognize themselves as consumers of the very products they design. But while the creative economy values children and their imagination in so much as they are believed to contribute future technologies, innovations, and commodities, the juxtaposition of *Corner Convenience* and Trayvon Martin's murder puts into stark relief that not all youth are granted the same access to childhood, to innocence, to imagination, or to their own futures. Although advocates often describe the critical potential of speculative technological design practices for exploring futures coming into being, practices such as design fiction encounter limits to this criticality. Design fiction as a speculative practice typically hinges on the diegetic prototype, as speculation centers around imagined technologies, innovations, and commodities. Consequently, these diegetic prototypes are always potentially subject to extraction by commodity capitalism into actual products at the expense of any critical potential for investigating the imagined world in which the diegetic prototype lives. While interested in critically exploring consumer goods, social media practices, and surveillance technologies, for instance, what *Corner Convenience* does not critically explore is a world without capitalism—the very force that impedes any such critical exploration. Depicted in *Corner Convenience*, after all, are speculative products on store shelves, potential customers, and technologies for transacting sales.

This limitation of design fiction's critical potential emerges from practitioners' persistent use of objects, products, and commodities as diegetic prototypes to anchor the imagined worlds they seek to explore. Discussion of such limits for speculative technological design practices, and speculative narrative more broadly, often consider how to imagine worlds without centering speculative objects that could be extracted as commodities.[150] Rather than privileging an imagination centered on gadgets and gizmos, then, practitioners of design fiction and speculative practices more broadly, if they are to engage the future critically while also resisting capitalism's eager extraction of commodities, might prioritize an imagination capable of exploring the political possibilities of speculative reorganizations of social relations, dynamics, and worlds.[151] Doing so encourages design fiction's critical potential, since there is no easy diegetic prototype ready for capitalist extraction as a commodity.

As Ruha Benjamin contends, "novel fictions that reimagine and rework all that is taken for granted about the current structure of the social world—alternatives to capitalism, racism, and patriarchy—are urgently needed."[152] Developing the imagination to speculate on alternate social worlds rather than a fixation on novel products offers one way to do so, especially if the social world constituted through capitalism and the creative labor economy is also inextricably constituted through patriarchy, white supremacy, cisnormativity, heteronormativity, ableism, and other oppressive and unjust systems of inequity and violence. Rather than developing the imagination only for the invention of new technologies, innovations, or commodities, the imaginations of children and adults alike could be directed toward social justice work in order to bring into the present more equitable future worlds, worlds that make room for those who have long been unable to imagine their own futures at all.

CONCLUSION

Much is believed to be at stake at the intersection of youth, digital media, and creativity.

But what is believed to be at stake is not wholly true to any natural or innate quality of actual youth subjects themselves.

Rather, as *The Digital Is Kid Stuff* has demonstrated, contemporary creative economy discourses in the United States traffic in images of naturally creative and naturally technological youth in order to negotiate the ambivalences and contradictions of a precarious creative labor economy made possible by digital technologies. In characterizing creative digital youth as the future of innovation, of the economy, and of the nation, images of creative digital youth ask us all to invest in their promise. But as their creative development is believed to depend greatly on careful and particular encounters with digital technologies, images of creative digital youth as youth at risk are also about the parents, educators, policymakers, and other adults responsible for ensuring the proper maturation of these developing subjects and their natural gifts. That is, discourses about the promise of creative digital youth and how to nurture them to contribute to a creative economy in an increasingly digital world are also about shaping the adults tasked to raise them to fit into that very world themselves.

In the process, images of creative digital youth negotiate and cement particular ideologies of creativity and creative value coherent with neoliberal economic and political conditions in early twenty-first-century American digital culture. Images of creative digital youth argue that creativity is inherently individualistic and in direct opposition to social conformity and dependence, best developed in and expressed through precarious situations. Images of creative digital youth assert that privatized technoscience and the self-governing of risk-taking is vital to produce innovation responsibly. Images of creative digital youth encourage self-branding as both deliberate market-driven self-fashioning as well as authentic identity discovery in an unstable work world constituted by short-term gigs and projects. And images of creative digital youth advocate the cultivation and disciplining of inventive imagination specifically to design novelties that extract economic value from youth itself for the future. As the chapters in this book have shown, these various beliefs about what creativity is, how it works, what it can do, and how to cultivate it are articulated and advanced through images of creative digital youth, shaping how we are to make sense of changes in subjecthood, education, labor, civic engagement, and the nation under the increasingly insecure and precarious conditions of the creative economy.

Creative economy discourses argue that creative digital youth are at risk—imperiled—without proper guidance and education by adults. Instead of fulfilling their potential for the future, youth may become no better than wolves with no control over their individuality, either swept up in the social conformity of a pack or cast out as isolated lone wolves. They may become reckless and irresponsible pyromaniacs and bioterrorists or may grow up too fearful to take risks to innovate. They may become deceptive scammers, catfish, and cons without any authentic sense of self-identity or intimate connections. Or they may become uninspired or distracted thinkers unable to harness their imaginations productively toward valuable invention. Against these images of improperly raised youth, the creative economy requires adults to raise creative, imaginative, self-branding, and responsibly risky digital youth into entrepreneurial and innovative laborers. Adults who fail to do so fail the future.

But as long as the creative economy traffics in the future as a mechanism to extract from youth ways to continue the underlying capitalist processes of exploitation, exclusion, and injustice of the past and present, what kind of future is really ever on offer? Although youth are generally imagined as naturally creative and naturally technological, not all populations of youth are imagined, explicitly or not, as part of the future that a creative economy undergirded by digital technologies promises. Only those whose youthful qualities are understood as valued and valuable for contributing to the creative economy have a celebrated place in that future. Youth without access to computing technologies, reliable internet infrastructures, as well as education and time demonstrate how technological facility is not natural but learned, excluding a population of youth conceived of as outside the bounds of digital culture. Youth who do not have the privilege of participating in creative industries or who refuse the mandate to "be creative" are deemed unoriginal, monotonous, and mindless. And youth denied the features believed to be essential to childhood and youth, including playfulness and innocence, have no opportunity to explore and imagine without endless threats of suspicion, surveillance, and violence.

Creativity is currently imagined as the endless driver of technological innovation and economic prosperity, putting youth and adults to work. But how might creativity be directed toward different ends? Beyond the valuing of youth insofar as we can render creative digital youth resources for a precarious creative labor economy that takes its continued operations, exclusions, and injustices for granted, creativity might not be so narrowly defined as only to produce instrumental, salable, and consumable novelty. To think about and create the future as not only made by extracting value from youth but instead as a future for youth to inhabit and flourish, particularly for youth who have historically been left outside of childhood and youth, requires acknowledging that we can and must continuously think otherwise about creativity itself—what it is, what it can do, and to what ends we might guide it. Creativity directed to undo this limiting, harmful, and unjust understanding of both creativity and its value is the creativity for the future that we need.

ACKNOWLEDGMENTS

While the cover and title page may indicate otherwise, this book is not completely the product of a sole author. And it is definitely not the output of an individual creative genius.

It has only been through my various encounters—deep as well as passing, recurring as well as singular, formal as well as surprising—with so many thinkers, mentors, interlocutors, and friends that I have been able to complete this book to the best of my ability.

My sincerest thanks to the thoughtful and supportive readers and editorial staff at the University of Minnesota Press. I am especially grateful to Leah Pennywark and Anne Carter for guiding me through the process of refining this book into its final form.

This book grew from a dissertation I developed under the great care and encouragement of Colin Milburn, John Marx, and Michael Ziser at the University of California, Davis. Financial support at the University of California, Davis, for this stage of the project's development included a UC Davis Provost's Dissertation Year Fellowship, a Margrit Mondavi Summer Fellowship, funding from the UC Davis Department of English, funding from the Mellon Research Initiative in Digital Cultures, funding from the UC Davis Office of Research Interdisciplinary Frontiers in the Humanities and Arts (IFHA) in Digital Humanities and Gamification, and funding from IMMERSe: The Research Network for Video Game Immersion, provided by the Social Sciences and Humanities Research Council of Canada. Additional financial support included a Phi Beta Kappa Northern California Association Graduate Scholarship.

I was fortunate to converse in person, over email, and during STS coffee times with many while a part of the UC Davis community while figuring out the foundations of this project. I owe many thanks to Ian Afflerbach, Russell Backman, Sophia Bamert, Gina Bloom, Stephanie Boluk, Evan Buswell, Jordan Carroll, Xan Chacko, Christina Cogdell,

Nicholas D'Avella, Joe Dumit, Kris Fallon, Jim Griesemer, James Housefield, William Hughes, Annette Hulbert, Mark Jerng, Caren Kaplan, Sawyer Kemp, Evan Lauteria, Patrick LeMieux, Stephanie Maroney, Michael Martel, Sarah McCullough, Roberta Millstein, Aaron Norton, Diana Pardo Pedraza, Simon Sadler, Ashley Sarpong, Leilani Serafin, Eric Smoodin, Meg Sparling, Alex Stalarow, Emma Leigh Waldron, Melissa Wills, Tobias Wilson-Bates, May Ee Wong, and Bryan Yazell.

My colleagues at the University of Texas at Dallas have been incredibly supportive, providing valuable feedback and reassurance throughout the book's maturation. I am exceptionally thankful to Anne Balsamo, Lisa Bell, Matt Brown, xtine burrough, Heidi Cooley, Juan Llamas-Rodriguez, Jessica Murphy, Sabrina Starnaman, Wendy Sung, and Hong-An Wu. Conversations with undergraduate and graduate students at UT Dallas have also contributed to this book, especially discussions with Chelsea Brtis, Clay Harper, Talia Henry, Cenk Köknar, Jack Murray, and Sam Owens.

I am grateful for my exchanges with many others who have helped with the shaping of this project over the years, including Mary Amasia, Marisa Cohn, Mark Cooper, Andrew Culp, Eva Della Lana, Paul Dourish, Chris Goetz, Lilly Irani, Will Jordan, Jordan Kraemer, Silvia Lindtner, Alexandra Lippman, Gavin Mueller, Jennifer Porst, Whit Pow, Aaron Trammell, Jacqueline Vickery, Jerry Zee, and Ozzie Zehner.

Shout-out to Alex Agloro, Amanda Phillips, Bo Ruberg, and Adrienne Shaw who, by their powers combined, form the best writing group ever.

Special thanks to the European University in St. Petersburg and Johannes Gutenberg University Mainz for invitations to share my work in progress and engage with their insightful and generous intellectual communities.

I know that there remain others toward whom I am deeply embarrassed and apologetic for failing to give thanks here.

Thank you nonetheless.

NOTES

Introduction

1. Po Bronson and Ashley Merryman, "The Creativity Crisis," *Newsweek*, 19 July 2010, 44–49.

2. Bronson and Merryman, 45.

3. Bronson and Merryman, 45.

4. Ken Robinson and Lou Aronica, *Creative Schools: The Grassroots Revolution That's Transforming Education* (New York: Penguin Books, 2015), 137.

5. Robinson and Aronica, 207.

6. Mark Yarm, "Does Screen Time Stunt Kids' Creativity?," in *The Science of Creativity*, ed. the Editors of *Time* (New York: Time USA, 2018), 70–74.

7. Yarm, 74.

8. Yarm, 74.

9. Philippe Ariès, *Centuries of Childhood: A Social History of Family Life*, trans. Robert Baldick (New York: Vintage Books, 1965); Joseph F. Kett, *Rites of Passage: Adolescence in America, 1790 to the Present* (New York: Basic Books, 1977); Daniel Blake Smith, *Inside the Great House: Planter Family Life in Eighteenth-Century Chesapeake Society* (Ithaca, N.Y.: Cornell University Press, 1980); Stevi Jackson, *Childhood and Sexuality* (Oxford: Blackwell, 1982); Linda A. Pollock, *Forgotten Children: Parent–Child Relations from 1500 to 1900* (New York: Cambridge University Press, 1983); Elliott West and Paula Petrik, eds., *Small Worlds: Children and Adolescents in America, 1850–1950* (Lawrence: University Press of Kansas, 1992); Harry Eiss, ed., *Images of the Child* (Bowling Green, Ohio: Bowling Green State University Popular Press, 1994); James Kincaid, *Child-Loving: The Erotic Child and Victorian Literature* (New York: Routledge, 1994); Viviana A. Zelizer, *Pricing the Priceless Child: The Changing Social Value of Children*, reprint ed. (Princeton, N.J.: Princeton University Press, 1994); Charles R. Acland, *Youth, Murder, Spectacle: The Cultural Politics of "Youth in Crisis"* (Boulder, Colo.: Westview Press, 1995); Wilma King, *Stolen Childhood: Slave Youth in Nineteenth-Century America* (Bloomington: Indiana University Press, 1995); Grace Palladino, *Teenagers: An American History* (New York: Basic Books, 1996); Joe Austin and Michael Nevin Willard, eds., *Generations of Youth: Youth Cultures and History in Twentieth-Century America* (New York: NYU Press, 1998); Henry Jenkins, ed., *The Children's Culture Reader* (New York: NYU Press, 1998); Thomas Hine, *The Rise and Fall of the American Teenager* (New York: HarperCollins, 1999); Nicholas Orme, *Medieval Children* (New Haven, Conn.: Yale University Press, 2003); Gary Cross, *The Cute and the Cool: Wondrous Innocence and Modern American Children's Culture* (New York: Oxford University Press, 2004); Rob Latham, *Consuming Youth: Vampires, Cyborgs, and the Culture of Consumption* (Chicago: University of Chicago Press, 2007); Lisa Cartwright, *Moral Spectatorship: Technologies of Voice and Affect in Postwar Representations of the Child* (Durham, N.C.: Duke

University Press, 2008); Maria Gutman and Ning de Coninck-Smith, *Designing Modern Childhoods: History, Space, and the Material Culture of Children* (New Brunswick, N.J.: Rutgers University Press, 2008); Sarah E. Chinn, *Inventing Modern Adolescence: The Children of Immigrants in Turn-of-the-Century America* (New Brunswick, N.J.: Rutgers University Press, 2009); Kathryn Bond Stockton, *The Queer Child, or Growing Sideways in the Twentieth Century* (Durham, N.C.: Duke University Press, 2009); Sally Shuttleworth, *The Mind of the Child: Child Development in Literature, Science, and Medicine, 1840–1900* (Oxford: Oxford University Press, 2010); Robin Bernstein, *Racial Innocence: Performing American Childhood and Race from Slavery to Civil Rights* (New York: NYU Press, 2011); Julie Passanante Elman, *Chronic Youth: Disability, Sexuality, and U.S. Media Cultures of Rehabilitation* (New York: NYU Press, 2014); J. Allan Mitchell, *Becoming Human: The Matter of the Medieval Child* (Minneapolis: University of Minnesota Press, 2014); Carly A. Kocurek, *Coin-Operated Americans: Rebooting Boyhood at the Video Game Arcade* (Minneapolis: University of Minnesota Press, 2015); Erica R. Meiners, *For the Children? Protecting Innocence in a Carceral State* (Minneapolis: University of Minnesota Press, 2016); Rebecca Onion, *Innocent Experiments: Childhood and the Culture of Popular Science in the United States* (Chapel Hill: University of North Carolina Press, 2016); Rebekah Sheldon, *The Child to Come: Life after the Human Catastrophe* (Minneapolis: University of Minnesota Press, 2016); Pamela R. Wojcik, *Fantasies of Neglect: Imagining the Urban Child in American Film and Fiction* (New Brunswick, N.J.: Rutgers University Press, 2016); Lauren S. Berliner, *Producing Queer Youth: The Paradox of Digital Media Empowerment* (New York: Routledge, 2018); Jules Gill-Peterson, *Histories of the Transgender Child* (Minneapolis: University of Minnesota Press, 2018); Hannah Dyer, *The Queer Aesthetics of Childhood: Asymmetries of Innocence and the Cultural Politics of Child Development* (New Brunswick, N.J.: Rutgers University Press, 2019).

10. Seymour Papert, *The Connected Family: Bridging the Digital Generation Gap* (Atlanta: Longstreet Press, 1996); Don Tapscott, *Growing Up Digital: The Rise of the Net Generation* (New York: McGraw-Hill, 1998); Marc Prensky, "Digital Natives, Digital Immigrants," *On the Horizon* 9, no. 5 (2001): 1–6; Sarah L. Holloway and Gill Valentine, *Cyberkids: Children in the Information Age* (New York: Routledge, 2003); J. D. Lasica, *Darknet: Hollywood's War against the Digital Generation* (Hoboken, N.J.: John Wiley and Sons, 2005); Howard Gardner and Katie Davis, *The App Generation: How Today's Youth Navigate Identity, Intimacy, and Imagination in a Digital World* (New Haven, Conn.: Yale University Press, 2013); Jean M. Twenge, *iGen: Why Today's Super-Connected Kids Are Growing Up Less Rebellious, More Tolerant, Less Happy—and Completely Unprepared for Adulthood—and What That Means for the Rest of Us* (New York: Atria Books, 2017).

11. Tapscott, *Growing Up Digital.*

12. Tapscott, 2.

13. Clay Shirky, *Here Comes Everybody: The Power of Organizing without Organizations,* revised ed. (New York: Penguin Books, 2009); Sherry Turkle, *Alone Together: Why We Expect More from Technology and Less from Each Other* (New York: Basic Books, 2011). For comparison of contemporary anxieties about youth and screens with similar nineteenth-century anxieties about youth and optical toys, see Meredith A. Bak, *Playful Visions: Optical Toys and the Emergence of Children's Media Culture* (Cambridge, Mass.: MIT Press, 2020).

14. David Buckingham, "Is There a Digital Generation?," in *Digital Generations: Children, Young People, and the New Media,* ed. David Buckingham and Rebekah Willett (Mahwah, N.J.: Lawrence Erlbaum Associates, 2013), 9.

15. John A. Vincent, "Understanding Generations: Political Economy and Culture in an Ageing Society," *British Journal of Sociology* 56, no. 4 (2005): 579–99.

16. McKenzie Wark, "Planet of Noise: So Who Are Generation X and Why Are They Saying These Terrible Things about Us," *Juice*, December 1993, 74–78.

17. Tapscott, *Growing Up Digital,* 9.

18. June Edmunds and Bryan S. Turner, *Generations, Culture and Society* (Philadelphia: Open University Press, 2002).

19. Michael Serazio, "Selling (Digital) Millennials: The Social Construction and Technological Bias of a Consumer Generation," *Television and New Media* 16, no. 7 (2015): 600.

20. Buckingham, "Is There a Digital Generation?," 3.

21. Prensky, "Digital Natives, Digital Immigrants"; John Perry Barlow, "A Declaration of the Independence of Cyberspace," Electronic Frontier Foundation, accessed 3 August 2020, http://eff.org/; Douglas Rushkoff, *Playing the Future: How Kids' Culture Can Teach Us to Thrive in an Age of Chaos* (New York: HarperCollins, 1996); Sherry Turkle, *Life on the Screen: Identity in the Age of the Internet* (New York: Simon & Schuster, 1995), 77.

22. danah boyd, *It's Complicated: The Social Lives of Networked Teens* (New Haven, Conn.: Yale University Press, 2014), 177. For literacy as a technology, see Anne Balsamo, "Public Interactives and the Design of Technological Literacies," in *Designing Culture: The Technological Imagination at Work* (Durham, N.C.: Duke University Press, 2011), 95–132.

23. For uneven youth participation with digital technologies, especially explicit attention to gender, race, class, and geography, see Sonia Livingstone, *Young People and New Media: Childhood and the Changing Media Environment* (Thousand Oaks, Calif.: SAGE Publications, 2002); Sonia Livingstone, "Internet Literacy: Young People's Negotiation of New Online Opportunities," in *Digital Youth, Innovation, and the Unexpected,* ed. Tara McPherson (Cambridge, Mass.: MIT Press, 2008), 101–22; *Children and the Internet* (Cambridge, UK: Polity, 2013); Jacqueline Ryan Vickery, *Worried about the Wrong Things: Youth, Risk, and Opportunity in the Digital World* (Cambridge, Mass.: MIT Press, 2017); Korina M. Jocson, *Youth Media Matters: Participatory Cultures and Literacies in Education* (Minneapolis: University of Minnesota Press, 2018); S. Craig Watkins et al., *The Digital Edge: How Black and Latino Youth Navigate Digital Inequality* (New York: NYU Press, 2018); and Morgan G. Ames, *The Charisma Machine: The Life, Death, and Legacy of One Laptop Per Child* (Cambridge, Mass.: MIT Press, 2019).

24. Jodi A. Byrd, "Tribal 2.0: Digital Natives, Political Players, and the Power of Stories," *Studies in American Indian Literatures* 26, no. 2 (2014): 57. See also Larry J. Zimmerman, Karen P. Zimmerman, and Leonard R. Bruguier, "Cyberspace Smoke Signals: New Technologies and Native American Ethnicity," in *Indigenous Cultures in an Interconnected World,* ed. Claire Smith and Graeme K. Ward (Vancouver: UBC Press, 2000), 69–86; Laurel Evelyn Dyson, Max Hendriks, and Stephen Grant, eds., *Information Technology and Indigenous People* (Melbourne: Information Science Publishing, 2006); Christian Sandvig, "Connection at Ewiiaapaayp Mountain: Indigenous Internet Infrastructure," in *Race after the Internet,* ed. Lisa Nakamura and Peter A. Chow-White (New York: Routledge, 2012), 168–200; Lisa Nakamura, "Indigenous Circuits: Navajo Women and the Racialization of Early Electronic Manufacture," *American Quarterly* 66, no. 4 (2014): 919–41; and Marisa Elena Duarte, *Network Sovereignty: Building the Internet across Indian Country* (Seattle: University of Washington Press, 2017).

25. Stephanie Ricker Schulte, "The '*WarGames* Scenario': Regulating Teenagers and Teenaged Technology," in *Cached: Decoding the Internet in Global Popular Culture*

(New York: NYU Press, 2013), 21–54; Meryl Alper, "'Can Our Kids Hack It with Computers?': Constructing Youth Hackers in Family Computing Magazines (1983–1987)," *International Journal of Communication* 8 (2014): http://ijoc.org/.

26. Neil Selwyn, "'Doing It for the Kids': Re-examining Children, Computers and the Information Society," *Media, Culture & Society* 25, no. 3 (2003): 353.

27. Mizuko Ito, *Engineering Play: A Cultural History of Children's Software* (Cambridge, Mass.: MIT Press, 2009).

28. Justine Cassell and Henry Jenkins, "Chess for Girls? Feminism and Computer Games," in *From Barbie to Mortal Kombat: Gender and Computer Games,* ed. Justine Cassell and Henry Jenkins (Cambridge, Mass.: MIT Press, 1998), 2–45.

29. Kocurek, *Coin-Operated Americans.*

30. Amy F. Ogata, *Designing the Creative Child: Playthings and Places in Midcentury America* (Minneapolis: University of Minnesota Press, 2013), 188.

31. Tom Peters, *Thriving on Chaos: Handbook for a Management Revolution* (New York: HarperCollins, 1988); Tom Peters, *Liberation Management: Necessary Disorganization for the Nanosecond Nineties* (New York: A. A. Knopf, 1992).

32. Richard Florida, *The Rise of the Creative Class: And How It's Transforming Work, Leisure, Community, and Everyday Life* (New York: Basic Books, 2002); Richard Florida, *Cities and the Creative Class* (New York: Routledge, 2005); Richard Florida, *The Flight of the Creative Class: The New Global Competition for Talent* (New York: HarperCollins, 2005); Richard Florida, *Who's Your City? How the Creative Economy Is Making Where to Live the Most Important Decision of Your Life* (New York: Basic Books, 2010).

33. Barack Obama, "Remarks by the President in State of Union Address," The White House, last modified 25 January 2011, accessed 3 August 2020, http://obamawhitehouse.archives.gov/.

34. Pascal Gielen, *Creativity and Other Fundamentalisms,* trans. Leo Reijnen (Heijningen, Netherlands: Jap Sam Books, 2013); Ogata, *Designing the Creative Child*; Sarah Brouillette, *Literature and the Creative Economy* (Stanford, Calif.: Stanford University Press, 2014); Angela McRobbie, *Be Creative: Making a Living in the New Culture Industries* (Cambridge, UK: Polity, 2016); Oli Mould, *Against Creativity* (London: Verso Books, 2018); Tyler Denmead, *The Creative Underclass: Youth, Race, and the Gentrifying City* (Durham, N.C.: Duke University Press, 2019); Michael L. Siciliano, *Creative Control: The Ambivalence of Work in the Culture Industries* (New York: Columbia University Press, 2021). I focus primarily on constructions of creativity as an individual personality trait in this book. While related, I distinguish innovation as the introduction of something regarded as a novelty into the market. This study is not a critical investigation into innovation but will discuss innovation as it is described as a product of creativity. For critical work on innovation, see Lucy Suchman and Libby Bishop, "Problematizing 'Innovation' as a Critical Project," *Technology Analysis & Strategic Management* 12, no. 3 (2000): 327–33.

35. Ogata, *Designing the Creative Child,* x.

36. Ogata, 33–34.

37. Fred Turner, *The Democratic Surround: Multimedia and American Liberalism from World War II to the Psychedelic Sixties* (Chicago: University of Chicago Press, 2013), 2.

38. Ogata, *Designing the Creative Child.*

39. Abraham H. Maslow, *Motivation and Personality,* 2nd ed. (New York: Harper & Row, 1970), 170; Abraham H. Maslow, *The Farther Reaches of Human Nature* (New York: Viking Press, 1971), 79; Abraham H. Maslow, *Toward a Psychology of Being,* 2nd ed. (New York: Van Nostrand Reinhold, 1982), 138.

40. Ogata, *Designing the Creative Child*, x.

41. Ogata, 187.

42. Zelizer, *Pricing the Priceless Child;* Lee Edelman, "The Future Is Kid Stuff," in *No Future: Queer Theory and the Death Drive* (Durham, N.C.: Duke University Press, 2004), 1–31.

43. Stanley Cohen, *Folk Devils and Moral Panics: The Creation of the Mods and Rockers,* 3rd ed. (New York: Routledge, 2002); Toby Miller, "A Risk Society of Moral Panic: The US in the Twenty-First Century," *Cultural Politics* 2, no. 3 (2006): 299–318; Vickery, *Worried about the Wrong Things.*

44. Acland, *Youth, Murder, Spectacle*, 10.

45. Stuart Hall et al., *Policing the Crisis: Mugging, the State and Law and Order,* 2nd ed. (New York: Palgrave Macmillan, 2013), 231.

46. Edelman, *No Future*, 11.

47. Bernstein, *Racial Innocence.* See also King, *Stolen Childhood;* and Meiners, *For the Children?*

48. José Esteban Muñoz, *Cruising Utopia: The Then and There of Queer Futurity* (New York: NYU Press, 2009), 95.

49. Joseph J. Fischel, *Sex and Harm in the Age of Consent* (Minneapolis: University of Minnesota Press, 2016), 217.

50. Stockton, *Queer Child.*

51. Gail Bederman, *Manliness and Civilization: A Cultural History of Gender and Race in the United States, 1880–1917* (Chicago: University of Chicago Press, 1995), 93.

52. Gill-Peterson, *Histories of the Transgender Child.*

53. Charles Baudelaire, *The Painter of Modern Life and Other Essays,* trans. Jonathan Mayne, reprinted 2nd ed. (New York: Phaidon Press, 1995), 5. For children and consumer culture, see Ellen Seiter, *Sold Separately: Children and Parents in Consumer Culture* (New Brunswick, N.J.: Rutgers University Press, 1993); Latham, *Consuming Youth;* Dennis Denisoff, ed., *The Nineteenth-Century Child and Consumer Culture* (Aldershot, UK: Ashgate, 2008); and Lisa Jacobson, ed., *Children and Consumer Culture in American Society: A Historical Handbook and Guide* (Westport, Conn.: Praeger, 2008).

54. Ogata, *Designing the Creative Child,* 33–34.

55. Seiter, *Sold Separately,* 71–72.

56. Mould, *Against Creativity,* 11, emphasis in original.

57. Andrew Ross, *Nice Work If You Can Get It: Life and Labor in Precarious Times* (New York: NYU Press, 2009), 17–19.

58. Ross, 19. For the history of creative economy policy, see Brouillette, "Creative Class and Cultural Governance," in *Literature and the Creative Economy,* 20–33; McRobbie, *Be Creative.*

59. George Yúdice, *The Expediency of Culture: Uses of Culture in the Global Era* (Durham, N.C.: Duke University Press, 2004), 16; Ross, *Nice Work If You Can Get It,* 17–19; McRobbie, *Be Creative,* 10. See also Nicholas Garnham, "From Cultural to Creative Industries: An Analysis of the Implications of the 'Creative Industries' Approach to Arts and Media Policy Making in the United Kingdom," *International Journal of Cultural Policy* 11, no. 1 (2005): 15–29; and Geert Lovink and Ned Rossiter, eds., *MyCreativity Reader: A Critique of Creative Industries* (Amsterdam: Institute of Network Cultures, 2007), http://networkcultures.org/.

60. Max Horkheimer and Theodor W. Adorno, "The Culture Industry: Enlightenment as Mass Deception," in *Dialectic of Enlightenment: Philosophical Fragments,* ed. Gunzelin Schmid Noerr and trans. Edmund Jephcott (Stanford, Calif.: Stanford University Press, 2002), 94–136. George Morgan and Pariece Nelligan trace a genealogy

binding culture with creativity beginning in early modern Europe through the development of an understanding of culture that could be actively cultivated. See George Morgan and Pariece Nelligan, *The Creativity Hoax: Precarious Work in the Gig Economy* (New York: Anthem Press, 2018), 16–23.

61. Ross, *Nice Work If You Can Get It*, 35.

62. Ross, 35.

63. Gielen, *Creativity and Other Fundamentalisms*.

64. Gielen, 41.

65. Brouillette, *Literature and the Creative Economy*, 2–3.

66. Alan McKinlay and Chris Smith, eds., *Creative Labour: Working in the Creative Industries* (London: Palgrave Macmillan, 2009); Gielen, *Creativity and Other Fundamentalisms*; Michael Curtin and Kevin Sanson, eds., *Precarious Creativity: Global Media, Local Labor* (Berkeley: University of California Press, 2016); Morgan and Nelligan, *Creativity Hoax*; Siciliano, *Creative Control*.

67. Angela McRobbie, *In the Culture Society: Art, Fashion and Popular Music* (London: Routledge, 1999), 27.

68. Sophie Hope and Jenny Richards, "Loving Work: Drawing Attention to Pleasure and Pain in the Body of the Cultural Worker," *European Journal of Cultural Studies* 18, no. 2 (2015): 123.

69. Brooke Erin Duffy, *(Not) Getting Paid to Do What You Love: Gender, Social Media, and Aspirational Work* (New Haven, Conn.: Yale University Press, 2017).

70. Gerald Raunig, "Anti-Precariousness Activism and Mayday Parades," trans. Aileen Derieg, *Transversal*, June 2004, http://transversal.at/.

71. McRobbie, *Be Creative*, 10–11.

72. McRobbie, 15, emphasis in original.

73. Ross, *Nice Work If You Can Get It*, 41.

74. Ross, 21.

75. Pierre Lévy, *Collective Intelligence: Mankind's Emerging World in Cyberspace*, trans. Robert Bononno (New York: Plenum Trade, 1997); Lawrence Lessig, *Free Culture: The Nature and Future of Creativity* (New York: Penguin Books, 2004); Clay Shirky, *Cognitive Surplus: How Technology Makes Consumers into Collaborators*, revised ed. (New York: Penguin Books, 2011). See also Ian Hargreaves and John Hartley, eds., *The Creative Citizen Unbound: How Social Media and DIY Culture Contribute to Democracy, Communities and the Creative Economy* (Bristol, UK: Policy Press, 2016).

76. Buckingham, "Is There a Digital Generation?," 9, emphasis in original.

77. Richard Barbrook and Andy Cameron, "Californian Ideology," in *Crypto Anarchy, Cyberstates, and Pirate Utopias*, ed. Peter Ludlow (Cambridge, Mass.: MIT Press, 2001), 369. See also Paulina Borsook, *Cyberselfish: A Critical Romp through the Terribly Libertarian Culture of High Tech* (New York: PublicAffairs, 2001); Richard Barbrook, *Imaginary Futures: From Thinking Machines to the Global Village* (Ann Arbor, Mich.: Pluto, 2007); Lincoln Dahlberg, "Cyber-Libertarianism 2.0: A Discourse Theory / Critical Political Economy Examination," *Cultural Politics* 6, no. 3 (2010): 331–56; Fred Turner, *From Counterculture to Cyberculture: Stewart Brand, the Whole Earth Network, and the Rise of Digital Utopianism* (Chicago: University of Chicago Press, 2006).

78. Schulte, *Cached*, 33.

79. Melissa Gregg, *Counterproductive: Time Management in the Knowledge Economy* (Durham, N.C.: Duke University Press, 2018), ii.

80. Schulte, *Cached*, 37.

81. Lilly Irani, "'Design Thinking': Defending Silicon Valley at the Apex of Global

Labor Hierarchies," *Catalyst: Feminism, Theory, Technoscience* 4, no. 1 (2018): http://catalystjournal.org/.

82. Jennifer S. Light, "When Computers Were Women," *Technology and Culture* 40, no. 3 (1999): 455–83; Thomas J. Misa, ed., *Gender Codes: Why Women Are Leaving Computing* (Hoboken, N.J.: Wiley, 2010); Janet Abbate, *Recoding Gender: Women's Changing Participation in Computing* (Cambridge, Mass.: MIT Press, 2012); Amy Sue Bix, *Girls Coming to Tech! A History of American Engineering Education for Women* (Cambridge, Mass.: MIT Press, 2014).

83. Nakamura, "Indigenous Circuits."

84. Minh-Ha T. Pham, *Asians Wear Clothes on the Internet: Race, Gender, and the Work of Personal Style Blogging* (Durham, N.C.: Duke University Press, 2015), 8.

85. Anita Say Chan, "Decolonial Computing and Networking Beyond Digital Universalism," *Catalyst: Feminism, Theory, Technoscience* 4, no. 2 (2018): http://catalystjournal.org/. See also Kavita Philip, Lilly Irani, and Paul Dourish, "Postcolonial Computing: A Tactical Survey," *Science, Technology, & Human Values* 37, no. 1 (2012): 3–29.

86. Irani, "'Design Thinking'"; Mary L. Gray and Siddharth Suri, *Ghost Work: How to Stop Silicon Valley from Building a New Global Underclass* (New York: Houghton Mifflin Harcourt, 2019); Pham, *Asians Wear Clothes on the Internet.*

87. David Morley and Kevin Robins, "Techno-Orientalism: Futures, Foreigners and Phobias," *New Formations* 16, no. 1 (1992): 136–56; Wendy Hui Kyong Chun, "Orienting the Future," in *Control and Freedom: Power and Paranoia in the Age of Fiber Optics* (Cambridge, Mass.: MIT Press, 2008), 171–246; David S. Roh, Betsy Huang, and Greta A. Niu, eds., *Techno-Orientalism: Imagining Asia in Speculative Fiction, History, and Media* (New Brunswick, N.J.: Rutgers University Press, 2015); Tara Fickle, *The Race Card: From Gaming Technologies to Model Minorities* (New York: NYU Press, 2019); Christopher B. Patterson, *Open World Empire: Race, Erotics, and the Global Rise of Video Games* (New York: NYU Press, 2020).

88. Chris Anderson, *Makers: The New Industrial Revolution* (New York: Crown Publishing, 2012), 31.

89. Steven M. Gelber, *Hobbies: Leisure and the Culture of Work in America* (New York: Columbia University Press, 1999), 281; Elaine Tyler May, "Security against Democracy: The Legacy of the Cold War at Home," *Journal of American History* 97, no. 4 (2011): 956. For contemporary Chinese nation-making and innovation, see Silvia M. Lindtner, *Prototype Nation: China and the Contested Promise of Innovation* (Princeton, N.J.: Princeton University Press, 2020).

90. Patterson, *Open World Empire,* 86.

91. Brouillette, *Literature and the Creative Economy.*

92. David Buckingham, *After the Death of Childhood: Growing Up in the Age of Electronic Media* (Cambridge, UK: Polity, 2000), 17.

93. Barbrook and Cameron, "Californian Ideology."

1. *Minecraft* and the Building Blocks of Creative Individuality

1. *Minecraft* was officially released in 2011.

2. Greg Lastowka, "Minecraft as Web 2.0: Amateur Creativity in Digital Games," in *Amateur Media: Social, Cultural and Legal Perspectives,* ed. Dan Hunter et al. (New York: Routledge, 2012), 159, emphasis in original.

3. Paul Owens, dir., *"Minecraft": The Story of Mojang* (2 Player Productions, 2012), DVD.

4. PBS Idea Channel, "Is Minecraft the Ultimate Educational Tool?," YouTube, uploaded 6 March 2013, http://youtube.com/.

5. Cathy Risberg, "More Than Just a Video Game: Tips for Using *Minecraft* to Personalize the Curriculum and Promote Creativity, Collaboration, and Problem Solving," *Illinois Association for Gifted Children Journal* 2 (2015): 44.

6. Risberg, 47.

7. Owen Hill, "Yes, We're Being Bought by Microsoft," Mojang, last modified 15 September 2014, accessed 2 August 2015, http://mojang.com/2014/09/yes-were-being-bought-by-microsoft.

8. For *Minecraft*, see also Nate Garrelts, *Understanding "Minecraft": Essays on Play, Community and Possibilities* (Jefferson, N.C.: McFarland, 2014); Hong-An Wu, "Video Game Prosumers: Case Study of a Minecraft Affinity Space," *Visual Arts Research* 42, no. 1 (2016): 22–37; Rob Gallagher, "Minecrafting Masculinities: Gamer Dads, Queer Childhoods and Father–Son Gameplay in a Boy Made of Blocks," *Game Studies: International Journal of Computer Games Research* 18, no. 2 (2018): http://gamestudies.org/; Bart Simon and Darren Wershler, "Childhood's End (or, We Have Never Been Modern, except in Minecraft)," *Cultural Politics* 14, no. 3 (2018): 289–303; and Daniel Dooghan, "Digital Conquerors: *Minecraft* and the Apologetics of Neoliberalism," *Games and Culture* 14, no. 1 (2019): 67–86.

9. Richard Florida, *The Rise of the Creative Class: And How It's Transforming Work, Leisure, Community, and Everyday Life* (New York: Basic Books, 2002); Barack Obama, "Remarks by the President in State of Union Address," The White House, last modified 25 January 2011, accessed 3 August 2020, http://obamawhitehouse.archives.gov/.

10. Pascal Gielen, *Creativity and Other Fundamentalisms*, trans. Leo Reijnen (Heijningen, Netherlands: Jap Sam Books, 2013); Amy F. Ogata, *Designing the Creative Child: Playthings and Places in Midcentury America* (Minneapolis: University of Minnesota Press, 2013); Sarah Brouillette, *Literature and the Creative Economy* (Stanford, Calif.: Stanford University Press, 2014); Angela McRobbie, *Be Creative: Making a Living in the New Culture Industries* (Cambridge, UK: Polity, 2016); George Morgan and Pariece Nelligan, *The Creativity Hoax: Precarious Work in the Gig Economy* (New York: Anthem Press, 2018); Oli Mould, *Against Creativity* (London: Verso Books, 2018); Tyler Denmead, *The Creative Underclass: Youth, Race, and the Gentrifying City* (Durham, N.C.: Duke University Press, 2019).

11. Ogata, *Designing the Creative Child.*

12. For discussions of youth, creativity, and digital culture, see Tara McPherson, ed., *Digital Youth, Innovation, and the Unexpected* (Cambridge, Mass.: MIT Press, 2008); David Buckingham and Rebekah Willett, eds., *Video Cultures: Media Technology and Everyday Creativity* (London: Palgrave Macmillan, 2009); Maaike Lauwaert, *The Place of Play: Toys and Digital Cultures* (Amsterdam: Amsterdam University Press, 2009); Mizuko Ito, *Engineering Play: A Cultural History of Children's Software* (Cambridge, Mass.: MIT Press, 2009); David Buckingham and Rebekah Willett, *Digital Generations: Children, Young People, and the New Media* (Mahwah, N.J: Lawrence Erlbaum Associates, 2013); and Patricia G. Lange, *Kids on YouTube: Technical Identities and Digital Literacies* (Walnut Creek, Calif.: Left Coast Press, 2014).

13. Scott Smith, "Could Minecraft Be the Next Great Engineering School?," *Quartz*, 30 November 2012, http://qz.com/; PBS Idea Channel, "Is Minecraft the Ultimate Educational Tool?"; Anthony Perez and Kim Jed, "Minecraft Blowing Up the Classroom; Educators Say the Game Can Teach Everything from Math to Genetics," *Southern California Public Radio*, 14 August 2013, http://scpr.org/; Shari Caton, "How Schools Are Using Gaming to Teach," *TechEdge*, May 2014, 12–13; James Drzewiecki, "Why Edu-

cators Should Use Minecraft in the Classroom," EducationWorld, last updated 2014, accessed 4 August 2020, http://educationworld.com/; Colin Gallagher, *"Minecraft" in the Classroom: Ideas, Inspiration, and Student Projects for Teachers* (San Francisco: Pearson Education, 2014); Alexandra Ossola, "Teaching in the Age of Minecraft," *The Atlantic*, 6 February 2015, http://theatlantic.com/.

14. Lauwaert, *Place of Play*, 40. See also Marsha Kinder, *Playing with Power in Movies, Television, and Video Games: From Muppet Babies to Teenage Mutant Ninja Turtles* (Berkeley: University of California Press, 1993); Ellen Seiter, *Sold Separately: Children and Parents in Consumer Culture* (New Brunswick, N.J.: Rutgers University Press, 1993); Dan Fleming, *Powerplay: Toys as Popular Culture* (Manchester, UK: Manchester University Press, 1996); Gary Cross, *Kids' Stuff: Toys and the Changing World of American Childhood* (Cambridge, Mass.: Harvard University Press, 2009); Ogata, *Designing the Creative Child;* Mark J. P. Wolf, ed., *Lego Studies: Examining the Building Blocks of a Transmedial Phenomenon* (New York: Routledge, 2014); and Meredith A. Bak, "Building Blocks of the Imagination: Children, Creativity, and the Limits of *Disney Infinity*," *Velvet Light Trap* no. 78 (2016): 53–64.

15. Mary Flanagan and Helen Nissenbaum, *Values at Play in Digital Games* (Cambridge, Mass.: MIT Press, 2014), 5.

16. Flanagan and Nissenbaum, 11.

17. John Locke, *Some Thoughts Concerning Education* (Menston, UK: Scolar Press, 1970), 177, emphasis in original.

18. Virginia Zimmerman, "Natural History on Blocks, in Bodies, and on the Hearth: Juvenile Science Literature and Games, 1850–1875," *Configurations* 19, no. 3 (2011): 407–30.

19. Jane McGonigal, *Reality Is Broken: Why Games Make Us Better and How They Can Change the World* (New York: Penguin Books, 2011); Patrick Jagoda, "Gamification and Other Forms of Play," *boundary 2* 40, no. 2 (2013): 113–44; Patrick Jagoda, "Gaming the Humanities," *differences* 25, no. 1 (2014): 189–215.

20. As in the contemporary interest in STEM education, economic and occupational classism is evident in the middle-class expectation that childhood exposure to construction toys should culminate in high-prestige and authoritative "white-collar" workers such as architects or engineers rather than becoming "blue-collar" construction workers or assemblers, which are regarded as lower- or working-class labor. For hierarchies of authority and prestige among engineers, technicians, and assemblers, see Beth A. Bechky, "Object Lessons: Workplace Artifacts as Representations of Occupational Jurisdiction," *American Journal of Sociology* 109, no. 3 (2003): 720–52.

21. Colin Fanning and Rebecca Mir, "Teaching Tools: Progresive Pedagogy and the History of Construction Play," in *Understanding "Minecraft": Essays on Play, Community and Possibilities*, ed. Nate Garrelts (Jefferson, N.C.: McFarland, 2014), 38.

22. TeamMojang, "Official Minecraft Trailer," YouTube, uploaded 6 December 2011, http://youtube.com/.

23. Gary Cross, *The Cute and the Cool: Wondrous Innocence and Modern American Children's Culture* (New York: Oxford University Press, 2004), 167.

24. Cross, *Kids' Stuff*, 8.

25. Cross, 60–66; Seiter, *Sold Separately*, 71; Ogata, *Designing the Creative Child*, 42–43.

26. Deborah Gage, "National Science Foundation Wants More Women Scientists and Engineers," *ZDNet*, 11 August 2010, http://zdnet.com/; Heather R. Huhman, "STEM Fields and the Gender Gap: Where Are the Women?," *Forbes*, 20 June 2012, http://forbes.com/; Katherine Beard, "Million Women Mentors Launched to Fill the

Gap of Women in STEM Fields," *U.S. News & World Report,* 4 January 2014, http://usnews.com/. For women and STEM, see Amy Sue Bix, *Girls Coming to Tech! A History of American Engineering Education for Women* (Cambridge, Mass.: MIT Press, 2014). For the exclusion of women from the history of gaming and computing, see Justine Cassell and Henry Jenkins, "Chess for Girls? Feminism and Computer Games," in *From Barbie to Mortal Kombat: Gender and Computer Games,* ed. Justine Cassell and Henry Jenkins (Cambridge, Mass.: MIT Press, 1998), 2–45; Jennifer S. Light, "When Computers Were Women," *Technology and Culture* 40, no. 3 (1999): 455–483; Lisa Nakamura, "Indigenous Circuits: Navajo Women and the Racialization of Early Electronic Manufacture," *American Quarterly* 66, no. 4 (2014): 919–941; and Carly A. Kocurek, *Coin-Operated Americans: Rebooting Boyhood at the Video Game Arcade* (Minneapolis: University of Minnesota Press, 2015).

27. Debbie Sterling, "Goldieblox: The Engineering Toy for Girls," Kickstarter, last modified 1 July 2013, accessed 4 August 2020, http://kickstarter.com/. For construction toys and gender, see Derek Johnson, "Chicks with Bricks: Building Creativity across Industrial Design Cultures and Gendered Construction Play," in *Lego Studies: Examining the Building Blocks of a Transmedial Phenomenon,* ed. Mark J. P. Wolf (New York: Routledge, 2014), 81–104.

28. "About Goldieblox: Meet Debbie Sterling—Goldieblox Founder," GoldieBlox, accessed 4 August 2020, http://goldieblox.com/; "Goldieblox Frequently Asked Questions," GoldieBlox, accessed 2 August 2015, http://goldieblox.com/pages/faq.

29. Katy Waldman, "Goldieblox: Great for Girls? Terrible for Girls? Or Just Selling Toys?," *Slate,* 26 November 2013, http://slate.com/; Lucia Graves, "The Revolution Will Not Be Goldieblox," *National Journal,* 28 November 2013, http://nationaljournal.com/; Andy Hinds, "Girl-Power Toy or Sexist Game?," *The Daily Beast,* 24 December 2014, http://thedailybeast.com/; Sandra Shpilberg, "What Goldieblox Is Telling My Girl, Which I Won't Let Her Hear," *Huffington Post,* 6 December 2017, http://huffingtonpost.com/; Kelly Faircloth, "Goldieblox Means Well but Doesn't Live up to the Hype," *Jezebel,* 11 February 2014, http://jezebel.com/.

30. Owens, *"Minecraft."*

31. David Chapman, "Minecraft Game Review," Common Sense Media, accessed 4 August 2020, http://commonsensemedia.org/.

32. Sean C. Duncan, *"Minecraft,* beyond Construction and Survival," *Well Played: A Journal on Video Games, Value and Meaning* 1, no. 1 (2011): 1–22; Lastowka, "Minecraft as Web 2.0."; PBS Idea Channel, "Is Minecraft the Ultimate Educational Tool?"; Kevin Schut, "The Virtualization of Lego," in *Lego Studies: Examining the Building Blocks of a Transmedial Phenomenon,* ed. Mark J. P. Wolf (New York: Routledge, 2014), 227–40; Rebekah J. Willett, "The Discursive Construction of 'Good Parenting' and Digital Media: The Case of Children's Virtual World Games," *Media, Culture & Society* 37, no. 7 (2015): 1060–15. For LEGO, see John Hughes's Brick Fetish website, last modified 2010, accessed 4 August 2020, http://brickfetish.com/; and Wolf, *Lego Studies.*

33. "Lego.com Minecraft Home," LEGO, accessed 4 August 2020, http://lego.com/.

34. Johnson, "Chicks with Bricks," 89.

35. Farah Miller and Emma Gray, "Lego Friends Petition: Parents, Women and Girls Ask Toy Companies to Stop Gender-Based Marketing," *Huffington Post,* 6 December 2017, http://huffpost.com/; Lori Day, "The Little Girl from the 1981 Lego Ad Is All Grown Up, and She's Got Something to Say," *Women You Should Know,* 11 February 2014, http://womenyoushouldknow.net/; Susana Polo, "What Does the Girl in the Most Internet Famous Vintage Lego Ad Think about Them Now?," *The Mary Sue,* 11 February 2014, http://themarysue.com/.

36. Owens, *"Minecraft."*

37. Fanning and Mir, "Teaching Tools," 52.

38. Alfred Gell, *Art and Agency: An Anthropological Theory* (Oxford: Oxford University Press, 1998), 30.

39. Fanning and Mir, "Teaching Tools," 52. See also Aaron L. Alcorn, "Flying into Modernity: Model Airplanes, Consumer Culture, and the Making of Modern Boyhood in the Early Twentieth Century," *History and Technology* 25, no. 2 (2009): 115–46; and Bob Rehak, "Materializing Monsters: Aurora Models, Garage Kits and the Object Practices of Horror Fandom," *Journal of Fandom Studies* 1, no. 1 (2012): 27–45.

40. Brouillette, *Literature and the Creative Economy*, 69. See also Melissa Gregg, *Counterproductive: Time Management in the Knowledge Economy* (Durham, N.C.: Duke University Press, 2018).

41. Abraham H. Maslow, *The Farther Reaches of Human Nature* (New York: Viking Press, 1971), 43.

42. Maslow, 64.

43. Abraham H. Maslow, *Toward a Psychology of Being*, 2nd ed. (New York: Van Nostrand Reinhold, 1982), 126; Abraham H. Maslow, *Motivation and Personality*, 2nd ed. (New York: Harper & Row, 1970), 217.

44. Maslow, *Toward a Psychology of Being*, 138.

45. Maslow, 107.

46. Maslow, *Motivation and Personality*, 170; Maslow, *Farther Reaches of Human Nature*, 79.

47. Recognizing this dynamic in expressions of creativity, psychological research by Mihaly Csikszentmihalyi advocated a systems model that examines creativity not as distinctly individual but emerging out of the interplay between individuals and their social contexts. See Mihaly Csikszentmihalyi, *Creativity: Flow and the Psychology of Discovery and Invention* (New York: HarperCollins, 1997).

48. Brouillette, *Literature and the Creative Economy*, 56.

49. Maslow, *Farther Reaches of Human Nature*, 43.

50. Abraham H. Maslow, *Eupsychian Management: A Journal* (Homewood, Ill.: Richard D. Irwin, 1965), 188.

51. Maslow, *Motivation and Personality*, 35–45.

52. Maslow, 100.

53. Brouillette, *Literature and the Creative Economy*, 57.

54. Maslow, *Eupsychian Management*, xi.

55. Abraham H. Maslow, "Eupsychia—the Good Society," *Journal of Humanistic Psychology* 1, no. 2 (1961): 4. In their study of Western utopian thought, Frank E. Manuel and Fritzie P. Manuel use Maslow's term "Eupsychia" to characterize imagined utopias committed to psychological well-being. See Frank E. Manuel and Fritzie P. Manuel, *Utopian Thought in the Western World* (Cambridge, Mass.: Harvard University Press, 1979), 4.

56. Maslow, "Eupsychia," 2.

57. Maslow.

58. My characterization of *Minecraft* as an island game relies on figurative conceptions of the island as a previously unmapped but bounded geography. While the procedurally generated worlds in *Minecraft* may be surrounded by water, players can specify different criteria for the makeup of virtual worlds in the game that may eliminate water entirely.

59. Ogata, *Designing the Creative Child*, 188.

60. For island narratives and inventive subjects, see Manuel and Manuel, *Utopian*

Thought in the Western World; J. C. Davis, *Utopia and the Ideal Society: A Study of English Utopian Writing, 1516–1700* (Cambridge: Cambridge University Press, 1981); Louis Marin, *Utopics: Spatial Play*, trans. Robert A. Vollrath (Atlantic Highlands, N.J.: Humanities Press, 1984); Martin Green, *The Robinson Crusoe Story* (University Park: Penn State University Press, 1990); and Richard H. Grove, *Green Imperialism: Colonial Expansion, Tropical Island Edens and the Origins of Environmental, 1600–1860* (Cambridge: Cambridge University Press, 1995).

61. Grove, *Green Imperialism*, 255. While originating in island settings, such narratives are not limited to literal islands and instead can take shape in other bounded spaces that serve a similar diegetic function, such as planets, cave interiors, and future temporalities. For example, Francis Godwin's fictional travel narrative *The Man in the Moone* (1638) transformed the island into the moon, while Edward Bellamy's utopian novel *Looking Backward, 2000–1887* (1888) rendered the island's spatial insularity into a temporal one by sending the protagonist from his time in 1887 into the future of 2000.

62. Although additional modes, such as Adventure Mode and Spectator Mode, are also available, players and critics often identify Survival Mode and Creative Mode as the main playing modes in *Minecraft*.

63. Keith Stuart, "*Journey* Claims Gamecity Prize 2012," *The Guardian*, 24 October 2012, http://theguardian.com/.

64. While most discussions of *Minecraft* gameplay focus on construction and survival, Amanda Phillips articulates a desire to explore the game's procedurally generated virtual environments. See Amanda Phillips, "(Queer) Algorithmic Ecology: The Great Opening Up of Nature to All Mobs," in *Understanding "Minecraft": Essays on Play, Community and Possibilities*, ed. Nate Garrelts (Jefferson, N.C.: McFarland, 2014), 106–20.

65. For narrative scripts, see Jon Turney, *Frankenstein's Footsteps: Science, Genetics and Popular Culture* (New Haven, Conn.: Yale University Press, 2000).

66. Colin Milburn, *Mondo Nano: Fun and Games in the World of Digital Matter* (Durham, N.C.: Duke University Press, 2015), 77.

67. Milburn, 103.

68. Gail Bederman, *Manliness and Civilization: A Cultural History of Gender and Race in the United States, 1880–1917* (Chicago: University of Chicago Press, 1995), 23.

69. Bederman, 27; Jodi A. Byrd, *The Transit of Empire: Indigenous Critiques of Colonialism* (Minneapolis: University of Minnesota Press, 2011), xx.

70. Mary Fuller and Henry Jenkins, "Nintendo and New World Travel Writing: A Dialogue," in *Cybersociety: Computer-Mediated Communication and Community*, ed. Steven G. Jones (Thousand Oaks, Calif.: SAGE Publications, 1995), 57–72; Alexander R. Galloway, "Allegories of Control," in *Gaming: Essays on Algorithmic Culture* (Minneapolis: University of Minnesota Press, 2006), 85–106; Jodi A. Byrd, "'Do They Not Have Rational Souls?': Consolidation and Sovereignty in Digital New Worlds," *Settler Colonial Studies* 6, no. 4 (2016): 423–37; Ligia (Licho) López López, Lars de Wildt, and Nikki Moodie, "'I Don't Think You're Going to Have Any Aborigines in Your World': Minecrafting *Terra Nullius*," *British Journal of Sociology of Education* 40, no. 8 (2019): 1037–54.

71. Green, *Robinson Crusoe Story*.

72. Davis, *Utopia and the Ideal Society*, 9.

73. Francis Bacon, *New Atlantis*, in *Three Early Modern Utopias: Thomas More: Utopia / Francis Bacon: New Atlantis / Henry Neville: The Isle of Pines*, ed. Susan Bruck (New York: Oxford University Press, 2008), 182–83. The Royal Society of London for

Improving Natural Knowledge, founded in 1660, modeled itself after Bacon's scientifically minded social utopia. See John Bender, *Ends of Enlightenment* (Stanford, Calif.: Stanford University Press, 2012), 26. Island narratives lampooning the Royal Society's exclusive insularity include Margaret Cavendish's *A Blazing World* (1666) and Jonathan Swift's *Gulliver's Travels* (1726).

74. Maslow, *Farther Reaches of Human Nature*, 60.

75. For games and utopian thought, see Bernard Suits, *The Grasshopper: Games, Life and Utopia* (Toronto: University of Toronto Press, 1978); and Elizabeth Nyman and Ryan Lee Teten, "Lost and Found and Lost Again: Island Utopias and Dystopias in the *Bioshock* Series," *Games and Culture* 13, no. 4 (2018): 370–84.

76. Stephanie Boluk and Patrick LeMieux, "Dwarven Epitaphs: Procedural Histories in *Dwarf Fortress*," in *Comparative Textual Media: Transforming the Humanities in the Postprint Era*, ed. N. Katherine Hayles and Jessica Pressman (Minneapolis: University of Minnesota Press, 2013), 138.

77. Daniel Defoe, *Robinson Crusoe* (New York: Oxford University Press, 2008), 50.

78. Defoe, 131.

79. Ian Watt, *The Rise of the Novel: Studies in Defoe, Richardson and Fielding*, 2nd ed. (Berkeley: University of California Press, 2001), 63. See also Ian Watt, *Myths of Modern Individualism: Faust, Don Quixote, Don Juan, Robinson Crusoe* (New York: Cambridge University Press, 1996); and Ulla Grapard and Gillian Hewitson, eds., *Robinson Crusoe's Economic Man: A Construction and Deconstruction* (New York: Routledge, 2012).

80. Manuel and Manuel, *Utopian Thought in the Western World*, 433.

81. Michael McKeon, *The Origins of the English Novel, 1600–1740* (Baltimore: Johns Hopkins University Press, 1987), 334.

82. Gayatri Chakravorty Spivak, "Theory in the Margin: Coetzee's *Foe* Reading Defoe's *Crusoe/Roxana*," *English in Africa* 17, no. 2 (1990): 1–23; Sheila Roberts, "'Post-Colonialism, or the House of Friday'—J. M. Coetzee's *Foe*," *Journal of Postcolonial Writing* 31, no. 1 (1991): 87–92; Ulla Grapard, "Robinson Crusoe: The Quintessential Economic Man?," *Feminist Economics* 1, no. 1 (1995): 33–52; Brett C. McInelly, "Expanding Empires, Expanding Selves: Colonialism, the Novel, and *Robinson Crusoe*," *Studies in the Novel* 35, no. 1 (2003): 1–21; Katrine Marçal, *Who Cooked Adam Smith's Dinner? A Story of Women and Economics*, trans. Saskia Vogel (New York: Pegasus Books, 2016). Many of these critiques position Defoe's text alongside J. M. Coetzee's novel *Foe* (1986), a retelling of *Robinson Crusoe* through Coetzee's fabricated perspective of Susan Barton, a female castaway.

83. Jean-Jacques Rousseau, *Emile: Or, on Education*, trans. Allan Bloom (New York: Basic Books, 1979); Maria Edgeworth and Richard Lovell Edgeworth, *Practical Education* (New York: Garland Publishing, 1974).

84. Rousseau, *Emile*, 184–85.

85. Manuel and Manuel, *Utopian Thought in the Western World*, 446.

86. Green, *Robinson Crusoe Story*.

87. David Spitz, "Power and Authority: An Interpretation of Golding's 'Lord of the Flies,'" *Antioch Review* 30, no. 1 (1970): 21–33; John F. Fitzgerald and John R. Kayser, "Golding's 'Lord of the Flies': Pride as Original Sin," *Studies in the Novel* 24, no. 1 (1992): 78–88; Minnie Singh, "The Government of Boys: Golding's *Lord of the Flies* and Ballantyne's *Coral Island*," *Children's Literature* 25, no. 1 (1997): 205–13.

88. Following *Minecraft*'s popularity, several digital games have used similar tensions between construction and survival to organize gameplay, including *Terraria* (Re-Logic, 2011), *Don't Starve* (Klei Entertainment, 2013), and *Rust* (Facepunch Studios, 2014).

89. Owens, "*Minecraft.*"

90. Christopher Goetz, "Tether and Accretions: Fantasy as Form in Videogames," *Games and Culture* 7, no. 6 (2012): 419–40.

91. Duncan, "*Minecraft,* beyond Construction and Survival," 9.

92. Joseph Hall, "Minecraft Game Being Hailed as Teaching Tool," *The Star,* 31 May 2013, http://thestar.com/.

93. Martin Heidegger, "The Question Concerning Technology," in *The Question Concerning Technology, and Other Essays,* ed. and trans. William Lovitt (New York: Harper Perennial, 1982), 17.

94. Peter Christiansen, "Players, Modders and Hackers," in *Understanding "Minecraft": Essays on Play, Community and Possibilities,* ed. Nate Garrelts (Jefferson, N.C.: McFarland, 2014), 31. For modding, see Julian Kücklich, "Precarious Playbour: Modders and the Digital Games Industry," *Fibreculture Journal* 5, no. 1 (2005): http://fibreculturejournal.org/; Hector Postigo, "Of Mods and Modders: Chasing Down the Value of Fan-Based Digital Game Modifications," *Games and Culture* 2, no. 4 (2007): 300–313; Olli Sotamaa, "On Modder Labour, Commodification of Play, and Mod Competitions," *First Monday* 12, no. 9 (2007): http://firstmonday.org/; Walt Scacchi, "Computer Game Mods, Modders, Modding, and the Mod Scene," *First Monday* 15, no. 5 (2010): http://firstmonday.org/; Tanja Sihvonen, *Players Unleashed! Modding "The Sims" and the Culture of Gaming* (Amsterdam: Amsterdam University Press, 2011); Evan W. Lauteria, "Ga(y)mer Theory: Queer Modding as Resistance," *Reconstruction: Studies in Contemporary Culture* 12, no. 2 (2012): http://reconstruction.digitalodu .com/; and Hanna Wirman, "Playing by Doing and Players' Localization of *The Sims 2,*" *Television & New Media* 15, no. 1 (2014): 58–67.

95. Paula K. Hooper, "Looking BK and Moving FD: Toward a Sociocultural Lens on Learning with Programmable Media," in *Digital Youth, Innovation, and the Unexpected,* ed. Tara McPherson (Cambridge, Mass.: MIT Press, 2008), 123.

96. Wallace Feurzeig et al., "Programming-Languages as a Conceptual Framework for Teaching Mathematics: Final Report on the First Fifteen Months of the Logo Project" (Bolt Beranek and Newman Inc., 1969).

97. Ito, *Engineering Play,* 150.

98. Smith, "Could Minecraft Be the Next Great Engineering School?"; Tom Cheshire, "Want to Learn Computer-Aided Design (CAD)? Play Minecraft," *Wired UK,* last modified 22 November 2012, http://www.wired.co.uk/; Pablo Abend and Benjamin Beil, "Editors of Play: The Scripts and Practices of Co-Creativity in *Minecraft* and *LittleBigPlanet,*" in *DiGRA '15—Proceedings of the 2015 DiGRA Conference: Diversity of Play: Games–Cultures–Identities* (Lüneburg, Germany: Digital Games Research Association, 2015), 53–56.

99. Kurt Squire, "From Content to Context: Videogames as Designed Experience," *Educational Researcher* 35, no. 8 (2006): 9.

100. "Minecraft: Learning Works for Kids," LearningWorks for Kids, accessed 4 August 2020, http://learningworksforkids.com/.

101. Defoe, *Robinson Crusoe,* 122.

102. Christiansen, "Players, Modders and Hackers," 33.

103. Christiansen, 35.

104. Christiansen, 33.

105. Defoe, *Robinson Crusoe,* 136.

106. Lastowka, "Minecraft as Web 2.0."

107. Owens, "*Minecraft.*"

108. "Official Minecraft Wiki: The Ultimate Resource for All Things Minecraft," Gamepedia, accessed 4 August 2020, http://minecraft.gamepedia.com/.

109. Esther MacCallum-Stewart, "'Someone Off the YouTubez': The Yogscast as Fan Producers," in *Understanding "Minecraft": Essays on Play, Community and Possibilities*, ed. Nate Garrelts (Jefferson, N.C.: McFarland, 2014), 148.

110. Christiansen, "Players, Modders and Hackers," 29.

111. Smith, "Could Minecraft Be the Next Great Engineering School?"

112. "Notch: Wolves Are a BAD Idea," Minecraft Forum, original post 31 March 2011, accessed 4 August 2020, http://minecraftforum.net/.

113. "Minecraft Forge Forums," Minecraft Forge, original post 31 March 2011, accessed 4 August 2020, http://minecraftforge.net/.

114. "Considering Dropping Forge," Better Than Wolves Forum, original post 23 November 2011, accessed 4 August 2020, http://sargunster.com/btwforum.

115. "Better Than Wolves Total Conversion!," Minecraft Forum, original post 10 April 2011, last modified 14 June 2019, accessed 4 August 2020, http://www.minecraftforum.net/.

116. "Better with Forge?," Feed the Beast, original post 18 December 2012, accessed 4 August 2020, http://feedthebeast.com/; "Better with Forge," Minecraft Forum, accessed 4 August 2020, http://minecraftforum.net/; "TFC/BTW Collab?," TerraFirmaCraft, original post 24 June 2014, accessed 4 August 2020, http://terrafirmacraft.com/; "RE: Notch—Maybe Wolves AREN'T Such a Bad Idea after All" YouChew, accessed 15 August 2015, http://youchew.net/; cube1234567890, "Whatever Happened to Better Than Wolves?," Reddit, original post 15 Feburary 2015, http://reddit.com/.

117. "Better with Forge?," Randomsteve, 17 December 2012, 6:29 p.m.

118. "Better with Forge," AlukaMak, 14 December 2012, 9:11 a.m.

119. Gilles Deleuze and Félix Guattari, "1914: One or Several Wolves?," in *A Thousand Plateaus: Capitalism and Schizophrenia*, trans. Brian Massumi (Minneapolis: University of Minnesota Press, 1987), 29.

120. cube1234567890, "Whatever Happened to Better Than Wolves?," DZCreeper, 16 February 2015, 4:34 a.m.

121. "Better Than Wolves Total Conversion!," FlowerChild, 9 April 2011, 10:40 p.m.

122. "Better with Forge," ShaRose, 14 December 2012, 9:28 a.m.

123. For online trolling, see Whitney Phillips, *This Is Why We Can't Have Nice Things: Mapping the Relationship between Online Trolling and Mainstream Culture* (Cambridge, Mass.: MIT Press, 2015); Pnina Fichman and Madelyn R. Sanfilippo, *Online Trolling and Its Perpetrators: Under the Cyberbridge* (Lanham, Md.: Rowman & Littlefield, 2016); and Anastasia Salter and Bridget Blodgett, *Toxic Geek Masculinity in Media: Sexism, Trolling, and Identity Policing* (New York: Palgrave Macmillan, 2017).

124. Watt, *Rise of the Novel*, 60.

125. Watt, 60.

126. Marçal, *Who Cooked Adam Smith's Dinner?*, 21.

127. Defoe, *Robinson Crusoe*, 112.

128. Watt, *Rise of the Novel*, 60; Fredric Jameson, *Archaeologies of the Future: The Desire Called Utopia and Other Science Fictions* (New York: Verso, 2005), 403.

129. Defoe, *Robinson Crusoe*, 235.

130. Defoe, 252–54.

131. Owens, *"Minecraft."*

132. Nate Garrelts, "Introduction: Why *Minecraft* Matters," in *Understanding "Minecraft": Essays on Play, Community and Possibilities*, ed. Nate Garrelts (Jefferson, N.C.: McFarland, 2014), 1.

133. Ossola, "Teaching in the Age of Minecraft."

134. Microsoft acquired MinecraftEdu in January 2016 and subsequently released *Minecraft: Education Edition* as its replacement title. See Christina Beck, "With Minecraftedu, Are Video Games the Future of Education?," *Christian Science Monitor*, 20 January 2016, http://csmonitor.com/.

135. Ossola, "Teaching in the Age of Minecraft."

2. *Make* Magazine and the Responsible Risks of DIY Innovation

1. The magazine title was initially stylized as *Make* or *MAKE* before becoming *Make:* starting with volume 40 (2016). I use *Make* for consistency.

2. Dale Dougherty, "Slow Made: Take It Easy," *Make* 13 (February 2008): 10. Maker Media Inc. began operating *Make* in 2013, which continued until filing for bankruptcy in 2019 and then relaunching as Make Community LLC.

3. William Gurstelle, "The Jam Jar Jet," *Make* 5 (February 2006): 102.

4. Gurstelle, 103.

5. Gurstelle, 103.

6. Gurstelle, 103.

7. For making in the United States, see Nicole Dawkins, "Do-It-Yourself: The Precarious Work and Postfeminist Politics of Handmaking (in) Detroit," *Utopian Studies* 22, no. 2 (2011): 261–84; Austin Toombs, Shaowen Bardzell, and Jeffrey Bardzell, "Becoming Makers: Hackerspace Member Habits, Values, and Identities," *Journal of Peer Production*, no. 5 (2014): http://peerproduction.net/; Sarah R. Davies, "Characterizing Hacking: Mundane Engagement in US Hacker and Makerspaces," *Science, Technology, & Human Values* 43, no. 2 (2017): 171–97; and Fred Turner, "Millenarian Tinkering: The Puritan Roots of the Maker Movement," *Technology and Culture* 59, no. 5 (2018): S160–82.

8. Dale Dougherty, "The Visible Hand," *Make* 16 (November 2008): 13. See also Mister Jalopy, "The Maker's Bill of Rights," *Make* 4 (November 2005): 157; Bruce Sterling, "The Interventionists: The 'Creative Class'—Tech Geeks and Fine Artists Are Jostling onto the Same Page," *Make* 7 (August 2006): 26–27; Gareth Branwyn, "Join the Robot Uprising!," *Make* 34 (April 2013): 8; and Ayah Bdeir, "littleBits Goes Big," *Make* 65 (November 2018): 12–17.

9. For making outside the United States, see Andrew Jackson, "Constructing at Home: Understanding the Experience of the Amateur Maker," *Design and Culture* 2, no. 1 (2010): 5–26; Denisa Kera, "Hackerspaces and DIYbio in Asia: Connecting Science and Community with Open Data, Kits and Protocols," *Journal of Peer Production*, no. 2 (2012): http://peerproduction.net/; Anna Seravalli, "Infrastructuring for Opening Production, from Participatory Design to Participatory Making?," in *Proceedings of the 12th Participatory Design Conference: Exploratory Papers, Workshop Descriptions, Industry Cases—Volume 2* (Roskilde, Denmark: Association for Computing Machinery, 2012), 53–56; Claudia Costa Pederson, "Situating Making in Contemporary Latin American Feminist Art," *Journal of Peer Production*, no. 8 (2016): http://peerproduction.net/; and Silvia M. Lindtner, *Prototype Nation: China and the Contested Promise of Innovation* (Princeton, N.J.: Princeton University Press, 2020).

10. "About Us—Maker Media: Leading the Maker Movement," Maker Media, accessed 1 October 2015, http://makermedia.com/. In addition to *Make*, Maker Media / Make Community LLC also produced consumer kits, has had a television series called

Make: television (PBS, 2009), and organized Maker Faires (i.e., public events showcasing makers).

11. Benedict Anderson, *Imagined Communities: Reflections on the Origin and Spread of Nationalism*, revised ed. (New York: Verso, 2006), 6.

12. For magazines and imagined communities, see Kenon Breazeale, "In Spite of Women: *Esquire* Magazine and the Construction of the Male Consumer," *Signs* 20, no. 1 (1994): 1–22; Carolyn Kitch, "Generational Identity and Memory in American Newsmagazines," *Journalism* 4, no. 2 (2003): 185–202; and Sheila M. Webb, "The Narrative of Core Traditional Values in Reiman Magazines," *Journalism & Mass Communication Quarterly* 83, no. 4 (2006): 865–82.

13. Sara Tocchetti, "DIYbiologists as 'Makers' of Personal Biologies: How MAKE Magazine and Maker Faires Contribute in Constituting Biology as a Personal Technology," *Journal of Peer Production*, no. 2 (2012): http://peerproduction.net/.

14. For *Mondo 2000*, see Vivian Sobchack, "New-Age Mutant Ninja Hackers: Reading *Mondo 2000*," *South Atlantic Quarterly* 92, no. 4 (1993): 569–84. For *Wired*, see Divina Frau-Meigs, "A Cultural Project Based on Multiple Temporary Consensus Identity and Community in *Wired*," *New Media & Society* 2, no. 2 (2000): 227–44; Fred Turner, *From Counterculture to Cyberculture: Stewart Brand, the Whole Earth Network, and the Rise of Digital Utopianism* (Chicago: University of Chicago Press, 2006); and Sarah E. Dempsey, "The Increasing Technology Divide: Persistent Portrayals of Maverick Masculinity in US Marketing," *Feminist Media Studies* 9, no. 1 (2009): 37–55. For diversity and Silicon Valley culture, see Christina Dunbar-Hester, *Hacking Diversity: The Politics of Inclusion in Open Technology Cultures* (Princeton, N.J.: Princeton University Press, 2019).

15. Richard Barbrook and Andy Cameron, "Californian Ideology," in *Crypto Anarchy, Cyberstates, and Pirate Utopias*, ed. Peter Ludlow (Cambridge, Mass.: MIT Press, 2001), 369. See also Paulina Borsook, *Cyberselfish: A Critical Romp through the Terribly Libertarian Culture of High-Tech* (New York: PublicAffairs, 2001); and Turner, *From Counterculture to Cyberculture*.

16. Borsook, *Cyberselfish*, 4.

17. Borsook; Turner, *From Counterculture to Cyberculture;* Richard Barbrook, *Imaginary Futures: From Thinking Machines to the Global Village* (Ann Arbor, Mich.: Pluto, 2007); Lincoln Dahlberg, "Cyber-Libertarianism 2.0: A Discourse Theory / Critical Political Economy Examination," *Cultural Politics* 6, no. 3 (2010): 331–56; Tocchetti, "DIYbiologists as 'Makers' of Personal Biologies."

18. *Maker Market Study and Media Report: An In-Depth Profile of Makers at the Forefront of Hardware Innovation* (Sebastopol, Calif.: O'Reilly, 2012), 24.

19. Douglas Thomas, *Hacker Culture* (Minneapolis: University of Minnesota Press, 2003); Tim Jordan and Paul A. Taylor, *Hacktivism and Cyberwars: Rebels with a Cause?* (New York: Routledge, 2004); O. Von Busch and K. Palmås, *Abstract Hacktivism: The Making of a Hacker Culture* (La Vergne, Tenn.: Lightning Source Inc., 2006); Tim Jordan, *Hacking: Digital Media and Technological Determinism* (Malden, Mass.: Polity, 2008); Faythe Levine and Cortney Heimerl, *Handmade Nation: The Rise of DIY, Art, Craft, and Design* (Princeton, N.J.: Princeton Architectural Press, 2008); Gabriella Coleman, *Coding Freedom: The Ethics and Aesthetics of Hacking* (Princeton, N.J.: Princeton University Press, 2012); Paul A. Taylor, *Hackers: Crime and the Digital Sublime* (New York: Routledge, 2012).

20. For hacking and youth, see Stephanie Ricker Schulte, "The '*WarGames* Scenario': Regulating Teenagers and Teenaged Technology," in *Cached: Decoding the Internet in Global Popular Culture* (New York: NYU Press, 2013), 21–54; and Meryl Alper,

"'Can Our Kids Hack It with Computers?': Constructing Youth Hackers in Family Computing Magazines (1983–1987)," *International Journal of Communication* 8 (2014): http://ijoc.org/.

21. *Makerspace Playbook: School Edition* (Berkeley, Calif.: Maker Ed, 2013), 5. The *Makerspace Playbook* is published by Maker Ed, a nonprofit organization created by Dougherty to support making in youth.

22. Joseph M. Reagle Jr., *Hacking Life: Systematized Living and Its Discontents* (Cambridge, Mass.: MIT Press, 2019).

23. Matt Ratto and Megan Boler, "Introduction," in *DIY Citizenship: Critical Making and Social Media,* ed. Matt Ratto and Megan Boler (Cambridge, Mass.: MIT Press, 2014), 9–11.

24. T. J. Jackson Lears, *No Place of Grace: Antimodernism and the Transformation of American Culture, 1880–1920* (Chicago: University of Chicago Press, 1994), 70–71; Eileen Boris, *Art and Labor: Ruskin, Morris, and the Craftsman Ideal in America* (Philadelphia: Temple University Press, 1986).

25. Steven M. Gelber, "Do-It-Yourself: Constructing, Repairing and Maintaining Domestic Masculinity," *American Quarterly* 49, no. 1 (1997): 68–69; Cathy Smith, "Handymen, Hippies and Healing: Social Transformation through the DIY Movement (1940s to 1970s) in North America," *Architectural Histories* 2, no. 1 (2014): http://journal.eahn.org/. See also Elaine Tyler May, "Security against Democracy: The Legacy of the Cold War at Home," *Journal of American History* 97, no. 4 (2011): 939–57. Intervening in this dominant tradition of DIY as a masculinized activity, women have also practiced home and technological repair. See Amy Bix, "Creating 'Chicks Who Fix': Women, Tool Knowledge, and Home Repair, 1920–2007," *WSQ: Women's Studies Quarterly* 37, no. 1 (2009): 38–60; and Daniela K. Rosner, "Making Citizens, Reassembling Devices: On Gender and the Development of Contemporary Public Sites of Repair in Northern California," *Public Culture* 26, no. 1 (2014): 51–77.

26. Aimi Hamraie and Kelly Fritsch, "Crip Technoscience Manifesto," *Catalyst: Feminism, Theory, Technoscience* 5, no. 1 (2019): http://catalystjournal.org/.

27. For gender and craft, see Steven M. Gelber, *Hobbies: Leisure and the Culture of Work in America* (New York: Columbia University Press, 1999). For women and craft, see Rozsika Parker, *The Subversive Stitch: Embroidery and the Making of the Feminine* (London: The Women's Press, 1984); Stella Minahan and Julie Wolfram Cox, "Stitch'nBitch: Cyberfeminism, a Third Place and the New Materiality," *Journal of Material Culture* 12, no. 1 (2007): 5–21; Elizabeth Groeneveld, "'Join the Knitting Revolution': Third-Wave Feminist Magazines and the Politics of Domesticity," *Canadian Review of American Studies* 40, no. 2 (2010): 259–77; Fiona Hackney, "Quiet Activism and the New Amateur: The Power of Home and Hobby Crafts," *Design and Culture* 5, no. 2 (2013): 169–93; Susan Luckman, *Craft and the Creative Economy* (New York: Palgrave Macmillan, 2015); and Samantha Close, "Knitting Activism, Knitting Gender, Knitting Race," *International Journal of Communication* 12 (2018): http://ijoc.org/.

28. "Play Hard, Play Soft: Make Is Crafting a New Magazine," *Make* 7 (August 2006): 10.

29. The projects common in *Make,* and in contrast to those featured in *Craft,* draw on the instructional publications historically intended for what John Lienhard calls "the savage boy inventor," which associated tinkering and experimentation with science and technology for boys and men, such as the book series *The Boy Mechanic* (1913) published by the magazine *Popular Mechanics* or *The Dangerous Book for Boys* (2006) by brothers Conn and Hal Iggulden. See John H. Lienhard, *Inventing Modern: Growing up with X-Rays, Skyscrapers, and Tailfins* (New York: Oxford University Press, 2003), 259.

See also Rebecca Onion, *Innocent Experiments: Childhood and the Culture of Popular Science in the United States* (Chapel Hill: University of North Carolina Press, 2016), 15.

30. "Play Hard, Play Soft," 10.

31. Dale Dougherty, "Craft: Volume 10 Is Our Last Issue in Print," *Make*, 11 February 2009, http://makezine.com/.

32. "Reader Input," *Make* 26 (May 2011): 12.

33. Luz Rivas, "Encouraging Girls to Hack and Make," *Make* 38 (March 2014): 13; Georgia Guthrie, "Where Are the Women?," *Make* 40 (July 2014): 52–53; Mike Senese, "Standing Out," *Make* 58 (September 2017): 18–23; "Culture and Creativity," *Make* 61 (March 2018): 7.

34. Dan Woods, "Bring DIY Inspiration to a Kid You Don't Know," *Make* 15 (July 2008): 28; Phillip Torrone, "Is It Time to Retool Public Libraries as Tech Shops?," *Make* 28 (November 2011): 28–29; *Makerspace Playbook;* Dale Dougherty, "I Fab a Dream," *Make* 50 (May 2016): 21.

35. Richard Sennett, *The Craftsman* (New Haven, Conn.: Yale University Press, 2008); Bernard Stiegler, *Taking Care of Youth and the Generations,* trans. Stephen Barker (Stanford, Calif.: Stanford University Press, 2010); Peter Korn, *Why We Make Things and Why It Matters: The Education of a Craftsman* (Boston: David R. Godine, 2013); Nina MacLaughlin, *Hammer Head: The Making of a Carpenter* (New York: W. W. Norton, 2015).

36. Stiegler, *Taking Care of Youth and the Generations,* 13.

37. Patrick Crogan, "Knowledge, Care, and Trans-Individuation: An Interview with Bernard Stiegler," *Cultural Politics* 6, no. 2 (2010): 161.

38. Cory Doctorow, "Are You the Scanner or the Barcode?," *Make* 22 (May 2010): 10.

39. Tim O'Reilly, "News from the Future," *Make* 5 (February 2006): 13.

40. Dale Dougherty, "Maker Friendly," *Make* 3 (August 2005): 7; Mister Jalopy, "The Maker's Bill of Rights"; O'Reilly, "News from the Future"; Bruce Sterling, "Hands On: Elegant Innovation from Lamps and Chainsaws to Saving the Planet," *Make* 6 (May 2006): 16–17; Charles Platt, "Upload," *Make* 12 (November 2007): 49; Saul Griffith, "The Power of Things," *Make* 14 (May 2008): 24–26; Cory Doctorow, "Selectable Output Control," *Make* 16 (November 2008): 14; "Are You the Scanner or the Barcode?"; Saul Griffith, "The Year of Cheap Robots That Make Cheap Robots," *Make* 31 (July 2012): 27; Kyle Wiens, "Right to Repair," *Make* 40 (July 2014): 12; Mike Senese, "Connected Everything," *Make* 64 (September 2018): 20–21; Dale Dougherty, "15 Years of *Make*:," *Make* 69 (July 2019): 6; Mike Senese, "The Cost of Convenience,"*Make* 72 (February 2020): 36–37; Forrest M. Mims III, "Solar Flares and EMP,"*Make* 72 (February 2020): 102–7; Dale Dougherty, "Makers: The Countermeasures for COVID-19," *Make* 73 (May 2020): 28–31.

41. George McKay, ed., *DIY Culture: Party and Protest in Nineties Britain* (London: Verso, 1998); Levine and Heimerl, *Handmade Nation;* Amy Spencer, *DIY: The Rise of Lo-Fi Culture* (London: Marion Boyars Publishing, 2008); Joan Tapper and Gale Zucker, eds., *Craft Activism: People, Ideas, and Projects from the New Community of Handmade and How You Can Join In* (New York: Potter Craft, 2011); Betsy Greer, *Craftivism: The Art of Craft and Activism* (Vancouver: Arsenal Pulp Press, 2014).

42. For individualism, see Daniel Shanahan, *Toward a Genealogy of Individualism* (Amherst: University of Massachusetts Press, 1992).

43. Philip Lamy, *Millennium Rage: Survivalists, White Supremacists, and the Doomsday Prophecy* (New York: Plenum, 1996); Rochelle Smith, "Antislick to Postslick: DIY Books and Youth Culture Then and Now," *Journal of American Culture* 33, no. 3 (2010): 207–16; Smith, "Handymen, Hippies and Healing"; Daniela K. Rosner and Fred Turner,

"Theaters of Alternative Industry: Hobbyist Repair Collectives and the Legacy of the 1960s American Counterculture," in *Design Thinking Research: Building Innovators*, ed. Hasso Plattner, Christoph Meinel, and Larry Leifer (Cham, Switzerland: Springer International Publishing, 2015), 59–69.

44. Lears, *No Place of Grace*, 83–84.

45. Lears, 70–71.

46. Lears, 84.

47. Lears, 72.

48. Dan Woods, "Announcing: Makers Market," *Make* 18 (May 2009): 15; Dale Dougherty, "Much More to Do—Five Years in, Make Is Just Getting Started," *Make* 21 (February 2010): 1; Mitch Altman, "Manufacture Your Project," *Make* 26 (May 2011): 32–37; Ryan P. C. Lawson, Esq., "What's in Your Toolbox?," *Make* 30 (May 2012): 17; David Merrill, "Going Pro," *Make* 33 (January 2013): 32–35; Alex Frommeyer, "Bring the Bids Back Home," *Make* 43 (January 2015): 12; D. C. Denison, "The Factory Finders," *Make* 54 (January 2017): 18. The magazine's commitment to encouraging makers to go commercial betrays *Make* contributors seeking to align themselves with the anti-establishment and DIY values of punk subculture. For the limits of countercultural politics and anti-consumerist critiques, see Joseph Heath and Andrew Potter, *The Rebel Sell: Why the Culture Can't Be Jammed* (Toronto: HarperCollins Canada, 2005).

49. Dougherty, "Much More to Do," 1.

50. Chris Anderson, *Makers: The New Industrial Revolution* (New York: Crown Publishing, 2012).

51. Dawkins, "Do-It-Yourself."

52. Susan Luckman, "The Aura of the Analogue in a Digital Age: Women's Crafts, Creative Markets and Home-Based Labour after Etsy," *Cultural Studies Review* 19, no. 1 (2013): 249–70.

53. Dougherty, "Visible Hand," 13.

54. William Lidwell, "MakeShift," *Make* 2 (May 2005): 188–89; Lee D. Zlotoff, "MakeShift: Impaled!," *Make* 12 (November 2007): 156–57; "MakeShift: Snowbound!," *Make* 22 (May 2010): 146–47.

55. Benjamin René Jordan, *Modern Manhood and the Boy Scouts of America: Citizenship, Race, and the Environment, 1910–1930* (Chapel Hill: University of North Carolina Press, 2016). For the intersection of making and disaster, apocalyptic, and survivalist thought, see Josef Nguyen, "How Makers and Preppers Converge in Premodern and Post-Apocalyptic Ruin," *Lateral: Journal of the Cultural Studies Association* 7, no. 2 (2018): http://csalateral.org/.

56. Lee D. Zlotoff, "MakeShift: Flood Panic," *Make* 6 (May 2006): 172–73.

57. Zlotoff, 172.

58. Lee D. Zlotoff, "MakeShift: Zombie Attack!," *Make* 25 (February 2011): 152–53; "MakeShift: Hot Water," *Make* 27 (August 2011): 154–55.

59. Ariel Levi Simons, "3 Rules for Successful Citizen Science," *Make* 31 (August 2012): 41.

60. Saul Griffith, "The Open Source Car: A Design Brief," *Make* 1 (February 2005): 44–46; Cory Doctorow, "Traitors to History: A Copyright-Controlled Museum Is a Crime against Humankind," *Make* 5 (February 2006): 16–17; Mitch Altman, "Patent-B-Gone: Inventor Mitch Altamn Explains Why He Open-Sourced His TV-B-Gone Kit," *Make* 12 (November 2007): 48; Phillip Torrone, "The {Unspoken} Rules of Open Source Hardware," *Make* 32 (November 2012): 12–14; Mike Senese, "Open Source Pushes On," *Make* 54 (January 2017): 8; Gareth Branwyn, "The Ripe Stuff," *Make* 57 (July 2017): 36–40. For open source politics, see Steve Weber, *The Success of Open Source* (New

York: Cambridge University Press, 2004); Christopher M. Kelty, *Two Bits: The Cultural Significance of Free Software* (Durham, N.C.: Duke University Press, 2008); Matteo Pasquinelli, *Animal Spirits: A Bestiary of the Commons* (Rotterdam: NAi Publishers, 2008); James Leach, Dawn Nafus, and Bernhard Krieger, "Freedom Imagined: Morality and Aesthetics in Open Source Software Design," *Ethnos: Journal of Anthropology* 74, no. 1 (2009): 51–71; Aaron Shaw, "Insurgent Expertise: The Politics of Free/Livre and Open Source Software in Brazil," *Journal of Information Technology & Politics* 8, no. 3 (2011): 253–72; John L. Sullivan, "Free, Open Source Software Advocacy as a Social Justice Movement: The Expansion of F/OSS Movement Discourse in the 21st Century," *Journal of Information Technology & Politics* 8, no. 3 (2011): 223–39; Dawn Nafus, "'Patches Don't Have Gender': What Is Not Open in Open Source Software," *New Media & Society* 14, no. 4 (2012): 669–83; Alison Powell, "Democratizing Production through Open Source Knowledge: From Open Software to Open Hardware," *Media, Culture & Society* 34, no. 6 (2012): 691–708; and Steven Mann, "Maktivism: Authentic Making for Technology in the Service of Humanity," in *DIY Citizenship: Critical Making and Social Media*, ed. Matt Ratto and Megan Boler (Cambridge, Mass.: MIT Press, 2014), 29–52.

61. Anne Balsamo, *Designing Culture: The Technological Imagination at Work* (Durham, N.C.: Duke University Press, 2011), 131.

62. Alan Irwin, *Citizen Science: A Study of People, Expertise and Sustainable Development* (New York: Routledge, 2002); Jason Corburn, *Street Science: Community Knowledge and Environmental Health Justice* (Cambridge, Mass.: MIT Press, 2005); Paul Atkinson, "Do It Yourself: Democracy and Design," *Journal of Design History* 19, no. 1 (2006): 1–10; Ji Sun Lee, "Technology Education for Woman by DIY Technology in Closing Gender Gap," in *Proceedings of the SIGCHI Conference on Human Factors in Computing Systems* (Florence, Italy: Association for Computing Machinery, 2008), 3447–52; Alessandro Delfanti, "Users and Peers. From Citizen Science to P2P Science," *Journal of Science Communication* 9, no. 1 (2010): http://jcom.sissa.it/; Victoria C. Stodden, "Open Science: Policy Implications for the Evolving Phenomenon of User-Led Scientific Innovation," *Journal of Science Communication* 9, no. 1 (2010): http://jcom.sissa.it/; Theresa Jean Tanenbaum et al., "Democratizing Technology: Pleasure, Utility and Expressiveness in DIY and Maker Practice," in *Proceedings of the SIGCHI Conference on Human Factors in Computing Systems* (Paris: Association for Computing Machinery, 2013), 2603–12; David A. Mellis and Leah Buechley, "Do-It-Yourself Cellphones: An Investigation into the Possibilities and Limits of High-Tech DIY," in *Proceedings of the SIGCHI Conference on Human Factors in Computing Systems* (Toronto: Association for Computing Machinery, 2014), 1723–32; Rosner, "Making Citizens, Reassembling Devices."

63. Clay Shirky, *Here Comes Everybody: The Power of Organizing without Organizations*, revised ed. (New York: Penguin Books, 2009), 57.

64. Juan Leguizamon, "Punk Science: Anarchy in the Laboratory," *Make* 31 (August 2012): 36. See also Jason Verlinde, "Downhill, Makers: Garage Ski Builders Are Outdoing the Pros," *Make* 10 (May 2006): 30–32; Forrest M. Mims III, "Country Scientist: Become an Amateur Scientist," *Make* 24 (November 2010): 26–28; Charles Platt, "Unreasonable Rocketeers," *Make* 32 (November 2012): 72–77; Mike Senese, "Subversive Science," *Make* 56 (May 2017): 7; Shannon Dosemagen, "Community Science," *Make* 70 (September 2019): 16–19.

65. Leguizamon, "Punk Science," 36.

66. Terrie Miller, "Citizen Weather Station," *Make* 5 (February 2006): 139–40; Dr. Shawn, "Build a Cloud Chamber," *Make* 9 (February 2007): 156–59; Gareth Branwyn,

"Three Test Tubes and the Truth," *Make* 31 (August 2012): 11; Erica Tiberia, "My Mini Mars Rover," *Make* 55 (March 2017): 28.

67. I use "workshop" to characterize maker, hacker, DIY, and other amateur scientific spaces. See Joseph Wachelder, "Democratizing Science: Various Routes and Visions of Dutch Science Shops," *Science, Technology & Human Values* 28, no. 2 (2003): 244–73; Jackson, "Constructing at Home"; Maxigas, "Hacklabs and Hackerspaces: Tracing Two Genealogies," *Journal of Peer Production*, no. 2 (2012): http://peerproduction.net/; and Andrew Richard Schrock, "'Education in Disguise': Culture of a Hacker and Maker Space," *InterActions: UCLA Journal of Education and Information Studies* 10, no. 1 (2014): http://interactions.gseis.ucla.edu/.

68. Hans-Jörg Rheinberger, "'Discourses of Circumstance': A Note on the Author in Science," in *Scientific Authorship: Credit and Intellectual Property in Science*, ed. Mario Biagioli and Peter Galison (New York: Routledge, 2003), 318.

69. Andrew Keen, *The Cult of the Amateur: How Today's Internet Is Killing Our Culture* (New York: Doubleday/Currency, 2007), 15.

70. Keen, 35.

71. Markus Schmidt, "Diffusion of Synthetic Biology: A Challenge to Biosafety," *Systems and Synthetic Biology* 2, nos. 1–2 (2008): 1–6; Janet Hope, *Biobazaar: The Open Source Revolution and Biotechnology* (Cambridge, Mass.: Harvard University Press, 2009); Iina Hellsten and Brigitte Nerlich, "Synthetic Biology: Building the Language for a New Science Brick by Metaphorical Brick," *New Genetics and Society* 30, no. 4 (2011): 375–97; Morgan Meyer, "Build Your Own Lab: Do-It-Yourself Biology and the Rise of Citizen Biotech-Economies," *Journal of Peer Production*, no. 2 (2012): http://peerproduction.net/; Alessandro Delfanti, "Tweaking Genes in Your Garage: Biohacking between Activism and Entrepreneurship," in *Activist Media and Biopolitics: Critical Media Interventions in the Age of Biopower*, ed. Wolfgang Sützl and Theo Hug (Inssbruck, Germany: Innsbruck University Press, 2012), 163–77; Ana Delgado, "DIYbio: Making Things and Making Futures," *Futures* 48 (2013): 65–73; Thomas Landrain et al., "Do-It-Yourself Biology: Challenges and Promises for an Open Science and Technology Movement," *Systems and Synthetic Biology* 7, no. 3 (2013): 115–26; Günter Seyfried, Lei Pei, and Markus Schmidt, "European Do-It-Yourself (DIY) Biology: Beyond the Hope, Hype and Horror," *BioEssays* 36, no. 6 (2014): 548–51.

72. Stew Magnuson, "Growing Public Interest in Genetic Science Sparks Some Bio-Security Concerns," *National Defense Industrial Association*, June 2010; Carl Zimmer, "Amateurs Are New Fear in Creating Mutant Virus," *New York Times*, 5 March 2012; Dustin T. Holloway, "Regulating Amateurs: How Should the Government Ensure the Safety and Responsibility of Do-It-Yourself Biologists?," *The Scientist*, 28 February 2013, http://the-scientist.com.

73. Gina Neff, *Venture Labor: Work and the Burden of Risk in Innovative Industries* (Cambridge, Mass.: MIT Press, 2012), 5. For risk societies, see Anthony Giddens, *The Consequences of Modernity* (Malden, Mass.: Polity, 1990); Ulrich Beck, *Risk Society: Towards a New Modernity*, trans. Mark Ritter (London: SAGE Publications, 1992); Stephen Crook, "Ordering Risks," in *Risk and Sociocultural Theory: New Directions and Perspectives*, ed. Deborah Lupton (New York: Cambridge University Press, 1999), 160–85; Mitchell Dean, *Governmentality: Power and Rule in Modern Society* (London: SAGE Publications, 1999); and Anthony Elliott, "Beck's Sociology of Risk: A Critical Assessment," *Sociology* 36, no. 2 (2002): 293–315.

74. Louis Althusser, "Ideology and Ideological State Apparatuses (Notes toward an Investigation)," in *Lenin and Philosophy and Other Essays*, trans. Ben Brewster (New York: Monthly Review Press, 1972), 173.

75. Bob Parks, "Garage Biotech: For a Safer World, Drew Endy Wants Everyone to Engineer Life from the Ground Up," *Make* 7 (August 2006): 44.

76. Cindi Katz, "Vagabond Capitalism and the Necessity of Social Reproduction," *Antipode* 33, no. 4 (2001): 714. See also Isabelle Bakker and Stephen Gill, eds., *Power, Production and Social Reproduction: Human In/security in the Global Political Economy* (New York: Palgrave Macmillan, 2003); Kate Bezanson and Meg Luxton, eds., *Social Reproduction: Feminist Political Economy Challenges Neo-Liberalism* (Montreal: McGill-Queen's University Press, 2006); and Susan Ferguson, "Intersectionality and Social-Reproduction Feminisms: Toward an Integrative Ontology," *Historical Materialism* 24, no. 2 (2016): 38–60.

77. Isabelle Bakker and Stephen Gill, "Ontology, Method, and Hypotheses," in *Power, Production and Social Reproduction: Human In/security in the Global Political Economy*, ed. Isabelle Bakker and Stephen Gill (New York: Palgrave Macmillan, 2003), 18.

78. Amy F. Ogata, *Designing the Creative Child: Playthings and Places in Midcentury America* (Minneapolis: University of Minnesota Press, 2013), 2.

79. Stiegler, *Taking Care of Youth and the Generations*, 1–3.

80. Stevi Jackson and Sue Scott, "Risk Anxiety and the Social Construction of Childhood," in *Risk and Sociocultural Theory: New Directions and Perspectives*, ed. Deborah Lupton (New York: Cambridge University Press, 1999), 86–87.

81. Jackson and Scott, 90–91. For youth and constructions of risk, see Charles R. Acland, *Youth, Murder, Spectacle: The Cultural Politics of "Youth in Crisis"* (Boulder, Colo.: Westview Press, 1995); Stanley Cohen, *Folk Devils and Moral Panics: The Creation of the Mods and Rockers*, 3rd ed. (New York: Routledge, 2002); Toby Miller, "A Risk Society of Moral Panic: The US in the Twenty-First Century," *Cultural Politics* 2, no. 3 (2006): 299–318; and Jacqueline Ryan Vickery, *Worried about the Wrong Things: Youth, Risk, and Opportunity in the Digital World* (Cambridge, Mass.: MIT Press, 2017).

82. Saul Griffith, "The Fairyland of Science: Magic Is in the Mind of a Fifth-Grader near You," *Make* 13 (February 2008): 38–39; Dale Dougherty, "Toy Stories," *Make* 28 (November 2011): 11; Saul Griffith, "A Curriculum of Toys," *Make* 28 (November 2011): 27; Phillip Torrone, "Zen and the Art of Making," *Make* 30 (May 2012): 28–29; AnnMarie Thomas, "Why Make?," *Make* 33 (January 2013): 12; Steve Davee, "What Sticks about Play and Bricks," *Make* 39 (May 2014): 12.

83. Griffith, "Fairyland of Science," 39.

84. Onion, *Innocent Experiments*, 4–5.

85. *Make*'s distrust of public schools aligns with contemporary anti-intellectualism. For U.S. public education during the Cold War, including anti-intellectual sentiment, see Andrew Hartman, *Education and the Cold War: The Battle for the American School* (New York: Palgrave Macmillan, 2008).

86. Dale Dougherty, "Learn by Making," *Make* 20 (November 2007): 13.

87. Dougherty, "Much More to Do," 1.

88. AnnMarie Thomas, "Real Tools for Kids," *Make* 29 (February 2012): 27.

89. Dale Dougherty and Gever Tulley, "Kid Safety Labels We Want to See," *Make* 7 (August 2006): 180.

90. Peter N. Stearns, *Anxious Parents: A History of Modern Childrearing in America* (New York: NYU Press, 2004), 37.

91. Jackson and Scott, "Risk Anxiety and the Social Construction of Childhood," 90–91.

92. Dougherty and Tulley, "Kid Safety Labels We Want to See."

93. Gever Tulley and Julie Spiegler, "Put Strange Stuff in the Microwave," *Make* 22

(May 2010): 166; "Lick a 9-Volt Battery," *Make* 25 (February 2011): 166; "Burn Things with a Magnifying Glass," *Make* 32 (November 2012): 159.

94. Phillip Torrone, "The Chemistry Gift Guide," *Make*, 23 November 2008, http://makezine.com/.

95. Torrone.

96. For "The Radioactive Boy Scout," see Ken Silverstein, *The Radioactive Boy Scout: The Frightening True Story of a Whiz Kid and His Homemade Nuclear Reactor* (New York: Villard, 2004).

97. Thomas, "Real Tools for Kids," 27.

98. Jackson and Scott, "Risk Anxiety and the Social Construction of Childhood," 89. For how children queer normative conceptions of development, see Kathryn Bond Stockton, *The Queer Child, or Growing Sideways in the Twentieth Century* (Durham, N.C.: Duke University Press, 2009).

99. Lee Edelman, *No Future: Queer Theory and the Death Drive* (Durham, N.C.: Duke University Press, 2004), 11.

100. Tim O'Reilly, "News from the Future," *Make* 2 (May 2005): 13.

101. "News from the Future," *Make* 5, 13.

102. *Makerspace Playbook*, 4.

103. Tim Anderson, "Heirloom Technology: Finding the Technology of the Future in the Forgotten Ideas of the Past," *Make* 1 (February 2005): 38–43; Dougherty, "Learn by Making"; Griffith, "Curriculum of Toys"; Thomas, "Real Tools for Kids"; Jessie Uyeda, "iJessup," *Make* 72 (February 2020): 22–25.

104. Saul Griffith, "Unhindered Creativity: Enable Kids to Invent Their Own Games," *Make* 8 (November 2006): 42.

105. Griffith, 43.

106. Cindi Katz, "The State Goes Home: Local Hyper-Vigilance of Children and the Global," *Social Justice* 28, no. 3 (2001): 51; Melinda Cooper, *Family Values: Between Neoliberalism and the New Social Conservatism* (New York: Zone Books, 2017), 137.

107. Griffith, "Curriculum of Toys," 27.

108. Robyn Miller, "Grandpop's Shop," *Make* 8 (November 2006): 37.

109. Charles Platt, "A Fusion Reactor for the Rest of Us," *Make* 3 (August 2005): 25–35; Bruce Sterling, "Everything, for Everybody, Every Time," *Make* 4 (November 2005): 26; Dr. Shawn, "Kitchen Counter DNA Lab: Extract, Purify, and Experiment with the Blueprint of Life," *Make* 7 (August 2006): 59–64; Mister Jalopy, "Workshops, Big and Very Small," *Make* 7 (August 2006): 178–79; Tom Owad, "A CNC Milling Machine for Less Than a Grand," *Make* 11 (August 2007): 92; Collin Cunningham, "The Arms of Assistance," *Make* 15 (August 2008): 137–38; Marc de Vinck, "Mini Fume Extractor," *Make* 19 (August 2009): 123–25; Andrew Lewis, "Copper Tool Tidy," *Make* 28 (October 2011): 130–31; Mike Senese, "Future of Home," *Make* 59 (November 2017): 8; Bob, Christine, and Jonathan Pappas, "Homeschool How-To," *Make* 73 (May 2020): 46–49.

110. Lisa Jacobson, *Raising Consumers: Children and the American Mass Market in the Early Twentieth Century* (New York: Columbia University Press, 2005); Teresa Michals, "Experiments before Breakfast: Toys, Education and Middle-Class Childhood," in *The Nineteenth-Century Child and Consumer Culture*, ed. Dennis Denisoff (Aldershot, UK: Ashgate, 2008), 29–42; Gary Cross, *Kids' Stuff: Toys and the Changing World of American Childhood* (Cambridge, Mass.: Harvard University Press, 2009); Ogata, *Designing the Creative Child*.

111. Kate Bezanson, *Gender, the State, and Social Reproduction: Household Insecurity in Neo-Liberal Times* (Toronto: University of Toronto Press, 2006), 11.

112. Mims, "Country Scientist."

113. Saul Griffith, "The Ultimate Tool Buying Guide," *Make* 3 (August 2005): 46. See also James Floyd Kelly, "Kickstart a Kids' Makerspace," *Make* 38 (March 2014): 28–29.

114. Dale Dougherty, "ReMake: America," *Make* 18 (May 2009): 1. See also Saul Griffith, "Making Things Work," *Make* 16 (November 2008): 26–27; Dougherty, "Much More to Do"; Saul Griffith, "DIT: Raising Our Collective Barn," *Make* 26 (May 2011): 27; Cory Doctorow, "The Half-Life of Stuff," *Make* 29 (February 2012): 31; Jose Gomez-Marquez, "Biozone," *Make* 56 (May 2017): 26–28; Dougherty, "15 Years of *Make:*."

115. Anderson, *Imagined Communities*, 67.

116. Susan Currie Sivek, "'We Need a Showing of All Hands': Technological Utopianism in Make Magazine," *Journal of Communication Inquiry* 35, no. 3 (2011): 187–209.

117. Dougherty, "Visible Hand," 13.

118. Lilly Irani, *Chasing Innovation: Making Entrepreneurial Citizens in Modern India* (Princeton, N.J.: Princeton University Press, 2019), 2.

119. Charles Peters, "A Neoliberal's Manifesto," *Washington Monthly* 15 (1983): 10.

120. "ReMake: America," *Make* 18 (May 2009): 45. See also Saul Griffith, "New Power Nation," *Make* 73 (May 2020): 16–21.

121. "ReMake: America," 45.

122. Neff, *Venture Labor*, 15.

123. Saul Griffith, "MENTORing Kids into Makers," *Make* 29 (February 2012): 16; William Gurstelle, "Security Is a Superstition," *Make* 35 (July 2013): 8; Forrest M. Mims III, "Under Suspicion," *Make* 54 (January 2017): 16–17; Michael Weinberg, "Devices and the Law,"*Make* 56 (May 2017): 42–43; Forrest M. Mims, III, "Clearing the Air," *Make* 57 (July 2017): 18–19.

124. Turner, *From Counterculture to Cyberculture*, 219.

125. Stephanie Ricker Schulte, "United States Digital Service: How 'Obama's Startup' Harnesses Disruption and Productive Failure to Reboot Government," *International Journal of Communication* 12 (2018): http://ijoc.org/.

126. Dunbar-Hester, *Hacking Diversity*, 3.

127. Dunbar-Hester, 4.

128. Michael Perdriel, "Off-Grid Laundry Machine," *Make* 18 (May 2009): 60–66.

129. William Gurstelle, "The Maker State: Safe Working Practices Give You the Freedom to Attempt Projects on the Edge," *Make* 11 (August 2007): 35.

130. For the nanny state, see Robert E. Goodin, "Permissible Paternalism: In Defense of the Nanny State," *Responsive Community* 1, no. 3 (1991): 42–51; and Marian Sawer, "Gender, Metaphor and the State," *Feminist Review* no. 52 (1996): 118–34.

131. Gurstelle, "Maker State," 35.

132. Crook, "Ordering Risks," 171.

133. Parks, "Garage Biotech"; William Gurstelle, "The Safe Workshop: Rules to Make By," *Make* 12 (November 2007): 44; Gurstelle, "Security Is a Superstition"; Kipp Bradford, "Void Your Warranty," *Make* 50 (May 2016): 45; Tim Deagan, "Workspace Fire Safety," *Make* 56 (May 2017): 22–25.

134. John Hartley, *Uses of Television* (New York: Routledge, 1999), 161.

135. Dahlberg, "Cyber-Libertarianism 2.0," 336.

136. Ratto and Boler, "Introduction," 11–12. See also Elizabeth Jacka, "'Democracy as Defeat': The Impotence of Arguments for Public Service Broadcasting," *Television & New Media* 4, no. 2 (2003): 177–91; Dahlberg, "Cyber-Libertarianism 2.0"; and Paul Dourish, "The Politics of Information and Participation: Digital Citizenship and Public Science," in *Critical Making: Science*, ed. Garnet Hertz (Hollywood, Calif.: Telharmonium Press, 2012), 6–13.

137. Ratto and Boler, "Introduction," 1–3. See also Jentery Sayers, ed., *Making Things*

and Drawing Boundaries: Experiments in the Digital Humanities (Minneapolis: University of Minnesota Press, 2018).

138. Shawn Connally, "We're All Alright," *Make* 10 (May 2006): 11.

139. Dale Dougherty and Mark Frauenfelder, "On to Year Two: Dale Dougherty and Mark Frauenfelder Look Back on Make's First Year,"*Make* 5 (February 2006): 11.

140. "Front Matter," *Make* 1 (February 2005): 8.

141. Julie Passanante Elman, *Chronic Youth: Disability, Sexuality, and U.S. Media Cultures of Rehabilitation* (New York: NYU Press, 2014), 17. Elman's rehabilitative citizenship draws on the conceptualization of infantile citizenship by Lauren Berlant. See Lauren Berlant, *The Queen of America Goes to Washington City: Essays on Sex and Citizenship* (Durham, N.C.: Duke University Press, 1997).

142. Michel Foucault, "Governmentality," in *The Foucault Effect: Studies in Governmentality*, ed. Graham Burchell, Colin Gordon, and Peter Miller (Chicago: University of Chicago Press, 1991), 87–104.

143. Gurstelle, "Maker State," 35. For constructions of thugs and the policing of Black youth, see Stuart Hall et al., *Policing the Crisis: Mugging, the State and Law and Order*, 2nd ed. (New York: Palgrave Macmillan, 2013); Michael P. Jeffries, *Thug Life: Race, Gender, and the Meaning of Hip-Hop* (Chicago: University of Chicago Press, 2011); Mark Anthony Neal, *Looking for Leroy: Illegible Black Masculinities* (New York: NYU Press, 2013); and Lakeyta M. Bonnette, *Pulse of the People: Political Rap Music and Black Politics* (Philadelphia: University of Pennsylvania Press, 2015).

144. Connally, "We're All Alright," 11.

145. Gurstelle, "Jam Jar Jet," 105.

146. Gurstelle, 109.

3. Instagram and the Creative Filtering of Authentic Selves

1. Jonah Engel Bromwich, "Paris Hilton Said She Invented the Selfie: We Set out to Find the Truth," *New York Times*, 20 November 2017, http://nytimes.com/; Jon Levine, "Paris Hilton Claims to Have Invented the Selfie and People Are Freaking," *The Wrap*, 20 November 2017, http://thewrap.com/; Chris Matyszczyk, "Paris Hilton Says She and Britney Spears Invented the Selfie," *CNET*, 20 November 2017, http://cnet.com/.

2. "The Instagram Community Hits 80 Million Users," Instagram, last modified 6 July 2012, accessed 31 March 2016, http://blog.instagram.com/post/28067043504/the-instagram-community-hits-80-million-users. Since its initial offerings of photographic content, Instagram has introduced additional content formats for users to create, including short-form videos and livestreaming.

3. "About Us," Instagram, accessed 31 March 2016, http://instagram.com/. Both Systrom and Krieger resigned from Instagram as CEO and CTO respectively on 24 September 2018, following disagreements with Instagram's parent company, Facebook.

4. "We're the 2011 App Store iPhone App of the Year!," Instagram, last modified 8 December 2011, accessed 31 March 2016, http://blog.instagram.com/post/13928169232/were-the-2011-app-store-iphone-app-of-the-year; "Instagram + Facebook," Instagram, accessed 31 March 2016, http://blog.instagram.com/post/20785013897/instagram-facebook; "Instagram's 2017 Year in Review," Instagram, last modified 29 November 2017, accessed 6 August 2020, http://about.instagram.com/blog/.

5. "Instagram Today: 100 Million People," Instagram, last modified 26 February 2013, accessed 31 March 2016, http://blog.instagram.com/post/44078783561/100-million.

6. José van Dijck, *The Culture of Connectivity: A Critical History of Social Media* (New York: Oxford University Press, 2013), 13.

7. "Instagram Today."

8. "Instagram," Google Play, accessed 31 March 2016, http://play.google.com/.

9. Pierre Lévy, *Collective Intelligence: Mankind's Emerging World in Cyberspace,* trans. Robert Bononno (New York: Plenum Trade, 1997); Henry Jenkins, *Convergence Culture: Where Old and New Media Collide* (New York: NYU Press, 2006); Clay Shirky, *Here Comes Everybody: The Power of Organizing without Organizations,* revised ed. (New York: Penguin Books, 2009); Clay Shirky, *Cognitive Surplus: How Technology Makes Consumers into Collaborators,* revised ed. (New York: Penguin Books, 2011).

10. Paolo Gerbaudo, *Tweets and the Streets: Social Media and Contemporary Activism* (London: Pluto Press, 2012); Zeynep Tufekci, *Twitter and Tear Gas: The Power and Fragility of Networked Protest* (New Haven, Conn.: Yale University Press, 2017); Sarah Florini, *Beyond Hashtags: Racial Politics and Black Digital Networks* (New York: NYU Press, 2019); Sarah J. Jackson, Moya Bailey, and Brooke Foucault Welles, *#HashtagActivism: Networks of Race and Gender Justice* (Cambridge, Mass.: MIT Press, 2020).

11. Shirky, *Here Comes Everybody,* 320. Since Instagram's widespread association with youth, newer social media platforms have also been associated with youth, including Snapchat, VSCO, and TikTok.

12. Nico Carpentier and Benjamin De Cleen, eds., *Participation and Media Production: Critical Reflections on Content Creation* (Newcastle, UK: Cambridge Scholars Publishing, 2008); Jodi Dean, *Democracy and Other Neoliberal Fantasies: Communicative Capitalism and Left Politics* (Durham, N.C.: Duke University Press, 2009); Bernard Stiegler, *Taking Care of Youth and the Generations,* trans. Stephen Barker (Stanford, Calif.: Stanford University Press, 2010); Evgeny Morozov, *The Net Delusion: The Dark Side of Internet Freedom* (New York: PublicAffairs, 2011); Geert Lovink, *Networks without a Cause: A Critique of Social Media* (Malden, Mass.: Polity, 2012); Jean M. Twenge, *iGen: Why Today's Super-Connected Kids Are Growing Up Less Rebellious, More Tolerant, Less Happy—and Completely Unprepared for Adulthood—and What That Means for the Rest of Us* (New York: Atria Books, 2017).

13. Sherry Turkle, *Alone Together: Why We Expect More from Technology and Less from Each Other* (New York: Basic Books, 2011); Sherry Turkle, *Reclaiming Conversation: The Power of Talk in a Digital Age* (New York: Penguin Books, 2015).

14. Nancy K. Baym, *Personal Connections in the Digital Age* (Malden, Mass.: Polity, 2015).

15. Justine Cassell and Meg Cramer, "High Tech or High Risk: Moral Panics about Girls Online," in *Digital Youth, Innovation, and the Unexpected,* ed. Tara McPherson (Cambridge, Mass.: MIT Press, 2007), 53–75; Mizuko Ito et al., *Hanging Out, Messing Around, and Geeking Out: Kids Living and Learning with New Media* (Cambridge, Mass.: MIT Press, 2009); David Buckingham and Helle Strandgaard Jensen, "Beyond 'Media Panics': Reconceptualising Public Debates about Children and Media," *Journal of Children and Media* 6, no. 4 (2012): 413–29; Jacqueline Ryan Vickery, *Worried about the Wrong Things: Youth, Risk, and Opportunity in the Digital World* (Cambridge, Mass.: MIT Press, 2017).

16. Joseph F. Kett, *Rites of Passage: Adolescence in America, 1790 to the Present* (New York: Basic Books, 1977); Grace Palladino, *Teenagers: An American History* (New York: Basic Books, 1996); Joe Austin and Michael Nevin Willard, eds., *Generations of Youth: Youth Cultures and History in Twentieth-Century America* (New York: NYU Press, 1998); Thomas Hine, *The Rise and Fall of the American Teenager* (New York: HarperCollins, 1999); Gary Cross, *The Cute and the Cool: Wondrous Innocence and Modern American Children's Culture* (New York: Oxford University Press, 2004); Kelly Schrum, *Some*

Wore Bobby Sox: The Emergence of Teenage Girls' Culture, 1920–1945 (New York: Palgrave Macmillan, 2004); Sarah E. Chinn, *Inventing Modern Adolescence: The Children of Immigrants in Turn-of-the-Century America* (New Brunswick, NJ: Rutgers University Press, 2009); Julie Passanante Elman, *Chronic Youth: Disability, Sexuality, and U.S. Media Cultures of Rehabilitation* (New York: NYU Press, 2014).

17. Erik H. Erikson, *Identity: Youth and Crisis* (New York: W. W. Norton, 1968); Reed Larson, "Secrets in the Bedroom: Adolescents' Private Use of Media," *Journal of Youth and Adolescence* 24, no. 5 (1995): 535–50; Susan Harter, *The Construction of the Self: A Developmental Perspective* (New York: Guilford Press, 1999); Jane Kroger, *Identity in Adolescence: The Balance between Self and Other* (New York: Routledge, 2004).

18. Jeffrey Jensen Arnett, "Adolescents' Uses of Media for Self-Socialization," *Journal of Youth and Adolescence* 24, no. 5 (1995): 522.

19. The Way Way Back, "12 Painfully Embarrassing Parents on Facebook," *BuzzFeed,* 14 June 2013, http://buzzfeed.com/; Brian Boone, "Grandparents Embarrassing Their Families on Social Media Is the Best Way to Celebrate Grandparents Day," Someecards, last modified 13 September 2015, accessed 31 March 2016, http://someecards.com /life/holidays/grandparents-day-grandparents-being-embarrassing-on-facebook; Lara Brown and Grace de Souza, "The 10 Worst Parental Crimes on Social Media," *The Guardian,* 12 December 2015, http://theguardian.com/; Susan Adcox, "10 Facebook No-Nos for Grandparents: Missteps Might Get You Unfriending, Even If You Are Family," *LiveAbout,* 4 January 2018, http://liveabout.com/.

20. My treatment of emerging social media platforms as adolescent is inspired by though not identical to Stephanie Ricker Schulte's discussion of teen technology discourses. For Schulte, teen technology discourses prevalent in the 1980s and 1990s surrounding networked computing framed both computer networks and their imagined users as teen-like, young, and potentially unruly entities requiring precise parental (or governmental) direction and supervision. See Stephanie Ricker Schulte, *Cached: Decoding the Internet in Global Popular Culture* (New York: NYU Press, 2013), 22.

21. Shayla Thiel Stern, *Instant Identity: Adolescent Girls and the World of Instant Messaging* (New York: Peter Lang, 2007); Carrie James, *Disconnected: Youth, New Media, and the Ethics Gap* (Cambridge, Mass.: MIT Press, 2014); Korina M. Jocson, *Youth Media Matters: Participatory Cultures and Literacies in Education* (Minneapolis: University of Minnesota Press, 2018).

22. danah boyd, *It's Complicated: The Social Lives of Networked Teens* (New Haven, Conn.: Yale University Press, 2014), 8.

23. danah boyd, "Why Youth (Heart) Social Network Sites: The Role of Networked Publics in Teenage Social Life," in *Youth, Identity, and Digital Media,* ed. David Buckingham (Cambridge, Mass.: MIT Press, 2007), 120. See also Lauren S. Berliner, *Producing Queer Youth: The Paradox of Digital Media Empowerment* (New York: Routledge, 2018).

24. Tobias Raun, ed., *Out Online: Trans Self-Representation and Community Building on YouTube* (New York: Routledge, 2016); Reid Lodge, "Trans Sites of Self-Exploration: From Print Autobiographies to Blogs," *Queer Studies in Media & Popular Culture* 2, no. 1 (2017): 49–71; Jon M. Wargo, "'Every Selfie Tells a Story . . .': LGBTQ Youth Lifestreams and New Media Narratives as Connective Identity Texts," *New Media & Society* 19, no. 4 (2017): 560–78; Lexi Webster, "'I Am I': Self-Constructed Transgender Identities in Internet-Mediated Forum Communication," *International Journal of the Sociology of Language,* no. 256 (2019): 129–46.

25. "National #Selfie Portrait Gallery," Moving Image, accessed 6 August 2020, http://moving-image.info/.

26. Kris Fallon, "Streams of the Self: The Instagram Feed as Narrative Autobiogra-

phy" (paper presented at the Interactive Narratives, New Media and Social Engagement International Conference, Toronto, 24–25 October 2014); Adam Levin, "The Selfie in the Age of Digital Recursion," *InVisible Culture*, no. 20 (2014): http://ivc.lib.rochester.edu/; Nicholas Mirzoeff, "How to See Yourself," in *How to See the World: An Introduction to Images, from Self-Portraits to Selfies, Maps to Movies, and More* (New York: Basic Books, 2016), 29–69; Karen ann Donnachie, "Selfies, #Me: Glimpses of Authenticity in the Narcissus' Pool of the Networked Amateur Self-Portrait," in *Rites of Spring*, ed. Julie Lunn (Perth: Black Swan Press, 2018), 61–76; Katrin Tiidenberg, *Selfies: Why We Love (and Hate) Them* (Bingley, UK: Emerald Publishing, 2018).

27. Alise Tifentale and Lev Manovich, "Selfiecity: Exploring Photography and Self-Fashioning in Social Media," in *Postdigital Aesthetics: Art, Computation and Design,* ed. David M. Berry and Michael Dieter (London: Palgrave Macmillan, 2015), 109–22.

28. Levin, "Selfie in the Age of Digital Recursion."

29. Edgar Gómez Cruz and Helen Thornham, "Selfies beyond Self-Representation: The (Theoretical) F(r)ictions of a Practice," *Journal of Aesthetics & Culture* 7, no. 1 (2015): http://tandfonline.com/.

30. Theresa M. Senft and Nancy K. Baym, "What Does the Selfie Say? Investigating a Global Phenomenon," *International Journal of Communication* 9 (2015): http://ijoc.org/.

31. Victoria Wollaston, "Selfies Are 'Damaging' and Leave Young People Vulnerable to Abuse, Claims Psychologist," *Daily Mail,* 23 August 2013, http://dailymail.co.uk/; Paul Martinka, "My Selfie with Brooklyn Bridge Suicide Dude," *New York Post,* 4 December 2013, http://nypost.com/; Carolyn Gregoire, "Study Links Selfies to Narcissism and Psychopathy," *Huffington Post,* 12 January 2015, http://huffingtonpost.com/. For how narcissism is used to vilify selfie practices, see Greg Goldberg, "Through the Looking Glass: The Queer Narcissism of Selfies," *Social Media + Society* 3, no. 1 (2017): http://journals.sagepub.com/.

32. Turkle, *Alone Together,* 12.

33. Shaka McGlotten, *Virtual Intimacies: Media, Affect, and Queer Sociality* (Albany, N.Y.: SUNY Press, 2013).

34. Catherine Moss, "Teenagers Are Taking Selfies at Funerals—and a New Tumblr Has the Entire Cringeworthy Collection," *Business Insider,* 29 October 2013, http://businessinsider.com/; Dino Grandoni, "Funeral Selfies Are the Latest Evidence Apocalypse Can't Come Soon Enough," *Huffington Post,* 6 December 2017, http://huffingtonpost.com/; Emma Cueto, "Selfies at Funerals Is a Trend Now: Are We Losing Our Humanity?," *Bustle,* 30 October 2013, http://bustle.com/.

35. Casey N. Cep, "In Praise of Selfies," *Pacific Standard,* 14 June 2015, http://psmag.com/; Kandice Rawlings, "Selfies and the History of Self-Portrait Photography," *OUPblog,* 21 November 2013, http://blog.oup.com/; Megan Garber, "The End of the Selfie Hype Cycle," *The Atlantic,* 1 October 2014, http://theatlantic.com/.

36. James Meese et al., "Selfies at Funerals: Mourning and Presencing on Social Media Platforms," *International Journal of Communication* 9 (2015): http://ijoc.org. For a similar approach to mourning on Facebook, see Jed R. Brubaker, Gillian R. Hayes, and Paul Dourish, "Beyond the Grave: Facebook as a Site for the Expansion of Death and Mourning," *The Information Society* 29, no. 3 (2013): 152–63.

37. Levin, "Selfie in the Age of Digital Recursion."

38. Donnachie, "Selfies, #Me," 66.

39. "FAQ," Instagram, accessed 31 March 2016, http://instagram.com/.

40. "FAQ."

41. "Instagram," Google Play.

42. Brooke Erin Duffy, *(Not) Getting Paid to Do What You Love: Gender, Social Media, and Aspirational Work* (New Haven, Conn.: Yale University Press, 2017), 187. See also Sut Jhally and Justin Lewis, "The Struggle for Media Literacy," in *The Spectacle of Accumulation: Essays in Culture, Media, and Politics,* ed. Sut Jhally (New York: Peter Lang, 2006), 225–37; Tobias Olsson, "Active and Calculated Media Use among Young Citizens: Empirical Examples from a Swedish Study," in *Digital Generations: Children, Young People, and New Media,* ed. David Buckingham and Rebekah Willett (Mahwah, N.J.: Lawrence Erlbaum Associates, 2006), 117; Steve Anderson and Anne Balsamo, "A Pedagogy for Original Synners," in *Digital Youth, Innovation, and the Unexpected,* ed. Tara McPherson (Cambridge, Mass.: MIT Press, 2008), 241–59; Sonia Livingstone, "Internet Literacy: Young People's Negotiation of New Online Opportunities," in *Digital Youth, Innovation, and the Unexpected,* ed. Tara McPherson (Cambridge, Mass.: MIT Press, 2008), 101–22; Shirky, *Here Comes Everybody;* Kristen Drotner and Kim Christian Schrøder, *Digital Content Creation: Perceptions, Practices, and Perspectives* (New York: Peter Lang, 2010); Henry Jenkins, Sam Ford, and Joshua Green, *Spreadable Media: Creating Value and Meaning in a Networked Culture* (New York: NYU Press, 2013); and Karine Nahon and Jeff Hemsley, *Going Viral* (Cambridge, UK: Polity, 2013).

43. Fallon, "Streams of the Self."

44. "Instagram," Google Play.

45. Fallon, "Streams of the Self," 59.

46. Levin, "Selfie in the Age of Digital Recursion."

47. Levin.

48. "573: Status Update," *This American Life,* 27 November 2015, http://thisamerican life.org/.

49. Tom Peters, *The Brand You 50 (Reinventing Work): Fifty Ways to Transform Yourself from an "Employee" into a Brand That Shouts Distinction, Commitment, and Passion!* (New York: Knopf Doubleday, 1999); Thomas Gad and Anette Rosencreutz, *Managing Brand Me: How to Build Your Personal Brand* (New York: Momentum Press, 2002); Erik Deckers and Kyle Lacy, *Branding Yourself: How to Use Social Media to Invent or Reinvent Yourself* (New York: Pearson Education, 2011); Robin Landa, *Build Your Own Brand: Strategies, Prompts and Exercises for Marketing Yourself* (Cincinnati: HOW Books, 2013).

50. Alice E. Marwick, *Status Update: Celebrity, Publicity, and Branding in the Social Media Age* (New Haven, Conn.: Yale University Press, 2013), 166.

51. Sarah Banet-Weiser, *Authentic™: The Politics of Ambivalence in a Brand Culture* (New York: NYU Press, 2012), 4.

52. Melissa Aronczyk, *Branding the Nation: The Global Business of National Identity* (New York: Oxford University Press, 2013); Katja Valaskivi, *Cool Nations: Media and the Social Imaginary of the Branded Country* (New York: Routledge, 2016).

53. For Cool Britannia, see Robert Hewison, *Cultural Capital: The Rise and Fall of Creative Britain* (London: Verso Books, 2014); and Jason Arday, *Cool Britannia and Multi-Ethnic Britain: Uncorking the Champagne Supernova* (New York: Routledge, 2019). For Cool Japan, see Mark McLelland, ed., *The End of Cool Japan: Ethical, Legal, and Cultural Challenges to Japanese Popular Culture* (New York: Routledge, 2016); and Jennifer Harris and Tets Kimura, eds., *Exporting Japanese Aesthetics: Evolution from Tradition to Cool Japan* (East Sussex, UK: Sussex Academic Press, 2020).

54. Andrew Wernick, *Promotional Culture: Advertising, Ideology and Symbolic Expression* (London: SAGE Publications, 1991), 181. See also Naomi Klein, *No Logo: Taking Aim at the Brand Bullies* (New York: Picador, 2000); Jonathan E. Schroeder and Miriam Salzer-Mörling, eds., *Brand Culture* (New York: Routledge, 2006); and Melissa

Aronczyk and Devon Powers, eds., *Blowing Up the Brand: Critical Perspectives on Promotional Culture* (New York: Peter Lang, 2010). For the history of branding as a material practice of slavery and marking ownership, see Simone Browne, "B®anding Blackness," in *Dark Matters: On the Surveillance of Blackness* (Durham, N.C.: Duke University Press, 2015), 89–128.

55. Tom Peters, "The Brand Called You," *Fast Company,* August–September 1997, 84.

56. Marwick, *Status Update,* 17.

57. Peters, "Brand Called You," 90.

58. Peters, 84. See Andrew Ross, *Nice Work If You Can Get It: Life and Labor in Precarious Times* (New York: NYU Press, 2009); Pascal Gielen, *Creativity and Other Fundamentalisms,* trans. Leo Reijnen (Heijningen, Netherlands: Jap Sam Books, 2013); Michael Curtin and Kevin Sanson, eds., *Precarious Creativity: Global Media, Local Labor* (Berkeley: University of California Press, 2016); and George Morgan and Pariece Nelligan, *The Creativity Hoax: Precarious Work in the Gig Economy* (New York: Anthem Press, 2018).

59. Lauren Berlant, *Cruel Optimism* (Durham, N.C.: Duke University Press, 2011), 24.

60. Peters, "Brand Called You," 94.

61. Duffy, *(Not) Getting Paid to Do What You Love,* 7, emphasis in original.

62. Duffy, 4–6.

63. Marwick, *Status Update,* 166.

64. Duffy, *(Not) Getting Paid to Do What You Love,* 3.

65. Marwick, *Status Update,* 12.

66. Tiziana Terranova, *Network Culture: Politics for the Information Age* (Ann Arbor: Pluto Press, 2004); José van Dijck and David Nieborg, "Wikinomics and Its Discontents: A Critical Analysis of Web 2.0 Business Manifestos," *New Media & Society* 11, no. 5 (2009): 855–74; Trebor Scholz, ed., *Digital Labor: The Internet as Playground and Factory* (New York: Routledge, 2012); Christian Fuchs et al., eds., *Internet and Surveillance: The Challenges of Web 2.0 and Social Media* (New York: Routledge, 2013). Even when social media work is compensated, as it often is within a business, such work is often feminized and relegated to reduced pay and status. See Brooke Erin Duffy and Becca Schwartz, "Digital 'Women's Work?': Job Recruitment Ads and the Feminization of Social Media Employment," *New Media & Society* 20, no. 8 (2017): 2972–89.

67. Brooke Erin Duffy and Elizabeth Wissinger, "Mythologies of Creative Work in the Social Media Age: Fun, Free, and 'Just Being Me,'" *International Journal of Communication* 11 (2017): 4653. See also Gabriella Lukács, *Invisibility by Design: Women and Labor in Japan's Digital Economy* (Durham, N.C.: Duke University Press, 2020).

68. Marwick, *Status Update,* 194.

69. John Hartley, *Uses of Television* (New York: Routledge, 1999), 178.

70. Sandra Weber and Claudia Mitchell, "Imaging, Keyboarding, and Posting Identities: Young People and New Media Technologies," in *Youth, Identity, and Digital Media,* ed. David Buckingham (Cambridge, Mass.: MIT Press, 2008), 27.

71. Weber and Mitchell, 39.

72. Weber and Mitchell, 39.

73. Weber and Mitchell, 43.

74. Banet-Weiser, *Authentic*^{TM}, 66.

75. Brooke Erin Duffy, "The Romance of Work: Gender and Aspirational Labour in the Digital Culture Industries," *International Journal of Cultural Studies* 19, no. 4 (2016): 451.

76. Anne Burns, "Self(ie)-Discipline: Social Regulation as Enacted through the

Discussion of Photographic Practice," *International Journal of Communication* 9 (2015): http://ijoc.org/; Son Vivienne, "'I Will Not Hate Myself Because You Cannot Accept Me': Problematizing Empowerment and Gender-Diverse Selfies," *Popular Communication* 15, no. 2 (2017): 126–40.

77. Janice A. Radway, "Girls, Reading, and Narrative Gleaning: Crafting Repertoires for Self-Fashioning within Everyday Life," in *Narrative Impact: Social and Cognitive Foundations,* ed. Melanie C. Green, Jeffrey J. Strange, and Timothy C. Brock (Mahwah, N.J.: Lawrence Erlbaum Associates, 2002), 185.

78. Larson, "Secrets in the Bedroom"; Jane D. Brown, Jeanne R. Steele, and Kim Walsh-Childers, eds., *Sexual Teens, Sexual Media: Investigating Media's Influence on Adolescent Sexuality* (Mahwah, N.J.: Lawrence Erlbaum Associates, 2001); Ashley D. Grisso and David Weiss, "What Are gURLS Talking About? Adolescent Girls' Construction of Sexual Identity on gURL.com," in *Girl Wide Web: Girls, the Internet, and the Negotiation of Identity,* ed. Sharon R. Mazzarella (New York: Peter Lang, 2005), 31–49; Cassell and Cramer, "High Tech or High Risk"; Stern, *Instant Identity;* Amy Adele Hasinoff, *Sexting Panic: Rethinking Criminalization, Privacy, and Consent* (Urbana: University of Illinois Press, 2015); Jessalynn Keller et al., "Mapping New Methodological Approaches to Girls' Media Studies: Reflections from the Field," *Journal of Children and Media* 7, no. 4 (2015): 528–35; Ashleigh Wade, "When Social Media Yields More Than 'Likes': Black Girls' Digital Kinship Formations," *Women, Gender, and Families of Color* 7, no. 1 (2019): 80–97.

79. Mary Celeste Kearney, *Girls Make Media* (New York: Routledge, 2006), 3; Alison Piepmeier, *Girl Zines: Making Media, Doing Feminism* (New York: NYU Press, 2009), 2.

80. Michele White, *The Body and the Screen: Theories of Internet Spectatorship* (Cambridge, Mass.: MIT Press, 2006).

81. Lisa Nakamura, *Digitizing Race: Visual Cultures of the Internet* (Minneapolis: University of Minnesota Press, 2008), 5. See also Lisa Nakamura and Peter A. Chow-White, eds., *Race after the Internet* (New York: Routledge, 2012).

82. Apryl A. Williams and Beatriz Aldana Marquez, "The Lonely Selfie King: Selfies and the Conspicuous Prosumption of Gender and Race," *International Journal of Communication* 9 (2015): 1781.

83. Williams and Marquez, 1781.

84. Minh-Ha T. Pham, *Asians Wear Clothes on the Internet: Race, Gender, and the Work of Personal Style Blogging* (Durham, N.C.: Duke University Press, 2015), 10–11.

85. Pham, 83.

86. For the gendered and racialized labor of negotiating beauty standards, see Ana Sofia Elias, Rosalind Gill, and Christina Scharff, eds., *Aesthetic Labour: Rethinking Beauty Politics in Neoliberalism* (London: Palgrave Macmillan, 2017).

87. Tarleton Gillespie, *Custodians of the Internet: Platforms, Content Moderation, and the Hidden Decisions That Shape Social Media* (New Haven, Conn.: Yale University Press, 2018), 209. See also Sarah T. Roberts, *Behind the Screen: Content Moderation in the Shadows of Social Media* (New Haven, Conn.: Yale University Press, 2019).

88. Gillespie, *Custodians of the Internet,* 5.

89. Katie Dupere, "#Curvy Forced Instagram to Rethink How It Polices Hashtags," *Mashable,* 24 July 2015, http://mashable.com/. For body positivity and Instagram, see Sofia P. Caldeira and Sander De Ridder, "Representing Diverse Femininities on Instagram: A Case Study of the Body-Positive @Effyourbeautystandards Instagram Account," *Catalan Journal of Communication & Cultural Studies* 9, no. 2 (2017): 321–37.

90. Lynn Schofield Clark, "Dating on the Net: Teens and the Rise of 'Pure' Relationships," in *Cybersociety 2.0: Revisiting Computer-Mediated Communication and Commu-*

nity, ed. Steven G. Jones (Thousand Oaks, Calif.: SAGE Publications, 1998); Susanna Stern, "Sexual Selves on the World Wide Web: Adolescent Girls' Home Pages as Sites for Sexual Self-Expression," in *Sexual Teens, Sexual Media: Investigating Media's Influence on Adolescent Sexuality,* ed. Jane D. Brown, Jeanne R. Steele, and Kim Walsh-Childers (Mahwah, N.J.: Lawrence Erlbaum Associates, 2001); Stern, *Instant Identity.*

91. The Chainsmokers, "#Selfie (Official Music Video)—the Chainsmokers," YouTube, uploaded 29 January 2014, http://www.youtube.com/.

92. Jefferson Pooley, "The Consuming Self: From Flappers to Facebook," in *Blowing Up the Brand: Critical Perspectives on Promotional Culture,* ed. Melissa Aronczyk and Devon Powers (New York: Peter Lang, 2010), 82; Marwick, *Status Update,* 167.

93. Marwick, *Status Update,* 250–51. For authenticity and self-presentation, see Erving Goffman, *The Presentation of Self in Everyday Life* (New York: Doubleday, 1959); Lionel Trilling, *Sincerity and Authenticity* (Cambridge, Mass.: Harvard University Press, 1972); and Howard Pickett, *Rethinking Sincerity and Authenticity: The Ethics of Theatricality in Kant, Kierkegaard, and Levinas* (Charlottesville: University of Virginia Press, 2017).

94. Banet-Weiser, *Authentic^{TM},* 61.

95. Duffy, "Romance of Work," 448–49.

96. Turkle, *Alone Together,* 12.

97. Katharina Lobinger and Cornelia Brantner, "In the Eye of the Beholder: Subjective Views on the Authenticity of Selfies," *International Journal of Communication* 9 (2015): 1850.

98. Marcus Banks, "True to Life: Authenticity and the Photographic Image," in *Debating Authenticity: Concepts of Modernity in Anthropological Perspective,* ed. Thomas Fillitz and A. Jamie Saris (New York: Berghahn Books, 2012), 161. Lorraine Daston and Peter Galison's concept of mechanical objectivity similarly identifies the emergence of photographic technologies alongside expectations of direct correspondence in representing reality. See Lorraine Daston and Peter Galison, "Mechanical Objectivity," in *Objectivity* (Brooklyn: Zone Books, 2007), 115–90.

99. Fallon, "Streams of the Self"; Levin, "Selfie in the Age of Digital Recursion"; Aaron Hess, "The Selfie Assemblage," *International Journal of Communication* 9 (2015): http://ijoc.org/.

100. Burns, "Self(ie)-Discipline."

101. Katrin Tiidenberg, "Boundaries and Conflict in a NSFW Community on Tumblr: The Meanings and Uses of Selfies," *New Media & Society* 18, no. 8 (2016): 1563–78.

102. Hess, "Selfie Assemblage."

103. Ana Elias, Rosalind Gill, and Christina Scharff, "Aesthetic Labour: Beauty Politics in Neoliberalism," in *Aesthetic Labour: Rethinking Beauty Politics in Neoliberalism,* ed. Ana Sofia Elias, Rosalind Gill, and Christina Scharff (London: Palgrave Macmillan, 2017), 3–49.

104. Thomas Gorton, "An Instagram Model Is Calling Bullshit on Her Fake Reality," *Dazed,* 3 November 2015, http://dazeddigital.com/; Elle Hunt, "Essena O'Neill Quits Instagram Claiming Social Media 'Is Not Real Life,'" *The Guardian,* 3 November 2015, http://theguardian.com/; Ella Ceron, "The Model Who Quit Social Media Reveals How Much Makeup Was behind Her Perfect Selfies," *Teen Vogue,* 20 November 2015, http://teenvogue.com/. O'Neill would subsequently delete this content entirely from her Instagram account.

105. Sherry Turkle, *Life on the Screen: Identity in the Age of the Internet* (New York: Simon & Schuster, 1995), 229.

106. Natalie Beach, "I Was Caroline Calloway," *The Cut*, 10 September 2019, http://thecut.com/.

107. Stephanie McNeal, "Caroline Calloway Says She Is Releasing a Book Called 'Scammer,'" *BuzzFeed News*, 15 January 2020, http://buzzfeednews.com/.

108. Lauren Rosewarne, *Cyberbullies, Cyberactivists, Cyberpredators: Film, TV, and Internet Stereotypes* (Santa Barbara, Calif.: Praeger, 2016), 201.

109. Leslie Rasmussen, "*Catfished*: Exploring Viewer Perceptions of Online Relationships," in *Reality Television: Oddities of Culture*, ed. Alison F. Slade, Amber J. Narro, and Burton P. Buchanan (New York: Lexington Books, 2014), 237–48.

110. Carolyn Marvin, *When Old Technologies Were New: Thinking About Electric Communication in the Late Nineteenth Century* (New York: Oxford University Press, 1990), 34–35.

111. Rosewarne, *Cyberbullies, Cyberactivists, Cyberpredators*, 90.

112. Rosewarne, 106. See also Qing Li, Donna Cross, and Peter K. Smith, eds., *Cyberbullying in the Global Playground: Research from International Perspectives* (Malden, Mass.: Wiley-Blackwell, 2012); Bailey Poland, *Haters: Harassment, Abuse, and Violence Online* (Lincoln, Neb.: Potomac Books, 2016); Anastasia Salter and Bridget Blodgett, *Toxic Geek Masculinity in Media: Sexism, Trolling, and Identity Policing* (New York: Palgrave Macmillan, 2017); Megan Condis, *Gaming Masculinity: Trolls, Fake Geeks, and the Gendered Battle for Online Culture* (Iowa City: University of Iowa Press, 2018); and Jacqueline Ryan Vickery and Tracy Everbach, eds., *Mediating Misogyny: Gender, Technology, and Harassment* (Cham, Switzerland: Palgrave Macmillan, 2018).

113. Oliver L. Haimson and Anna Lauren Hoffmann, "Constructing and Enforcing 'Authentic' Identity Online: Facebook, Real Names, and Non-Normative Identities," *First Monday* 21, no. 6 (2016): http://firstmonday.org/; Maggie MacAulay and Marcos Daniel Moldes, "Queen Don't Compute: Reading and Casting Shade on Facebook's Real Names Policy," in *Queer Technologies: Affordances, Affect, Ambivalence*, ed. Katherine Sender and Adrienne Shaw (New York: Routledge, 2016), 6–22.

114. Tobias Raun and Cáel M. Keegan, "Nothing to Hide: Selfies, Sex, and the Visibility Dilemma in Trans Male Online Cultures," in *Sex in the Digital Age* (New York: Routledge, 2018), 89–100.

115. Christopher E. M. Lloyd and Mark D. Finn, "Authenticity, Validation and Sexualisation on Grindr: An Analysis of Trans Women's Accounts," *Psychology & Sexuality* 8, nos. 1–2 (2017): 158–69.

116. Hess, "Selfie Assemblage," 1635.

117. Hess, 1635.

118. Lobinger and Brantner, "In the Eye of the Beholder."

119. Donnachie, "Selfies, #Me," 71.

120. Fallon, "Streams of the Self."

121. Jin Kang and Lewen Wei, "Let Me Be at My Funniest: Instagram Users' Motivations for Using Finsta (a.k.a., Fake Instagram)," *Social Science Journal* 57, no. 1 (2020): 58–71; Sijia Xiao et al., "Random, Messy, Funny, Raw: Finstas as Intimate Reconfigurations of Social Media," in *Proceedings of the 2020 CHI Conference on Human Factors in Computing Systems* (Honolulu: Association for Computing Machinery, 2020), 1–13.

122. Sofia Dewar et al., "Finsta: Creating 'Fake' Spaces for Authentic Performance," in *Extended Abstracts of the 2019 CHI Conference on Human Factors in Computing Systems* (Glasgow: Association for Computing Machinery, 2019), 1–6.

123. Kaya Yurieff, "Instagram Star Isn't What She Seems: But Brands Are Buying In," *CNN*, 25 June 2018, http://cnn.com/.

4. Design Fiction and the Imagination of Technological Futures

1. "Creative Science Foundation—CSF—a Partnership with You to Invent the Future," Creative Science Foundation, accessed 7 August 2020, http://creative-science.org/, emphasis in original.

2. "A Brief History of CSF—Creative Science Foundation," Creative Science Foundation, accessed 7 August 2020, http://creative-science.org/; "Meetings—Creative Science Foundation," Creative Science Foundation, accessed 7 August 2020, http://creative-science.org/.

3. "Brief History of CSF"; "The Foundation—Creative Science Foundation," Creative Science Foundation, accessed 7 August 2020, http://creative-science.org/.

4. "New Creatives—Creative Science Foundation," Creative Science Foundation, accessed 7 August 2020, http://creative-science.org/.

5. "Foundation."

6. "New Creatives."

7. "Creative Science Foundation."

8. Bruce Sterling, "Imaginary Gadgets 0004: Design Fiction," *Wired*, 23 May 2009, http://www.wired.com/.

9. Anthony Dunne, *Hertzian Tales: Electronic Products, Aesthetic Experience, and Critical Design* (Cambridge, Mass.: MIT Press, 2008), xvii.

10. Throughout the chapter, I primarily focus on several related speculative technological design practices with particular focus on design fiction as a prominent example.

11. Futures studies is also known as "futurism" or "futurology."

12. Lawrence R. Samuel, *Future: A Recent History* (Austin: University of Texas Press, 2009), 1.

13. Brian David Johnson and Sandy Winkelman, *21st Century Robot* (Sebastopol, Calif.: Maker Media Inc., 2014), 229.

14. Samuel, *Future*.

15. Edward Cornish and Members and Staff of the World Future Society, *The Study of the Future: An Introduction to the Art and Science of Understanding and Shaping Tomorrow's World* (Washington, D.C.: World Future Society, 1977), 80.

16. Cornish, 90–91.

17. Wendell Bell, *Foundations of Futures Studies, Volume 1: History, Purposes, and Knowledge*, revised ed. (New Brunswick, N.J.: Transaction Publishers, 2003), 154. See also Roy Amara, "The Futures Field: Searching for Definitions and Boundaries," *The Futurist* 15, no. 1 (1981): 25.

18. Cornish, *Study of the Future*, 51.

19. Edward Cornish, *Futuring: The Exploration of the Future* (Bethesda, Md.: World Future Society, 2004), 215.

20. Wendy Brown, "Neoliberalism and the End of Liberal Democracy," in *Edgework: Critical Essays on Knowledge and Politics* (Princeton, N.J.: Princeton University Press, 2009), 42; Sarah Brouillette, *Literature and the Creative Economy* (Stanford, Calif.: Stanford University Press, 2014), 38.

21. For traditional histories of design beginning with William Morris, see George H. Marcus, *Masters of Modern Design: A Critical Assessment* (New York: Monacelli Press, 2005); Nicholas Pevsner, *Pioneers of Modern Design: From William Morris to Walter Gropius*, revised and expanded ed. (New Haven, Conn.: Yale University Press, 2005); and Stephen Eisenman et al., *Design in the Age of Darwin: From William Morris to Frank Lloyd Wright* (Evanston, Ill.: Northwestern University Press, 2008).

22. Kjetil Fallan, *Design History: Understanding Theory and Method* (New York: Berg, 2010), x.

23. Daniela K. Rosner, *Critical Fabulations: Reworking the Methods and Margins of Design* (Cambridge, Mass.: MIT Press, 2018), 24. See also Lilly Irani, "'Design Thinking': Defending Silicon Valley at the Apex of Global Labor Hierarchies," *Catalyst: Feminism, Theory, Technoscience* 4, no. 1 (2018): http://catalystjournal.org/.

24. For design history, see Clive Dilnot, "The State of Design History, Part I: Mapping the Field," *Design Issues* 1, no. 1 (1984): 4–23; Clive Dilnot, "The State of Design History, Part II: Problems and Possibilities," *Design Issues* 1, no. 2 (1984): 3–20; Adrian Forty, *Objects of Desire* (New York: Pantheon Books, 1986); John A. Walker and Judy Attfield, *Design History and the History of Design* (London: Pluto Press, 1989); David Irwin, "Art Versus Design: The Debate, 1760–1860," *Journal of Design History* 4, no. 4 (1991): 219–32; Richard Buchanan, Dennis Doordan, and Victor Margolin, "Introduction: Telling the History of Design," *Design Issues* 11, no. 1 (1995): 1–3; and Guy Julier, "From Visual Culture to Design Culture," *Design Issues* 22, no. 1 (2006): 64–76; and Fallan, *Design History*.

25. Fallan, *Design History*, 49. See also Arturo Escobar, *Designs for the Pluriverse: Radical Interdependence, Autonomy, and the Making of Worlds* (Durham, N.C.: Duke University Press, 2018).

26. Guy Julier, *The Culture of Design*, 2nd ed. (London: SAGE Publications, 2008), 22.

27. Guy Julier, *Economies of Design* (Los Angeles: SAGE Publications, 2017), 52.

28. Julier, 3.

29. Julier, *Culture of Design*, 4.

30. Herbet A. Simon, *The Sciences of the Artificial* (Cambridge, Mass.: MIT Press, 1969), 55.

31. Gerald Nadler, "A Timeline Theory of Planning and Design," *Design Studies* 1, no. 5 (1980): 299–307; Ezio Manzini, "Prometheus of the Everyday: The Ecology of the Artificial and the Designer's Responsibility," *Design Issues* 9, no. 1 (1992): 5–20; Victor Margolin, "Design, the Future and the Human Spirit," *Design Issues* 23, no. 3 (2007): 4–15; Tony Fry, *Design Futuring: Sustainability, Ethics and New Practice* (New York: Berg Publishers, 2008).

32. Stuart Reeves, Murray Goulden, and Robert Dingwall, "The Future as a Design Problem," *Design Issues* 32, no. 3 (2016): 6.

33. Margolin, "Design, the Future and the Human Spirit," 4.

34. Anne Balsamo, *Designing Culture: The Technological Imagination at Work* (Durham, N.C.: Duke University Press, 2011), 49.

35. Tony Fry, *A New Design Philosophy: An Introduction to Defuturing* (Sydney: University of New South Wales Press, 1999), xi.

36. Christina Cogdell, *Eugenic Design: Streamlining America in the 1930s* (Philadelphia: University of Pennsylvania Press, 2010), 4.

37. Cogdell, 5.

38. Aimi Hamraie, *Building Access: Universal Design and the Politics of Disability* (Minneapolis: University of Minnesota Press, 2017), 6.

39. Hamraie, 5. See also Sasha Costanza-Chock, *Design Justice: Community-Led Practices to Build the Worlds We Need* (Cambridge, Mass.: MIT Press, 2020).

40. Samuel, *Future*, 185.

41. Torie Bosch, "Sci-Fi Writer Bruce Sterling Explains the Intriguing New Concept of Design Fiction," *Slate*, 2 March 2012, http://slate.com/.

42. Thomas F. Gieryn, *Cultural Boundaries of Science: Credibility on the Line* (Chicago: University of Chicago Press, 1999), 22.

43. Gieryn, 1.

44. Cornish, *Study of the Future*, 51.

45. Bell, *Foundations of Futures Studies*, 188.

46. Bell, 188.

47. C. P. Snow, *The Two Cultures* (New York: Cambridge University Press, 1993). For responses seeking to elaborate on or dismiss Snow, see Frank Raymond Leavis, *Two Cultures? The Significance of C. P. Snow* (New York: Cambridge University Press, 2013); E. O. Wilson, *Consilience: The Unity of Knowledge* (New York: Knopf Doubleday, 1999); and Stephen Jay Gould, *The Hedgehog, the Fox, and the Magister's Pox: Mending the Gap between Science and the Humanities* (New York: Three Rivers Press, 2003).

48. David A. Roos, "Matthew Arnold and Thomas Henry Huxley: Two Speeches at the Royal Academy, 1881 and 1883," *Modern Philology* 74, no. 3 (1977): 316–24.

49. Bruce Archer, "The Three Rs," *Design Studies* 1, no. 1 (1979): 18. See also Simon, *Sciences of the Artificial;* and Nigel Cross, "Designerly Ways of Knowing," *Design Studies* 3, no. 4 (1982): 221–27.

50. Archer, "Three Rs," 20.

51. Archer, 20.

52. For critique of an "ideology of need" in design, see Tony Fry, "Against an Essential Theory of 'Need': Some Considerations for Design Theory," *Design Issues* 8, no. 2 (1992): 41–53.

53. "Creative Science Foundation."

54. For science fiction, see Darko Suvin, *Metamorphoses of Science Fiction: On the Poetics of a Literary Genre* (New Haven, Conn.: Yale University Press, 1979); Marleen S. Barr, *Lost in Space: Probing Feminist Science Fiction and Beyond* (Chapel Hill: University of North Carolina Press, 1993); Camille Bacon-Smith, *Science Fiction Culture* (Philadelphia: University of Pennsylvania Press, 2000); Alan Sandison and Robert Dingley, *Histories of the Future: Studies in Fact, Fantasy and Science Fiction* (New York: Palgrave, 2000); Eugene Thacker, "The Science Fiction of Technoscience: The Politics of Simulation and a Challenge for New Media Art," *Leonardo* 34, no. 2 (2001): 155–58; Fredric Jameson, *Archaeologies of the Future: The Desire Called Utopia and Other Science Fictions* (New York: Verso, 2005); Istvan Csicsery-Ronay Jr., *The Seven Beauties of Science Fiction* (Middletown, Conn.: Wesleyan University Press, 2008); Seo-Young Chu, *Do Metaphors Dream of Literal Sleep? A Science-Fictional Theory of Representation* (Cambridge, Mass.: Harvard University Press, 2010); Patricia Melzer, *Alien Constructions: Science Fiction and Feminist Thought* (Austin: University of Texas Press, 2010); Raymond Williams, *Tenses of Imagination: Raymond Williams on Science Fiction, Utopia and Dystopia* (New York: Peter Lang, 2010); andré m. carrington, *Speculative Blackness: The Future of Race in Science Fiction* (Minneapolis: University of Minnesota Press, 2016); and Sami Schalk, *Bodyminds Reimagined: (Dis)ability, Race, and Gender in Black Women's Speculative Fiction* (Durham, N.C.: Duke University Press, 2018).

55. Bell, *Foundations of Futures Studies*, 317. See also Cornish, *Study of the Future*, 111; and Daniel Pargman et al., "The (Un)sustainability of Imagined Future Information Societies," in *CHI '17: Proceedings of the 2017 SIGCHI Conference on Human Factors in Computing Systems: Explore, Innovate, Inspire* (Denver: Association for Computing Machinery, 2017), 774.

56. Cornish, *Study of the Future*, 112.

57. Herman Kahn, *Thinking about the Unthinkable: Scenarios and Metaphors* (New York: Horizon, 1962), 143.

58. Kahn, 145.

59. Kahn, 174.

60. Wendell Bell and Jeffrey K. Olick, "An Epistemology for the Futures Field: Problems and Possibilities of Prediction," *Futures* 21, no. 2 (1989): 115–35.

61. Alvin Toffler, *Future Shock* (New York: Bantam Books, 1970). Marking the fiftieth anniversary of *Future Shock*'s publication, *After Shock* was published in 2020 and includes contemporary futurists reflecting on developments since Toffler's influential work as well as looking into the future. See John Schroeter, ed., *After Shock: The World's Foremost Futurists Reflect on 50 Years of "Future Shock"—and Look Ahead to the Next 50* (Bainbridge Island, Wash.: John August Media LLC, 2020).

62. Charles Eames, "Architecture 1 and 2, University of California, Berkeley," in *An Eames Anthology: Articles, Film Scripts, Interviews, Letters, Notes, Speeches*, ed. Daniel Ostroff (New Haven, CT: Yale University Press, 2015), 125. See also Nathan Shedroff and Chris Noessel, "Make It So: Learning from Sci-Fi Interfaces," in *Proceedings of the International Working Conference on Advanced Visual Interfaces* (Capri Island, Italy: Association for Computing Machinery, 2012), 7–8.

63. Balsamo, *Designing Culture*, 52.

64. Wolfgang Jonas, "A Scenario for Design," *Design Issues* 17, no. 2 (2001): 64–80.

65. Bruce Sterling, *Shaping Things* (Cambridge, Mass.: MIT Press, 2005), 30.

66. Bosch, "Sci-Fi Writer Bruce Sterling."

67. Julian Bleecker, "Design Fiction: A Short Essay on Design, Science, Fact and Fiction" (Near Future Laboratory, 2009), 8.

68. Bleecker, 6.

69. Johnson and Winkelman, *21st Century Robot*. See also Brian David Johnson, *Science Fiction Prototyping: Designing the Future with Science Fiction* (San Rafael, Calif.: Morgan & Claypool, 2011).

70. Balsamo, *Designing Culture*, 51.

71. Anthony Dunne and Fiona Raby, *Speculative Everything: Design, Fiction, and Social Dreaming* (Cambridge, Mass.: MIT Press, 2013), 70.

72. Cornish, *Futuring*, 93.

73. Sterling, *Shaping Things*, 34.

74. Kahn, *Thinking about the Unthinkable*, 145.

75. Brian Sutton-Smith, *The Ambiguity of Play* (Cambridge, Mass.: Harvard University Press, 1997), 151.

76. Robin Bernstein, *Racial Innocence: Performing American Childhood and Race from Slavery to Civil Rights* (New York: NYU Press, 2011), 4.

77. Hannah Dyer, *The Queer Aesthetics of Childhood: Asymmetries of Innocence and the Cultural Politics of Child Development* (New Brunswick, N.J.: Rutgers University Press, 2019), 4.

78. Teresa Michals, "Experiments before Breakfast: Toys, Education and Middle-Class Childhood," in *The Nineteenth-Century Child and Consumer Culture*, ed. Dennis Denisoff (Aldershot, UK: Ashgate, 2008), 36.

79. Maria Edgeworth and Richard Lovell Edgeworth, *Practical Education* (New York: Garland Publishing, 1974), 604.

80. Edgeworth and Edgeworth, 643–44.

81. Edgeworth and Edgeworth, 641–42.

82. Edgeworth and Edgeworth, 643.

83. Michals, "Experiments before Breakfast," 36.

84. Sutton-Smith, *Ambiguity of Play*, 129.

85. William Wordsworth, *The Collected Poems of William Wordsworth*, revised ed. (London: Wordsworth Editions, 1994), 91.

86. Wordsworth, 701.

87. Sally Shuttleworth, *The Mind of the Child: Child Development in Literature, Science, and Medicine, 1840–1900* (Oxford: Oxford University Press, 2010), 74.

88. Harriet Martineau, *Household Education* (London: Edward Moxon, 1849), 247, 29.

89. Martineau, 163.

90. Gary Cross, *The Cute and the Cool: Wondrous Innocence and Modern American Children's Culture* (New York: Oxford University Press, 2004), 37.

91. Gary Cross, *Kids' Stuff: Toys and the Changing World of American Childhood* (Cambridge, Mass.: Harvard University Press, 2009), 9.

92. Cross, *The Cute and the Cool*, 17. For youth, rebellion, and style, see Dick Hebdige, *Subculture: The Meaning of Style* (New York: Routledge, 1979).

93. Cross, *The Cute and the Cool*, 139.

94. Nicola Nixon, "Cyberpunk: Preparing the Ground for Revolution or Keeping the Boys Satisfied?," *Science Fiction Studies* 19, no. 2 (1992): 219–35; Jane Donawerth, *Frankenstein's Daughters: Women Writing Science Fiction* (Syracuse, N.Y.: Syracuse University Press, 1997); Bacon-Smith, *Science Fiction Culture;* Justine Larbalestier, *The Battle of the Sexes in Science Fiction* (Middletown, Conn.: Wesleyan University Press, 2002); Helen Merrick, *The Secret Feminist Cabal: A Cultural History of Science Fiction Feminisms* (Seattle: Aqueduct Press, 2009); Jordan S. Carroll, "Reading *Playboy* for the Science Fiction," *American Literature* 87, no. 2 (2015): 331–58.

95. Balsamo, *Designing Culture*, 31–32. See also Ruth Oldenziel, *Making Technology Masculine: Men, Women and Modern Machines in America, 1870–1945* (Amsterdam: Amsterdam University Press, 1999).

96. Barr, *Lost in Space;* Melzer, *Alien Constructions.*

97. Alondra Nelson, ed., *Afrofuturism: A Special Issue of Social Text* (Durham, N.C.: Duke University Press, 2002); Isiah Lavender III, ed., *Black and Brown Planets: The Politics of Race in Science Fiction* (Jackson: University Press of Mississippi, 2014); carrington, *Speculative Blackness;* Schalk, *Bodyminds Reimagined.* For Blackness and contemporary technological usage, see André Brock Jr., *Distributed Blackness: African American Cybercultures* (New York: NYU Press, 2020); and Kishonna L. Gray, *Intersectional Tech: Black Users in Gaming* (Baton Rouge: Louisiana State University Press, 2020).

98. Amy F. Ogata, *Designing the Creative Child: Playthings and Places in Midcentury America* (Minneapolis: University of Minnesota Press, 2013), xix.

99. Ogata, 25.

100. Steve Mannheim, *Walt Disney and the Quest for Community* (New York: Routledge, 2016).

101. Mannheim, 46.

102. Johnson and Winkelman, *21st Century Robot*, xii.

103. David Kirby, "The Future Is Now: Diegetic Prototypes and the Role of Popular Films in Generating Real-World Technological Development," *Social Studies of Science* 40, no. 1 (2010): 41–70.

104. David A. Kirby, *Lab Coats in Hollywood: Science, Scientists, and Cinema* (Cambridge, Mass.: MIT Press, 2011), 195.

105. Bleecker, *Design Fiction*, 35.

106. Bleecker, 41.

107. Kirby, *Lab Coats in Hollywood*, 199–200.

108. For discursive dimensions of invention, see Carolyn Marvin, *When Old Technologies Were New: Thinking about Electric Communication in the Late Nineteenth Century* (New York: Oxford University Press, 1990); Bruno Latour, *Aramis or the Love of Technology,* trans. Catherine Porter (Cambridge, Mass.: Harvard University Press,

1996); Erkki Huhtamo, "From Kaleidoscomaniac to Cybernerd: Notes toward an Archaeology of the Media," *Leonardo* 30, no. 3 (1997): 221–24; Lisa Gitelman, *Scripts, Grooves, and Writing Machines: Representing Technology in the Edison Era* (Stanford, Calif.: Stanford University Press, 1999); Alain Pottage and Brad Sherman, *Figures of Invention: A History of Modern Patent Law* (New York: Oxford University Press, 2010); and Ghislain Thibault, "The Automatization of Nikola Tesla: Thinking Invention in the Late Nineteenth Century," *Configurations* 21, no. 1 (2013): 26–52.

109. Sterling, *Shaping Things*, 29. For gadgets and gadgetry, see Jean Baudrillard, *The System of Objects*, trans. James Benedict (New York: Verso, 2005); Michael Simeone, "Why We Will Not Be Posthuman: Gadgets as a Technocultural Form," *Configurations* 19, no. 3 (2011): 336–56; William Merrin, "The Rise of the Gadget and Hyperludic Media," *Cultural Politics* 10, no. 1 (2014): 1–20; and Jean Baudrillard, *The Consumer Society: Myths and Structures*, trans. Chris Turner, revised ed. (Los Angeles: SAGE Publications, 2016).

110. Sterling, "Imaginary Gadgets 0004."

111. Sterling.

112. Bleecker, *Design Fiction*, 7.

113. Suvin, *Metamorphoses of Science Fiction*, 63.

114. Thacker, "Science Fiction of Technoscience," 158.

115. Thacker, 158.

116. Anthony Dunne and Fiona Raby, *Design Noir: The Secret Life of Electronic Objects* (London: August, 2001), 58.

117. Dunne and Raby, 58. The dominant historical narrative of critical design favors a practice developing out of human-computer interaction design intervention that typically begins with Dunne and Raby at the Royal College of Art in the late 1990s. For histories complicating this narrative of critical design, see Cilla Robach, "Critical Design: Forgotten History or Paradigm Shift," in *Shift: Design as Usual—or a New Rising?*, ed. Monika Sarstad and Helen Emanuelsson (Stockholm: Arvinius, 2005), 30–41; and Rosner, *Critical Fabulations*. For the meaning of "critical" in critical design, see Jeffrey Bardzell and Shaowen Bardzell, "What Is Critical about Critical Design?," in *CHI '13: Proceedings of the SIGCHI Conference on Human Factors in Computing Systems* (Paris: Association for Computing Machinery, 2013), 3297–3306.

118. There are other critical design frameworks centered on fabricating fictional objects, such as alternatives design, speculative design, counterfunctional design, material speculation, and discursive design. See James Auger, "Speculative Design: Crafting the Speculation," *Digital Creativity* 24, no. 1 (2013): 11–35; James Pierce and Eric Paulos, "Counterfunctional Things: Exploring Possibilities in Designing Digital Limitations," in *DIS 2014: Proceedings of the 2014 Conference on Designing Interactive Systems* (Vancouver: Association for Computing Machinery, 2014), 375–84; Ron Wakkary et al., "Material Speculation: Actual Artifacts for Critical Inquiry," in *Proceedings of The Fifth Decennial Aarhus Conference on Critical Alternatives* (Aarhus, Denmark: Aarhus University Press, 2015), 97–108; Bill Gaver and Heather Martin, "Alternatives: Exploring Information Appliances through Conceptual Design Proposals," in *CHI '00: Proceedings of the SIGCHI Conference on Human Factors in Computing Systems* (The Hague: Association for Computing Machinery, 2000): 209–16; and Bruce M. Tharp and Stephanie M. Tharp, *Discursive Design: Critical, Speculative, and Alternative Things* (Cambridge, Mass.: MIT Press, 2019).

119. Rosner, *Critical Fabulations*, 17.

120. Kirby, "Future Is Now," 46.

121. Kirby, 46.

122. Julian Bleecker, "Design Fiction + Advanced Designing + Trust in Volume Quarterly," *Near Future Laboratory,* 22 December 2010, http://nearfuturelaboratory.com/.

123. Bleecker.

124. Bleecker.

125. For examples of human–computer interaction and user interface designers pursuing the gestural interface popularized in *Minority Report* or, at least, referencing *Minority Report* to describe gestural and touchless interfaces without mention of the dystopian elements of the film, see Andrew D. Wilson, "TouchLight: An Imaging Touch Screen and Display for Gesture-Based Interaction," in *Proceedings of the 6th International Conference on Multimodal Interfaces* (State College, Penn.: Association for Computing Machinery, 2004), 69–79; Eric Lee, Marius Wolf, and Jan Borchers, "Improving Orchestral Conducting Systems in Public Spaces: Examining the Temporal Characteristics and Conceptual Models of Conducting Gestures," in *Proceedings of the SIGCHI Conference on Human Factors in Computing Systems* (Portland, Ore.: Association for Computing Machinery, 2005): 731–40; Nicolas Villar et al., "The ColorDex DJ System: A New Interface for Live Music Mixing," in *Proceedings of the 7th International Conference on New Interfaces for Musical Expression* (New York: Association for Computing Machinery, 2007), 264–69; Ismo Rakkolainen, "Mid-Air Displays Enabling Novel User Interfaces," in *Proceedings of the 1st ACM International Workshop on Semantic Ambient Media Experiences* (Vancouver: Association for Computing Machinery, 2008), 25–30; and Jiaqing Lin et al., "Free Hand Interface for Controlling Applications Based on Wii Remote IR Sensor," in *Proceedings of the 9th ACM SIGGRAPH Conference on Virtual-Reality Continuum and Its Applications in Industry* (Seoul: Association for Computing Machinery, 2010), 139–42.

126. Lisa Nakamura, *Digitizing Race: Visual Cultures of the Internet* (Minneapolis: University of Minnesota Press, 2008); Simone Browne, *Dark Matters: On the Surveillance of Blackness* (Durham, N.C.: Duke University Press, 2015); Ruha Benjamin, ed., *Captivating Technology: Race, Carceral Technoscience, and Liberatory Imagination in Everyday Life* (Durham, N.C.: Duke University Press, 2019); Ruha Benjamin, *Race after Technology: Abolitionist Tools for the New Jim Code* (Medford, Mass.: Polity, 2019).

127. Similarly, the Technovelgy website catalogs commercial products that appear to be realizations of technologies described in science fiction novels, films, and other media, many of them dystopian or apocalyptic. While Technovelgy attempts to make links, those recorded are not necessarily claims for causality, influence, or inspiration. See Bill Christensen, "Timeline of Science Fiction Ideas, Technology and Inventions," Technovelgy: Where Science Meets Fiction, accessed 7 August 2020, http://technovelgy.com/.

128. Rodrigo Freese Gonzatto et al., "The Ideology of the Future in Design Fictions," *Digital Creativity* 24, no. 1 (2013): 36.

129. Matt Malpass, *Critical Design in Context: History, Theory, and Practices* (London: Bloomsbury, 2017), 108.

130. Bleecker, *Design Fiction,* 7.

131. Bleecker, 7.

132. "Centre of Talented Youth of Ireland Summer School—Creative Science Foundation," Creative Science Foundation, accessed 7 August 2020, http://creative-science.org/.

133. "Centre of Talented Youth of Ireland Summer School."

134. "Centre of Talented Youth of Ireland Summer School."

135. My conception of extracting youth is inspired by Rob Latham's articulation of consuming youth. See Rob Latham, *Consuming Youth: Vampires, Cyborgs, and the Culture of Consumption* (Chicago: University of Chicago Press, 2007).

136. Wilma King, *Stolen Childhood: Slave Youth in Nineteenth-Century America* (Bloomington: Indiana University Press, 1995); Bernstein, *Racial Innocence;* Sarah E. Chinn, "Enslavement and the Temporality of Childhood," *American Literature* 92, no. 1 (2020): 33–59.

137. Jacob Breslow, "Adolescent Citizenship, or Temporality and the Negation of Black Childhood in Two Eras," *American Quarterly* 71, no. 2 (2019): 474.

138. For a brief history of SFIS, see ASU School for the Future of Innovation in Society, *Annual Report, 2015–2016,* 2016, http://sfis.asu.edu/. ASU has continued to brand itself as an educational institution interested in the future through the founding of the College of Global Futures in July 2020, bringing SFIS together with the School of Sustainability and the School of Complex Adaptive Systems. See "About— College of Global Futures," Arizona State University, accessed 7 August 2020, http:// collegeofglobalfutures.asu.edu/.

139. ASU School for the Future of Innovation in Society, *Annual Report, 2016–2017,* 2017, http://sfis.asu.edu/.

140. "Student FAQs: School for the Future of Innovation in Socety," School for the Future of Innovation in Society, Arizona State University, accesed 7 August 2020, http:// sfis.asu.edu/.

141. "Student FAQs."

142. Bruce Sterling, "EMERGE Conference, Phoenix: Sterling, Bleecker, Candy, Neal Stephenson, Stewart Brand, and Many Others," *Wired,* 25 Februarry 2012, http://www .wired.com/.

143. Bruce Sterling, "Design Fiction: Near Future Laboratory, 'Corner Convenience,'" *Wired,* 4 March 2012, http://www.wired.com/.

144. Julian Bleecker, "Corner Convenience // The Near Future // Design Fiction," *Near Future Laboratory,* 4 March 2012, http://nearfuturelaboratory.com/.

145. Kasia Cieplak-Mayr von Baldegg, "The High-Tech Crap You Might Find at the Corner Store Tomorrow," *The Atlantic,* 20 March 2012, http://theatlantic.com/.

146. Bruce Sterling, "Design Fiction: Object-Oriented Futures at Emerge 2012," *Wired,* 5 April 2012, http://www.wired.com/.

147. Charlotte Bell, "The Inner City and the 'Hoodie,'" *Wasafiri* 28, no. 4 (2013): 38–44; Mimi Thi Nguyen, "The Hoodie as Sign, Screen, Expectation, and Force," *Signs: Journal of Women in Culture and Society* 40, no. 4 (2015): 791–816; Osmud Rahman, "The Hoodie: Consumer Choice, Fashion Style and Symbolic Meaning," *International Journal of Fashion Studies* 3, no. 1 (2016): 111–33.

148. For critical discussion of Trayvon Martin's murder, see Ange-Marie Hancock, "Trayvon Martin, Intersectionality, and the Politics of Disgust," *Theory & Event* 15, no. 3 (2012): http://muse.jhu.edu/; George Yancy and Janine Jones, eds., *Pursuing Trayvon Martin: Historical Contexts and Contemporary Manifestations of Racial Dynamics* (New York: Lexington Books, 2013); Kenneth J. Fasching-Varner et al., eds, *Trayvon Martin, Race, and American Justice: Writing Wrong* (Rotterdam, Netherlands: Sense Publishers, 2014); Bryan J. McCann, "On Whose Ground? Racialized Violence and the Prerogative of 'Self-Defense' in the Trayvon Martin Case," *Western Journal of Communication* 78, no. 4 (2014): 480–99; Adam Hodges, "Ideologies of Language and Race in US Media Discourse about the Trayvon Martin Shooting," *Language in Society* 44, no. 3 (2015): 401–23; Lamar Johnson and Nathaniel Bryan, "Using Our Voices, Losing Our Bodies: Michael Brown, Trayvon Martin, and the Spirit Murders of Black Male Professors in the Academy," *Race Ethnicity and Education* 20, no. 2 (2017): 163–77; Devon Johnson, Patricia Y. Warren, and Amy Farrell, eds., *Deadly Injustice: Trayvon Martin, Race, and the Criminal Justice System* (New York: NYU Press, 2015); Safiya Umoja Noble, "Teach-

ing Trayvon," *The Black Scholar* 44, no. 1 (2014): 12–29; Joshua Reeves, "License to Kill: Trayvon Martin and the Logic of Exception," *Cultural Studies* ↔ *Critical Methodologies* 15, no. 4 (2015): 287–91; and Franklin Nii Amankwah Yartey, "Race, Solidarity and Dissent in the Trayvon Martin Case: A Critical Analysis," *Visual Studies* 31, no. 1 (2016): 50–62; and Breslow, "Adolescent Citizenship."

149. Breslow, "Adolescent Citizenship," 474.

150. Colin Milburn, "Greener on the Other Side: Science Fiction and the Problem of Green Nanotechnology," *Configurations* 20, no. 1 (2012): 53–87; Mark Blythe et al., "Anti-Solutionist Strategies: Seriously Silly Design Fiction, " in *CHI '16: Proceedings of the 2016 CHI Conference on Human Factors in Computing Systems* (San Jose, Calif.: Association for Computing Machinery, 2016), 4968–78.

151. Ruha Benjamin, "Racial Fictions, Biological Facts: Expanding the Sociological Imagination through Speculative Methods," *Catalyst: Feminism, Theory, Technoscience* 2, no. 2 (2016): http://catalystjournal.org/; Marisol de la Cadena and Mario Blaser, eds., *A World of Many Worlds* (Durham, N.C.: Duke University Press, 2018); Escobar, *Designs for the Pluriverse.*

152. Benjamin, "Racial Fictions, Biological Facts." In this capacity, Alexis Lothian identifies the stories in the 2015 science fiction anthology *Octavia's Brood: Science Fiction Stories from Social Justice Movements* edited by Walidah Imarisha and adrienne maree brown as "science fiction prototypes" by activists and organizers imagining worlds without war, capitalism, or prison. See Alexis Lothian, *Old Futures: Speculative Fiction and Queer Possibility* (New York: NYU Press, 2018), 19; and Walidah Imarisha and adrienne maree brown, eds., *Octavia's Brood: Science Fiction Stories from Social Justice Movements* (Chico, Calif.: AK Press, 2015).

INDEX

ableism: in design, 133, 160–61; and
digital culture, 11, 64, 109, 147. *See
also* difference
access: and ableism in design, 133; to
childhood, 152, 158; and class privilege, 6, 19–20, 115; and DIY science,
74, 81, 83, 90–91; through science fiction prototypes, 146–47; to technology, 164
Acland, Charles R., 10
adolescents, 4–6, 16, 93–94, 119, 143,
196n20; and selfies, 100–101, 104,
108–9, 111–13, 124–25; and socialization, 21, 23, 89, 95–99, 122. *See
also* children; digital generation
discourse; teenagers
Adorno, Theodor, 14
advertising, 13, 107, 144; in *Make* magazine, 69; and self-branding culture,
94, 108; to young people, 1, 5, 33
affirmative design, 148–50, 153
alphabet dice, 32–33
alternatives design, 208n118
Althusser, Louis, 73
AlukaMak, 53–54
Amabile, Teresa, 37
amateurization of technoscience, 21–23,
60, 70–75, 79, 84, 87–91, 190n67
Anderson, Benedict, 62, 84
Anderson, Chris, 19, 69
apocalypse, 69–70, 188n55, 209n127
app generation, 4. *See also* digital generation discourse
Arab Spring, 96
arcade culture, 7, 33. *See also* digital
gaming culture
Archer, Bruce, 135–36
Arizona State University (ASU), 153–55,

158; College of Global Futures,
210n138; School for the Future of
Innovation in Society, 152, 210n138
Arnett, Jeffrey Jensen, 97
Arnold, Matthew, 135
Aronica, Lou, 1
artificiality, 21–23, 95, 113–20, 123–25;
and appropriateness, 121–22. *See also*
authenticity
Arts and Crafts Movement, 64, 68
aspirational labor, 106, 108, 115
Atwood, Margaret, 144
authenticity, 21–23, 113–20, 123–25;
and appropriateness, 121–22; in
individual development, 37, 95, 164,
201n93. *See also* artificiality
autonomy, 88, 91, 107–8, 143; and creativity, 3, 9, 14–16, 21–22, 30, 34; in
survival narratives, 38–41, 44, 53–56,
70. *See also* individualism

Baby Boomers, 5. *See also* generational
discourse
Bacon, Francis: *New Atlantis,* 22, 30,
40–41, 180n73
Badham, John: *WarGames,* 6
Balenciaga, 123
Ballantyne, R. M.: *The Coral Island,* 44
Balsamo, Anne, 132, 137–39, 143–44
Banet-Weiser, Sarah, 108, 115
Banks, Marcus, 115–16
Barbie. *See* @socalitybarbie
Barbrook, Richard, 17, 20, 63
Barlow, John Perry, 5
Baudelaire, Charles, 12
Bauhaus, 9
Beach, Natalie, 118, 122
becoming-wolf, 53–54

Index

JOSEF NGUYEN is assistant professor of critical media studies at the University of Texas at Dallas.